ADVICE & CONSENT

ADVICE
&
CONSENT

Clarence Thomas, Robert Bork and the Intriguing History of the Supreme Court's Nomination Battles

Senator Paul Simon

National
Press
Books

Washington, D.C.

Library of Congress Cataloging-in-Publication Data

Simon, Paul, 1928-
Advice and Consent: Clarence Thomas, Robert Bork and the
Intriguing History of the Supreme Court's Nomination Battles
Paul Simon
328 pp. 15.25 x 22.85 cm.
Includes biographical references and index
ISBN 0-915765-98-5: $23.95
1. Judges–United States–Selection and appointment–History.
2. United States. Congress. Senate–History.
3. United States. Supreme Court–History.
I. Title.
KF8776.S56   1992
347.73'14–dc20
[347.30714]
92-16107   CIP

PRINTED IN THE UNITED STATES OF AMERICA

*To all those who have courageously stood
for freedom and opportunity
when it was not popular to do so.*

Also by Paul Simon

Winners and Losers (1989)

Let's Put America Back to Work (1987)

Beginnings (1986)

The Glass House (1984)

The Once and Future Democrats (1982)

The Tongue-Tied American (1980)

The Politics of World Hunger (with Arthur Simon, 1973)

You Want to Change the World? So Change It (1971)

Protestant-Catholic Marriages Can Succeed (with Jeanne Hurley Simon, 1967)

A Hungry World (1966)

Lincoln's Preparation for Greatness (1965)

Lovejoy: Martyr to Freedom (1964)

The President "shall have power, by and with the advice and consent of the senate, to . . . appoint ambassadors, other public ministers and consuls, judges of the supreme court, and all other officers of the United States . . ."

–Article II, Constitution of the United States

Acknowledgments

I am grateful to many people for their help.

My primary reader and critic, my wife Jeanne, not only read the first very rough draft that I typed on an old manual typewriter, she also assisted in other ways. For example, I apparently am the first writer to go through the records of the secret sessions of the Senate Judiciary Committee of 1874, but they were all written by hand. My wife typed those records for me, no simple chore. And she provided invaluable editorial suggestions.

Particularly helpful in editorial improvement were my brother, Arthur Simon, and Judy Wagner.

On all the books I have written, librarians have been of immense help in suggesting resources, books and materials. Nowhere is this better illustrated than the Library of Congress where Robert Gee and others there, including Harold Moore, Emily Carr and John Edmonds, were helpful on everything from finding resources and making editorial suggestions, to finding a cubbyhole where I could type.

State historians in several states helped me track down information. I am grateful for that, as well as the contributions they are making to preserving our heritage.

Joel Joseph and Alan Sultan of National Press Books have been both encouraging and helpful. I appreciate the cooperation of the publisher on everything but one item: the title of the book. It is too much like the Allen Drury book title, in my opinion, but on this issue the publisher prevailed.

Jackie Williams waded through my typing and scribbling to produce the final copy, and Christopher Ryan chased down research minutia.

Among others who helped in some way, listed in alphabetical order, are Henry Abraham, Nancy Bandy, Heather Booth, David Carle, Beth Donohue, Jonathan Epstein, Pamela Huey, Susan Kaplan, Jeremy Karpatkin, Deborah Leavy, John Marty, Vincent Michelot, David O'Brien, Todd Pruzan, Marcus Raskin, John Y. Simon, Kim Sinclair, Philippa Strum and Laurence Tribe. There were also a few who provided information who cannot be listed, for reasons that will be apparent to the reader. I am grateful to all of them, but conclusions and errors are mine, not theirs.

My hope is that as a result of this book, the phrase "liberty and justice for all" can become a little more of a reality.

Contents

Foreword

_____

by Laurence H. Tribe

The author is Tyler Professor of Constitutional Law, Harvard University.

The Supreme Court confirmation process—once a largely behind-the-scenes affair—has lately moved front-and-center onto the public stage. In a virtual daytime soap opera between 1987 and 1991, the Nation witnessed the spectacle of Robert Bork's defeat after a battle that was bitter and politicized on both sides; Douglas Ginsburg's withdrawal under pressure from the Reagan Administration after disclosures that he had smoked marijuana while a law professor; the nomination and Senate approval of two "stealth" candidates (perhaps in reaction to the increased scrutiny accorded judicial nominees) in the persons of Anthony Kennedy and David Souter; and the confirmation of Clarence Thomas from Pinpoint, Georgia, who was driven by Senate questioning to assert that he had never in his legal career discussed the merits of *Roe v. Wade* as a decision of constitutional law.

Some lament the new visibility of the nomination process, and it has undoubtedly produced changes in the way that nominees are selected and packaged by the White House and in the manner that nominees present themselves to the Senate and the Nation. Confirmation by sound-bite is indeed lamentable, but we should not confuse the role of publicists, handlers, and spin-doctors with the effort to understand who these nominees really are. Their power over our lives is, after all, enormous.

Careful scrutiny of the judicial philosophies as well as the personal characters of nominees for the Nation's highest court is a critical element of the Senate's constitutional function of advice and consent. If the appointment of a particular nominee would move the Court in a substantive direction that a Senator conscientiously determines would exacerbate what that Senator views as an already excessive conservative *or* liberal bias on the Court, then the Senator can and should vote against confirmation. To do otherwise is to trivialize the Supreme Court's historical role as an autonomous third branch of government and that it is not simply a mouthpiece of the President.

Indeed, if there is any complaint to be made about the experience of recent confirmations, it is not that nominees have been the unfair victims of televised witch-hunts or "high-tech lynchings," but that the Senate has been too supine and deferential to the Administration and its hand-picked nominees. The hearings have been attention-grabbing public drama, but all too often the Senate has simply rolled over and, after going through the perfunctory — albeit highly visible — motions, proved in the end to be a willing co-conspirator in the President's Court-packing strategy.

The History of Court-Packing

A quick survey of recent appointments is revealing. Prior to Richard Nixon, the last Republican President to fill any Supreme Court vacancies was Dwight Eisenhower in the 1950s, who appointed jurists as diverse as Earl Warren and John M. Harlan, William J. Brennan Jr. and Potter Stewart. Subsequently, Presidents Kennedy and Johnson appointed four Justices in the early 1960s, ranging on the political spectrum from Byron White to Thurgood Marshall. Since 1969, however, eleven Supreme Court appointments in a row—from Warren Burger in 1969 to Clarence Thomas in 1991—have been made by Republican Presidents applying increasingly ideological criteria, with the Senate dutifully confirming all these nominees except Judge Bork. Despite decades of divided government, the current Supreme Court is one of the least philosophically diverse Courts in American history and can hardly be said to reflect the range of mainstream constitutional and legal views. Any Court this lopsided—in any direction—is bound to overlook vital issues, engage in relatively shallow and constricted internal debate, and deprive the future of the great dissents that have so often been destined to become the law long after they have been issued.

Contrary to what some have claimed, the single-minded presidential search for ideological purity is itself quite new. Washington's Federalist appointees, for example, were as different as James Iredell and Samuel Chase, who found themselves on opposite sides of such landmark and deeply divisive cases as *Chisholm v. Georgia,* which established (before it was overruled by the Eleventh Amendment) that the Supreme Court had jurisdiction over a private citizen's suit for damages against a State, filed without the State's consent. Franklin Delano Roosevelt's appointees were as diverse as Hugo Black and Felix Frankfurter, William O. Douglas and Robert H. Jackson. Prior to Richard Nixon's nominees, the Justices elevated by Republican Presidents in this century included (in addition to the Eisenhower selections noted above) Oliver Wendell Holmes, Charles Evans Hughes, and Benjamin Cardozo—true giants of American law.

The all-but-admitted Court-packing efforts of Presidents Reagan and Bush have been remarkable not merely because they manifest so little respect for the Court as an independent third branch, but also because they have proven relatively successful. Beginning with the Republican Senate's unfortunate attempt to impeach Justice Samuel Chase in 1804 and 1805—largely on the ground that, as a Federalist, his judicial philosophy was inconsistent with the new mood on Capitol Hill—the Senate historically has played a vigorous role in ensuring ideological diversity on the Supreme Court. Even a Republican Senate rejected President Herbert Hoover's nominee John Parker as out-of-step with labor and civil rights issues, forcing Hoover instead to name the more moderate Owen Roberts to the Court in 1930. And conservatives who today applaud the string of Reagan and Bush Justices were vehement only decades ago that the Senate possessed the constitutional prerogative to impeach liberals like Chief Justice Warren and Justice Douglas on the basis of their records as sitting Justices.

To grasp the truly unprecedented nature of the contemporary pattern—with the most recent eleven Supreme Court vacancies filled by Republican Presidents—it is necessary to realize that only four times in all of American history have Presidents of a single political party named more than ten Justices in a row. In a Federalist era, George Washington and John Adams chose thirteen Justices from 1789 to 1801; in a Republican era, Presidents from Lincoln to Arthur selected fourteen Justices between 1862 and 1882; and in a Democratic era Roosevelt and Truman appointed thirteen Justices from 1937 to 1949. But 39 of these 40 Justices were confirmed by Senates of the President's own party! Only once during any of these prior strings of single-party nominations to the Supreme Court did a Senate in which the opposition party held a majority acquiesce in the President's choice for the Court—in 1880, when Justice William Woods was name by Republican President Rutherford B. Hayes and confirmed by a Democratic Senate.

The latest Republican series of eleven Justices in a row is in stark contrast to this historical pattern: the latest nominees were confirmed with the "advice and consent" of only three Republican Senates but *eight* Democratic Senates. Never before in U.S. history has a divided government been willing for so long to let the Executive Branch remake the Judicial Branch so uniformly in the Executive's own image. The complacency—complicity would not be too strong a word—on Capitol Hill seems attributable in part to the modern emergence of the historically inaccurate myths that the President is entitled to "deference" regarding the judicial philosophy of his nominees, and that there is a "presumption" in favor of a nominee's confirmation (as if the nomination were for a mere cabinet post, or as if a nominee's defeat were akin to a criminal conviction), which can be rebutted only by clear proof of some startling impropriety or gross shortfall in the candidate's qualifications.

This is all wrong, it seems to me. If there is any "deference," it ought to be to the *Constitution,* and if there is any "presumption," it should rest against attempts to tilt the overall ideological make-up of the Supreme Court too far in any one direction.

The Senate's Role

In light of this momentous shift in the Senate's approach to — some might say abdication of — its solemn constitutional duties, Senator Paul Simon's book could not come at a better time. His is a critically important insider's account of the confirmation process from a previously silent perspective. There has already appeared in print a quite partisan indictment of the confirmation process by a defeated nominee, Robert Bork. Senator Simon's balanced and fair-minded work affords us all an opportunity to view the same system from the other side of the Judiciary Committee hearing table — and with considerably less distortion and vitriol. His book will be all the more useful in light of revisions in the confirmation process being proposed by all quarters in the wake of Clarence Thomas's appointment.

The main lesson I would draw from the experience of recent confirmations is that the Senate *must* once again take its constitutional "advice and consent" role seriously and must treat the Supreme Court with the respect it deserves, if the judiciary is to flourish as the truly independent instititution that the Framers intended and that a constitutional democracy presupposes. But treating the Court with respect does not mean surrounding nominees to that august body with a shield that precludes meaningful inquiry into how they would approach constitutional or statutory problems. And it surely doesn't mean permitting nominees who have staked out strong positions in prior articles and speeches to disavow them as mere musings or as political posturing without considerably more explanation of what those nominees meant when they wrote or said those things, and, if they no longer believe what they seemed to believe in the past, how and why their legal views have changed.

Stealth Nominees

The Court and the Nation cannot afford any more "stealth" nominees who steadfastly decline to answer substantive questions the Senate might pose on the oft-invoked ground that the matter might come before the Court during their possible tenure. This easy refrain does not provide a valid excuse for stonewalling, no matter how frequently it is repeated.

The notion that a Supreme Court Justice will be more open-minded or less prone to prejudgment if the Senate and the public are prevented from knowing what tentative conclusions that Justice has already reached is simply untenable. No one would dream of suggesting that sitting Justices must recuse themselves on matters as to which their own prior writings, in Supreme Court opinions or elsewhere, have revealed their initial views. On the contrary, the adversary system works best when all concerned, and not just those who nominated the judge, know what there is to be known about that judge's starting predispositions on a pending issue. And let's stop pretending that such predispositions do not exist. It hardly fosters fairness to claim that a mind is completely neutral when in fact a lifetime of experiences has unavoidably inclined it one way or the other, and to equate an *open* mind with a *blank* one insults the intelligence of all concerned. Hence, regardless of the propriety of evasive tactics by nominees in the past, the determined Court-packing by the Reagan and Bush Administrations makes an inquiry into the judicial philosophy of future candidates absolutely essential if the Supreme Court is ever again to discharge a fully effective checking function in our system of government.

Thoroughly examining candidates' judicial philosophies need not mean badgering witnesses or insisting that they declare their views on abstract legal topics that can be meaningfully discussed only in the context of particular factual settings. Nor need such examination mean drastic changes in the format of Judiciary Committee hearings. It is unclear that much could be achieved by extending the time spent ritualistically questioning nominees or even — in the interest of replacing ritual with substance — by according a greater role to congressional staff in cross-examining them. If anything, perhaps less effort should be devoted to attempting to corner candidates with cleverly phrased questions that cannot be evaded by the calculated pirouettes that White House advisors have choreographed.

A nominee whose record is too pale to read with the naked eye or whose views are shrouded in fog too dense for anything but the klieg lights of national television to pierce is probably ill-suited for a lifetime seat on the Supreme Court in any event. If this is so, it follows that Senators should try to assess nominees' likely approaches to important legal issues before the hearings even begin — on the basis of the nominees' records, the criteria by which they were selected by the President, and other available information. Some might maintain that Senators must remain "open-minded" about a candidate until the nomination hearing is over — as if the President were equally "open-minded" when he selected the candidate in the first place. In most cases, of course, a Senator would be wise to withhold final judgment — and not just pretend to do so — until all the evidence is in. But, to my mind, it is dangerous as well as naive for Senators to pretend that nothing about a nominee is knowable until he or she has testified — particularly when the President either has direct knowledge of the nominee's legal views or has, at worst, made a highly educated guess about those views.

By now, it should be clear that certain issues — in our time, abortion, affirmative action, drugs, and the death penalty, for example — play so prominent a role in the national consciousness that they badly distort the legal landscape in which the Supreme Court moves. Just as those issues can warp legal doctrines when they arise in particular cases — in the way that successive appeals by death-row inmates have led the Court to curtail the rights of all criminal defendants to federal habeas corpus, or in the way the abortion gag rule case, *Rust v. Sullivan,* led the Supreme Court to bend free speech principles and restraints on the power of government to place conditions on public subsidies — those issues can also give us a badly skewed perspective on the confirmation process.

I do not fault those who would have the Senate focus intently on those questions in an era when judicial candidates are nominated in the first place with a keen eye towards their views on the matters in question. But the legal landscape is not always dominated by a small set of issues — and, even when it is, the salient issues frequently change before the Justice selected with those issues in mind has left the Court. It is possible that — just as Frankfurter and Douglas differed dramatically in their later years over the role of the Court in protecting civil and political liberties from governmental incursion, when at the time of their nominations both were strong supporters of judicial deference to economic regulation — judges who today seem so ideologically similar might prove quite diverse when the topics change to, say, organ transplants, genetic engineering, computerized bulletin boards, or the application of U.S. and international law to outer space. By that time, the country may finally have elected a President who does not impose a narrow ideological filter on his or her judicial appointments, but who seeks instead a combination of virtues ranging from depth of learning and breadth of experience to great legal acumen and social vision. If that were to occur, the need for Senate vigilance might well be lessened.

World's Greatest Deliberative Body

For now, however, the Senate is obligated to inquire closely into nominees' substantive views in order to prevent the Court from becoming an even more monolithic mirror of the Executive Branch's legal philosophy. Indeed, the Senate is as much to blame as the President for the current sorry state of affairs in which the Senate's confirmation timidity is exceeded only by its *post-hoc* handwringing over the results of the nomination process. Although voters can fortify the courage of individual Senators and punish those who betray the public's trust, the Senate does itself and the country a great disservice if, instead of affirmatively seeking to fulfill its historical and constitutionally ordained role as a true partner in the system of advice and consent, it is moved to respond to the public's will only by crude electoral calculations. The Senate of Daniel Webster and John C. Calhoun was known as the world's "Greatest Deliberative Body"; this book by one of the Senate's most thoughtful members is a step toward making that honorific appropriate once again.

Part I

Overview

1

Introduction

Outside of presidential elections, no political battle has greater impact on our nation's long-term future than the periodic struggle between the President and the Senate as to who will sit on the United States Supreme Court. *Advice & Consent* is a story of those battles, with some conclusions on how we can do better.

This book is *not* a history of the Supreme Court. The best single-volume history of the Court is *Justices and Presidents* by Henry Abraham. Nor is this book a history of presidential appointments in other fields and the Senate's role in those appointments. Joseph Harris has written such a book, *The Advice and Consent of the Senate.*

The Clarence Thomas hearings confirmed to the nation that something is wrong with the way we handle Supreme Court nominations. This book is an analysis of what has happened historically that is right and wrong in the processing of Supreme Court nominations.

Supreme Court justices are appointed for life and are called upon to make decisions that affect the lives of all Americans. The principles of "one man, one vote" and "separate but equal" and the constitutional right to an abortion were decided by the Supreme Court, not by the President or Congress.

Because of the televised hearings and particularly the dramatic Clarence Thomas/Anita Hill encounter, there is a greater public understanding of the significance of Supreme Court appointments, and at least some greater understanding of the impact of Court decisions on our daily lives. The public became absorbed in the Thomas/Hill live "soap opera," and the impact of those hearings has reverberated far beyond the important single voice and vote on the Supreme Court. In my home state of Illiniois, for example, Senator Alan Dixon lost his seat primarily because of his vote for Judge Thomas. This is one of the many manifestations of the impact of what took place in October 1991.

I begin this book with our most recent experiences, particularly the Robert Bork and Clarence Thomas confirmation hearings. Then I go back to the earliest confirmation battles to put these current struggles into historical perspective. I examine what those who founded our nation meant when they wrote "advice and consent" into the Constitution.

Do we have indications of how they envisioned the power of the presidency and the power of the Senate balancing each other? How has this relationship worked historically? There are periods in which the President and the Senate worked well together. There are other times when the Senate was too dominant, and also times when the President paid almost no attention to the Constitution's requirement for consultation with the Senate. What factors should the Senate weigh as it looks at nominees? There are those who suggest the Senate has no business weighing political and constitutional philosophy. What can we learn about this from history?

There are similarities in these battles between the President and the Senate, yet each circumstance is different, sometimes because of the cast of characters and sometimes because of outside forces, such as the technology of television.

The Bork and Thomas nominations are examined more carefully than the others because each in its own way is a classic confrontation in a world that is dramatically different than when the Senate battled over George Washington's nomination of John Rutledge. I examine how we in the Senate played or misplayed our role in those hearings, and I explore the question of whether Clarence Thomas or Anita Hill told us the truth.

Finally, I see what can be learned from more than two centuries of this encounter.

Perhaps you will discover that history is more fascinating than you thought. And you will gain a better sense of perspective through which to judge more recent happenings. With that sense of perspective, we can view the decision-making for Supreme Court nominations not as a political game to be exercised by competing political parties or different branches of government, but what in fact it is: an awe-inspiring opportunity to defend basic freedoms and to provide justice to future generations.

2

The Sweep of History

From George Washington's nomination of John Jay to George
Bush's nomination of Clarence Thomas, Supreme Court
nominees have received more careful scrutiny and have caused
more controversy than any other presidential appointments.

Rightfully so.

Unlike a cabinet member or similar nominee, a Supreme
Court Justice is not selected to be a member of the President's
team. Rather, the President is choosing a watchdog for the
Constitution who sometimes decides against the executive
branch, sometimes against the legislative branch and sometimes
against both.

As early as 1835, Frenchman Alexis deTocqueville wrote,
after a visit through our nation: "Scarcely any political question
arises in the United States that is not resolved sooner or later into
a judicial question."[1] What deTocqueville saw then is still true
today. Little wonder that the Senate watches carefully who is

appointed to the Supreme Court, to sit in that decision-making chair for the remainder of his or her life.

Occasionally the Supreme Court is called upon to stand not only against the executive and legislative branches, but also against public opinion. Sometimes it fails that test. In 1942, shortly after the start of World War II, in one of the most clear-cut federal actions in violation of the Constitution, President Franklin D. Roosevelt ordered the removal of 120,000 Japanese-Americans and their relatives (three-fourths of them born in the United States) from the West Coast on security grounds. Not one had been found guilty of committing an act of sabotage; not one had even been charged with any such crime. They were given one to three days to sell all their property and belongings, to put everything into one suitcase and be moved into camps in the interior of the United States. In a 6-3 ruling, the Supreme Court called the President's action legal. Later, all three branches of government would recognize that the action, taken at a moment of national hysteria, violated the Constitution. In 1942 the Supreme Court failed that test. (The only member of Congress to speak out formally against the action was Senator Robert A. Taft of Ohio.)

That case, *Korematsu v. United States,* illustrates the need for a Supreme Court that is willing to be courageously independent. Justices Frank Murphy and Robert Jackson, appointed by FDR, ruled with great boldness against public opinion and the President who appointed them. Justice Owen Roberts, appointed by President Herbert Hoover, cast the third courageous negative vote. In his strong dissent, Justice Murphy said the action was based on the "assumption of racial guilt" and that it "falls into the ugly abyss of racism."

The *Korematsu* decision also illustrates the huge impact the Supreme Court can have on the lives of people and on the destiny of the nation. Likewise, the *Dred Scott* decision of 1857 made freedom regional and slavery national; a slave remained a slave even if he or she went to a free state. That decision headed the nation toward a civil war. And in 1982, journalist and American observer Theodore H. White commented about the dramatic changes that had been achieved through government in the immediately preceding years, saying, "In all these events, the governor and throttle of the motor remained the Supreme Court of the United States, as political an institution as Congress or the presidency. The Supreme Court's role in the transformation starts . . . with its historic decision on May 17, 1954, on school desegregation, known as *Brown v. Board of Education of Topeka.*"[2]

The extreme (the correct word) importance of the position of Supreme Court Justice makes it imperative that the Senate not take casually its responsibility to advise the President. Once on the Court, these men and one woman are somewhat isolated. Senators do not lobby members of the judiciary on rulings to be made. The great decision is: Who sits on the Court? From that decision flows much of the course of the nation.

Approximately one-fifth of those who have been nominated by Presidents for the Supreme Court have failed to be confirmed, a far higher figure than for any other office. During the nineteenth century, one-fourth were rejected.

Diversity

For a good portion of our history, geography dominated the choice of Justices as much as or more than political philosophy. Geography more properly played a role in the days when members of the Supreme Court "rode circuit," conducting trials in the geographical area assigned. Gradually there grew an assumption that a state or a region had an entitlement to a seat. "They are crowding Ohio on us a little too thick," commented a Senator in 1881 when another Ohioan was nominated to the Court.[3] However, by the 1930s, when Herbert Hoover nominated Benjamin Cardozo, the fact that he would be the third New Yorker on the Court received little attention. Today geography is a minor consideration, and for most Senators it is not a consideration at all.

Early Presidents sought diversity on the Court, and by that they meant Justices from all regions of the country. Today diversity has different meanings, and we have achieved a diversity that would have shocked many of those who met in Philadelphia in 1787. When they wrote the Constitution, neither African-Americans nor women could vote. On February 1, 1865 — shortly before Abraham Lincoln's death — an African-American, Dr. John S. Rock, was admitted to practice before the U. S. Supreme Court, an action that stunned many. One hundred and two years later, Thurgood Marshall, already a legal giant, took a seat on the Supreme Court, having been nominated by President Lyndon Johnson. On March 3, 1879, Belva Lockwood became the first woman to be admitted to practice before the Supreme Court. In 1934, FDR named an Ohio Supreme Court Justice, Florence E. Allen, to the U. S. Court of Appeals, the first woman to serve on the federal bench. Forty-seven years later President Ronald Reagan nominated Sandra Day O'Connor to the Supreme Court. Diversity as the Constitution-writers could not imagine had come to the Court.

Independence

While geographical diversity was one reason for involving the Senate in Supreme Court appointments, a greater concern dominated the thinking of early American leaders: the necessity of having a judiciary that stood firmly independent of the executive branch. Their bitter experiences under the British system with its sometimes supine judiciary caused the construction of the cooperative effort between the executive and legislative branches.

That cooperation has varied. Some Presidents, including George Washington, worked with the Senate closely but retained the decisive role in the process. Washington's procedure is best illustrated, not with a Supreme Court appointment, but with the choice of Minister to France. The Senate designated James Madison and James Monroe as a committee of two to talk to the President on behalf of the Senate, urging Washington to name Aaron Burr as Minister to France. Washington refused, saying that "he had made it an invariable rule never to appoint to a high and responsible office a man whose integrity he was not assured."[4] He said he would be willing to name either Madison or Monroe. When the Senate caucus tried a second time, Washington made clear that he stood firm, a position history vindicates. Washington worked with the Senate, but like later Presidents, retained the final decision.

Some decades later, the Senate became too dominant a force in the selection process, going beyond the role envisioned for it. In a fight over a Supreme Court nomination, President James Garfield wrote that the contest "will settle the question whether the President is the registering clerk of the Senate or the Executive of the United States."[5] From time to time the Supreme Court itself has played a quiet but effective role in picking successors, reaching its high point during the chief justiceship of William Howard Taft. And there have been occasions, including recent periods, in which the President and his staff have consulted almost not at all with the Senate.

Politics, Politics

In making the nomination decision, political philosophy has been the primary consideration for some Presidents but not with others. President Gerald Ford viewed it as "a mistake [for Presidents] to appoint people to the Court on ideological grounds." He said such appointments "denigrate the nominee and the Court."[6] Many Presidents have nominated people with whom they differed philosophically, including the majority of Presidents of this century. Taft, Wilson, Harding, Hoover, FDR, Truman, Eisenhower and Nixon nominated at least one person from the other political party; and Coolidge and Kennedy nominated candidates with whom they differed philosophically, though they were of the same political party.

A few Presidents have said political philosophy was not a factor even when it clearly dominated the decision-making. Some Presidents have looked to legal expertise as a qualifying factor. When Washington named the first Supreme Court on September 24, 1789, all but one, James Wilson, had judicial experience. After his retirement, Justice Lewis F. Powell Jr. answered a question about Chief Justices and the reason for their selection:

> The first three Chief Justices were conspicuous leaders in both fields [law and politics] at a time when the ablest lawyers also dominated the Government. [Chief Justice] Stone, the scholar, also was unique. Among the other Chief Justices, I think it is fair to say that Chase, Taft, Vinson, Warren and possibly White attained distinction—and the chief justiceship—primarily through political office. In my view, Marshall, Taney, Waite, Fuller and Hughes, despite political activity and service, attained prominence initially as lawyers of wide reputation. They were primarily not politicians.[7]

Personal friendship has been a factor, as President Harry Truman's appointments strikingly illustrate.

Age has been a factor both for those appointed and for some who have turned down the offer of appointments. Presidents Reagan and Bush sought younger appointees, while President Grant nominated seventy-four-year-old Caleb Cushing for Chief Justice, at a time when the average life span for an American male was about forty. Theodore Roosevelt nominated sixty-two-year-old Oliver Wendell Holmes Jr., and he served almost three decades on the Court. At the time of the Holmes nomination, the average American male lived to be forty-six. Charles Evans Hughes became Chief Justice at sixty-eight. When Roger Taney was sworn in as Chief Justice, he was two days shy of being sixty years old and "delicate in health."[8] He served as Chief Justice twenty-eight years.

Until recently, Presidents frequently named key people within their administrations to the Supreme Court. Since 1968 only Arthur Goldberg and William Rehnquist fit that pattern.

Political Philosophy

Whatever factors are weighed by a President, one thing is clear and is contrary to widely held opinion: When Presidents have tried to shape the Supreme Court through choosing someone of a particular political and philosophical bent, they have generally been successful in doing that. Presidents have argued that you cannot know what someone will do when he or she is on the Court, and it is true that how someone will rule on a specific case is not always predictable. In his typically blunt fashion, Truman said, "Packing the Supreme Court simply can't be done .... I've tried it and it won't work."[9] But Truman did not really try.

Presidents determined to set the Court on a particular philosophical course have been able to do that when vacancies on the Court occurred. There are exceptions to that general rule, and the exceptions launch academic debate on the validity of the assertion. Nominees are not blank slates when they come onto the Court, and their course on the Court, with rare exceptions, generally can be predicted by the views they held prior to the assumption of the seat. Robert G. Ingersoll, the nineteenth century political leader and orator, noted: "We must remember that we have to make judges out of men, and by being made judges their prejudices are not diminished and their intelligence is not increased."[10]

A non-judicial nominee illustrates the reality. When Earl Butz came before the Senate Agriculture Committee for confirmation as Secretary of Agriculture, Senator Hubert Humphrey said to him:

> I am worried about your economic philosophy .... Your bonds and stocks [are] to your credit .... You have earned everything that you have. You can put all that in escrow, but I don't think you can put your philosophy in escrow.[11]

The Senate approved Butz, and he implemented the philosophy Humphrey feared.

Whatever consideration the President uses in selecting the nominee would appear to be a reasonable ground for the Senate to weigh in the process of advice and consent, with one exception. That exception is the shrewd political calculation some Presidents have made about what will help them in the next election. Senators have not been immune from the same temptation, but it is a temptation, whether exercised by a President or a Senator, that often ill serves the nation. Other than that, whatever factors the President weighs in making a choice are just as appropriate for the Senate to consider.

Political philosophy and constitutional philosophy, as examples, should be weighed by the United States Senate. Andrew Jackson's choice for Chief Justice, Roger Taney, wrote that critics are inaccurate who say that "no consideration should be given to the views of the appointee on the subject of politics, taking politics in its highest and philosophical sense as involving the theories of human rights and the principles of government."[12] Few students of history would differ with Taney, but editorial writers, media commentators and Senators who have not looked at history can easily reach a different conclusion. While some say, "The Senate should consider a Supreme Court nominee the same way it considers a Secretary of Transportation," that argument fails to weigh the immense importance of the Court position to be filled and that the President is not simply naming someone to his or her administration.

Two decades ago Yale law scholar Charles Black wrote:[13]

> If a President should desire . . . to change entirely the character of the Supreme Court . . . nothing would stand in his way except the United States Senate. Few constitutional questions are then of more moment than the question whether a Senator properly may, or even at sometimes in duty must, vote against a nominee to that Court, on the ground that the nominee holds views which . . . are likely, in the Senator's judgment, to be very bad for the country . . . . A Senator not only may but generally ought to vote in the negative, if he firmly believes on reasonable grounds, that the nominee's views on the large

issues of the day will make it harmful to the country for him to sit and vote on the Court.

Then Black added this significant line (emphasis his): "He who *advises* gives or withholds his advice on the basis of *all* the relevant considerations bearing on a decision."[14]

One of the most careful scholars of the Court, Joseph Harris, writes: "It is entirely appropriate for the Senate, as well as the President, to consider the social and economic philosophy of persons nominated to the Supreme Court. With the changed conditions of the Court, considerations of this kind are more pertinent than the legal attainments and experience of nominees."[15]

Looking at our history, it is difficult to disagree with Prof. A. E. Howard of the University of Virginia Law School: "Good public policy will argue in favor of thorough senatorial review."[16] A 1971 memorandum by three law professors who researched the issue reached this conclusion:

> It is the Senate's affirmative responsibility to examine a nominee's political and constitutional philosophy, and to confirm his nomination only if he has demonstrated a clear commitment to the fundamental values of our Constitution—the rule of law, the liberty of the individual, and the equality of all persons.[17]

Those who have asserted the right and responsibility of the Senate to look at political philosophy include the current Chief Justice, William Rehnquist. Before he went to the Supreme Court, Rehnquist wrote:

> Until the Senate restores its practice of thoroughly informing itself of the judicial philosophy of a Supreme Court nominee before voting to confirm him, it will have a hard time convincing doubters that it could make effective use of any additional part in the selection process.

He then commented on the confirmation of Justice Charles Evans Whittaker, saying it "reveals a startling dearth of inquiry or even concern over the views of the new Justice on constitutional interpretation."[18] Written thirteen years before Rehnquist went on the Court, its logic still stands.

Coming Before the Committee

A major change has occurred in how the Senate takes up Supreme Court nominations. Until 1929 it closed to the public even the floor debate on the nominations on the theory that Senators could speak with greater candor without reporters and the public present. But distorted reports of Senate action eventually changed that. Judiciary Committee hearings have gradually grown in importance. For most of our early history there were none.

The first Court nominee to testify before the Judiciary Committee was Harlan Fiske Stone in 1925. As Attorney General, Stone had investigated Senator Burton Wheeler of Montana, not an act to endear him to the Senate. While the request to testify came in part out of hostility, Stone handled the situation well. When President Herbert Hoover nominated John Parker and a controversy arose, Parker requested of the Judiciary Committee chairman, Senator George Norris, the right to appear before the Judiciary Committee. Norris turned him down. Felix Frankfurter, a professor at Harvard when nominated by FDR, declined an invitation to appear before a Senate Judiciary subcommittee on the basis that he did not want to be absent from class, but he made it clear that if the subcommittee really wanted him to testify, he would. He appeared on the last day of hearings. Frankfurter became the second Supreme Court nominee to appear before the committee. When Truman nominated Attorney General Tom Clark to the Court, the Judiciary Committee held hearings but did not call Clark. Senator Robert Taft of Ohio used this on the Senate floor in speaking against Clark, saying the Judiciary Committee should have called him to testify. When

President John F. Kennedy nominated Justice Byron White, the entire hearing lasted less than two hours.

Today it is unthinkable that the Judiciary Committee would not call a nominee before it or that a hearing would last only two hours. The hearings are lengthy, detailed and, as today's public expects, televised. Although one recent study by the Twentieth Century Task Force on Judicial Selection recommended that Supreme Court nominees not appear, its report received little support.

Before a confirmation hearing, the Senate Judiciary Committee now gives a nominee a detailed questionnaire that primarily requests information on financial interests, decisions (in the case of a judge), and articles and books or public statements. Earlier in our history, the Senate required none of this.

Two other factors have changed in the Senate process since the early days of the nation. One is that organizations now take an active role in voicing their opinions, from the highly influential American Bar Association reports to the sometimes raucous efforts of those on both left and right. How much influence they have is difficult to gauge, but this author's impression is that the two sides have balanced each other in terms of political effectiveness, and the net result has been less than decisive. Senator Arlen Specter of Pennsylvania, commenting on the Bork nomination, said: "I believe that the Senate was not significantly influenced, if it was influenced at all, by the media advertising campaigns."[19] Attempts by organizations to influence the decision go back to the post-Civil War period and have gradually escalated, reaching their high points in the Herbert Hoover nomination of John Parker, the battles over Justice Brandeis and Justice Fortas, and most recently in the Robert Bork and Clarence Thomas nominations.

One other major change in the Senate cannot be calculated but has played a role: the election of more Senators who take their lead from the pollsters rather than personal conviction. Some argue — and they may be correct — that the polls that went against Bork played the decisive role in his defeat, while in the case of Thomas his narrow margin of victory can be attributed to polls taken after the hearing that showed a majority of Americans favoring his acceptance by the Senate.

Combine that factor with televised hearings, and it is clear the Senate climate has changed markedly. Senators could vote for or against President Grant's nomination of George Williams for Chief Justice with virtually no concern about the reaction in their home states. That is no longer the case. In 1992 at least one Senator, Alan Dixon of Illinois, lost a primary largely because of his vote for Judge Thomas; and another Senator, Arlen Specter of Pennsylvania, faces significantly greater opposition in his home state because of his stand on the Thomas nomination.

While neither the Constitution nor the laws of the land have a requirement that Supreme Court Justices be attorneys, all have been. It is highly unlikely that will change, although it is conceivable that some day a journalist like Irving Dilliard, formerly with the *St. Louis Post-Dispatch,* who became a student of Court history and a champion of civil liberties, might be named to a seat. Justice Hugo Black urged the appointment of a non-lawyer to the Supreme Court. But in a 1975 hearing, Senator Edward Kennedy asked Robert Meserve, former president of the American Bar Association, "Would a non-lawyer automatically be stamped as nonqualified [by the Bar Association]?" Meserve responded: "I think the chances are very good that a non-lawyer would not be regarded as having that [necessary] professional standing . . . . I doubt that such an extraordinary case could arise."[20]

Keeping a Distance

One strong thread runs through our history: great respect for the separation of powers among the three branches that gives the Supreme Court independence. It started with the Constitutional Convention in Philadelphia, and George Washington carried on with that spirit. It has been respected more often than not. Because of close friendships or political ties, sometimes the lines have been blurred. Examples are Lyndon Johnson and Justice Abe Fortas, Abraham Lincoln and Justice David Davis, Warren

Harding and Chief Justice William Howard Taft. But more typical is the response of President Dwight Eisenhower, who had nominated Earl Warren as Chief Justice. Warren invited Eisenhower to the swearing-in ceremony. As future Chief Justice Warren Burger recalled, "The President responded by saying that because of his strong belief in both the reality and the importance of public perception of separation of powers, he would come if invited by the Court. Justice Black then officially invited him."[21] Eisenhower came.

The need for independence by the Court is not questioned by any serious student of American government.

But how to achieve that, and at the same time maintain quality and political balance on the Court, is a question Presidents and Senators have weighed for more than two hundred years.

When the Constitution created the major office of Supreme Court Justice, it also created a system for appointment that would result in some of the major political brawls in our nation's history.

Endnotes

1. Alexis deTocqueville, *Democracy in America*, Ed. Phillips Bradley (New York: Knopf, 1945), p. 180.
2. Theodore H. White, *America in Search of Itself* (New York: Harper and Row, 1982), p. 120.
3. "The Contested Confirmation of Stanley Matthews," by Harold M. Helfman, *Bulletin of the Historical and Philosophical Society of Ohio,*" July 1950, quoting from the *Cincinnati Commercial,* February 2, 1881.
4. Joseph P. Harris, *Advice and Consent of the Senate* (New York: Greenwood Press, 1968), reprint of University of California Press, 1953, p. 42.
5. James Garfield, letter to Burke A. Hinsdale, April 4, 1881, quoted in Harris, p. 86.
6. Former President Gerald Ford, interview with David M. O'Brien, *Supreme Court Yearbook 1989* (Washington: Supreme Court Historical Society), "Filling Justice William O. Douglas's Seat: President Gerald R. Ford's Appointment of Justice John Paul Stevens," p. 20.
7. "Of Politics and the Court," by Justice Lewis F. Powell, Jr. *Supreme Court Year Book 1982* (Washington: Supreme Court Historical Society), address by Justice Powell to the American College of Trial Lawyers, August 8, 1981.
8. Hampton, Carson, *History of the Supreme Court of the United States* (New York: Burt Franklin, 1902), Vol. I., p. 291.
9. President Harry Truman, quoted by Laurence Tribe, *God Save This Honorable Court* (New York: Random House, 1985), p. 51.
10. Robert G. Ingersoll, speech in Washington, October 22, 1883, quoted by H. L. Mencken, *New Dictionary of Quotations* (New York: Knopf, 1942), p. 620.
11. *Nomination of Earl L. Butz,* Senate Committee on Agriculture and Forestry, p. 57, quoted in address by G. Calvin McKenzie to the Southwest Political Science Association, 1977, p. 9.

12. Charles Warren, *The Supreme Court in United States History, 1836-1918* (Boston: Little, Brown, 1935). Vol. 2, pp. 4-5.

13. "A Note on Senatorial Consideration of Supreme Court Nominee," by Charles L. Black, Jr., *Yale Law Journal,* March 1970, Vol. 79, No. 4, p. 657.

14. *Ibid., p. 659.*

15. Harris, p. 313.

16. Statement of Prof. A. E. Howard before the Subcommittee on Separation of Powers, Senate Judiciary Committee, 1976, p. 3.

17. Memorandum of Paul Brest and Thomas C. Grey of Stanford University and Arnold M. Paul of Michigan State University to Senator Birch Bayh and Senator John V. Tunney, October 21, 1971, Senate Judiciary Committee Records.

18. "The Making of A Supreme Court Justice," William H. Rehnquist, *Harvard Law Record*, October 8, 1959, Vol. 29, No. 2.

19. "On the Confirmation of a Supreme Court Justice," by Senator Arlen Specter, *Northwestern University Law Review,* 1990, Vol. 84, Nos. 3 and 4, p. 1,043.

20. *Advice and Consent on Supreme Court Nominations,* Subcommittee on Separation of Powers, Senate Judiciary Committee (Washington: Government Printing Office, 1976), p.6.

21. "My Predecessor: Earl Warren," by Chief Justice Warren Burger, *Supreme Court Yearbook 1989* (Washington: Supreme Court Historical Society), p. 17.

Part II

Recent History

3

The Bork Battle

When Ronald Reagan ran for President, he pledged to nominate a woman to the United States Supreme Court. It would, however, have to be someone who met his philosophical criteria, since he had spent much of his political speech-making warming up crowds with criticisms of the Court. Five months after Reagan became President, Justice Potter Stewart announced that he would retire.

A member of the Arizona Court of Appeals, Sandra Day O'Connor, a former state legislator, quickly became one of the primary possibilities. Fellow Arizonans Justice Rehnquist and Senator Barry Goldwater pushed her nomination, as did others. President Ford had considered her when he nominated Justice Stevens. When Reagan announced the O'Connor choice, not only did he received support from Goldwater but also from Senator Edward Kennedy. The nomination was rightfully viewed as a step forward for women. O'Connor had experienced the prejudices that women face. After graduating third in her law school class at Stanford, she could get a job only as a legal secretary while males far behind her in the same class received generous offers from law firms. She soon moved to working for county government as an attorney.

Her conservative credentials pleased conservatives, and liberals were pleased to see a woman on the Court. One study describes her as "a solid professional who held vaguely conservative views."[1] Because her anti-abortion views were somewhat undefined, Rev. Jerry Falwell, heading a group called "Moral Majority," called her nomination "a disaster" and urged all "good Christians" to convey their feelings to Senators.[2] Barry Goldwater responded: "Every good Christian ought to kick Falwell right in the ass."[3] The Judiciary Committee approved her 17-0 and the Senate, 99-0.

A New Chief Justice

A more difficult but also successful nomination followed when Chief Justice Burger resigned in 1986, and the President named Associate Justice Rehnquist, the most conservative member of the Court, to the chief justiceship. Reagan knew that the nomination would invite oratorical sparks, but he also calculated correctly that the Rehnquist nomination would be approved. My major concern was that the Court's most conservative voice would be elevated to the position of Chief Justice, the symbol of justice for the nation. Several Senate colleagues and I felt that in this symbolic role minorities and the powerless of the nation could not look to him as their champion, their symbol of justice.

The closest Rehnquist came to having problems occurred when Kennedy pursued him for challenging minority voters at two precincts in southwest Phoenix several years before he went on the Court. People submitted affidavits on this, and Rehnquist either denied the validity of the claims in the affidavits or in some cases said he could not remember details of things that happened, in some instances twenty years earlier. The most effective witness regarding this was James Brosnahan, a San Francisco attorney.

Rehnquist at first felt he should not attend a Judiciary Committee hearing, citing Justice Minton as an example. Minton served on the Appellate Court when Truman nominated him and declined to appear before the Judiciary Committee. White House staff persuaded Rehnquist that he had to do it. Rehnquist and another nominee resented what one called the "wordy, convoluted questions" of Senator Arlen Specter, Republican of Pennsylvania. At one point Rehnquist told the White House staff, "I'm not going one word further with that guy." They cautioned patience and he followed their advice. A later nominee, Robert Bork, told the White House staff, "I don't understand where he's coming from." While Specter's questions at times were "wordy and convoluted," Specter does solid homework, and they probably resented most the "attack style that he uses."

The Committee approved Rehnquist 13-5. I voted against the nomination, as did Senators Joe Biden of Delaware, Kennedy, Howard Metzenbaum of Ohio and Patrick Leahy of Vermont–all Democrats.

The Senate approved Rehnquist as Chief Justice 65-33. While many Senators continue to differ with the Chief Justice in political philosophy, and a rerun in the Senate vote would not produce a significantly different result, there is general agreement that he has handled the administrative aspects of the position with great skill.

To fill the vacant spot as Associate Justice, Reagan nominated Appellate Court Justice Antonin Scalia, recognized for his ability, scholarship and self-deprecating sense of humor. He faced criticism from Senators Dennis DeConcini, Democrat of Arizona, and Specter for being evasive in answering questions, but without great difficulty he received a unanimous vote of approval, both in the Committee and on the Senate floor. A French student of U.S. politics called the handling of the Scalia nomination by the Senate "strangely eventless considering the profile of the nominee and the political atmosphere of the time."[4] Later, in a speech on a college campus, Scalia called Senate Judiciary hearings on Supreme Court nominations "an absurd spectacle."[5] (Sometimes "spectacles" help us to see things more clearly.) In the same speech, the *Legal Times* reported: "Perhaps Scalia's most controversial comments came in response to a question from a woman in the audience. She asked Scalia what she was supposed to tell her granddaughter about who was protecting her rights when the Supreme Court was mainly male. There was reportedly a gasp from the audience when Scalia seemed to shrug off the question with a sarcastic remark that the questioner's granddaughter would simply have to rely on her male relatives for protection." It is probable that if Scalia were up for reconfirmation today, there would be at least a scattering of votes against him. Some Senators feel that he has been more rigidly conservative than they had anticipated. I would include myself in that number. But on some issues, such as First Amendment cases, his is not a totally predictable vote.

The "Swing Seat" Opens Up

The "swing seat" on the Court often was Justice Powell, and in June 1987, he announced his retirement. Because Chief Justice Burger generally would be labeled a conservative, Burger's replacement by Scalia as a vote on the Court, when Rehnquist moved to Chief Justice, did not cause as much concern among many Court observers as the replacement for the Powell seat.

Reagan chose a man long talked about for the Court, a man of unquestioned intellectual skills and long a favorite of the right wing of the Republican Party, Appellate Court Justice Robert Bork. Once a poll-watcher for Socialists, he gradually drifted rightward, delivering literature for Adlai E. Stevenson in 1952 on the Bork trek to the right. In making the announcement the President described Bork as "well prepared, evenhanded and openminded."[6] Although he had been confirmed unanimously for the Appellate Court, his move to the highest court immediately set off fireworks.

Whether in a speech such as one at the University of Michigan questioning whether free speech and freedom of the press have gone too far, or an address at Catholic University suggesting that the Supreme Court had created rights—specifically the right to use contraceptives and the right of a woman to have an abortion—that are not in the Constitution, Bork had stimulated the thinking of his audiences—and he obviously enjoyed that. However, most of us in the Senate knew him more by reputation than from reading what he wrote. I had read a little–and like reading William Buckley–found Bork thought-provoking even when I disagreed, though his style is much more ponderous than the Buckley prose.

Robert Bork criticized the "one man, one vote" decision of the Court, as well as civil rights rulings. Sometimes he appeared to make extreme statements either to please the audience or to stimulate discussion. Those talks gave him a following—and led to difficulty. In the *National Catholic Reporter,* Father Robert Drinan, a former U.S. House member and a professor of law at Georgetown University, wrote:

> Bork's anti-civil rights positions are almost unbelievable. He wrote in 1971 that the Supreme Court was wrong in 1948 when it ruled that the 14th amendment forbade state-court enforcement of racially restrictive convenants .... Bork has even stated that the Supreme Court's decision in 1966 striking down Virginia's poll tax was "wrongly decided."[7]

One Yale observer called Bork "intensely cynical about the law and the possibility for what it can do"—and that appealed to some and repelled others.[8] One writer commented that Bork's problem was not his conservatism, but that he "looked like a warrior in that cause."[9]

Preparing for the Judiciary Committee hearings on Bork was not easy because of the volume of opinions, articles and speeches he had authored. Deborah Leavy headed my staff effort on this, working with volunteer lawyers and law school faculty members, carefully going through the mountain of material. Then they would give a smaller bundle to me, which I read, marked up, and sometimes sent back for more research. Questioning by Committee members proceeds on the basis of seniority, alternating between Democrats and Republicans. In many hearings, the material left for questioning by a junior member of the Committee is slim, sometimes so slim that no questions are asked. In the case of the Bork hearings, the opportunities were so plentiful that we could have doubled the size of the Committee and still had ample material for serious questioning.

In his book, *The Tempting of America,* Bork gives his view of what happened in the Judiciary Committee. According to Bork, liberal groups organized in opposition put on a massive national advertising campaign to defeat him. He charges that these groups pressured enough senators to waver in their support and finally vote against him. What is not stated in the book is that his supporters also mounted a strong campaign for Bork, and backing him were the powerful and vigorous lobbying efforts of the White House as well as the additional outside lobbyists hired through the administration. The much-talked-about television advertising campaign against Bork by People for the American Way consisted of $165,000 in paid commercials in seven cities and on Cable News Network. This amount is less than is spent on television advertising in most House races. Nina Totenberg of National Public Radio observed: "The process was affected by the advertising campaign against him, but my guess is that the effect was minimal."[10] I agree with her conclusion.

From my perspective — one with which Bork would disagree — what defeated Robert Bork in the Judiciary Committee hearings was Robert Bork. If a vote had been taken when the hearings began, he would have emerged with a 9-5 or 8-6 majority on the Committee. I would have been in the minority, although I had not announced any position because I was willing to be persuaded that Bork was more open than I sensed from reading his record and his writings.

There were twelve days of hearings, more than for any nominee in the history of nominations to the Court except for Justice Brandeis (though the acrimony in the Brandeis nomination exceeded that of the Bork nomination).

Former President Gerald Ford, who had declined to nominate Bork to the Court, testified first, calling him a person who "is uniquely qualified to sit on the U.S. Supreme Court."[11]

The opening statements by Senators began with words of praise from Republican Senator Strom Thurmond of South Carolina. Then Senator Kennedy sounded a trumpet call for the nation to do battle:

> Robert Bork falls short of what Americans demand of a man or woman as a Justice on the Supreme Court. Time and again, in his public record over more than a quarter of a century, Robert Bork has shown that he is hostile to the rule of law and the role of the courts in protecting individual liberty . . . . He has consistently demonstrated his hostility towards equal justice for all . . . . In Robert Bork's America, there is no room at the inn for blacks, and no place in the Constitution for women, and in our America there should be no seat on the Supreme Court for Robert Bork.[12]

In turn, the Committee members indicated their leaning. Republican members of the Committee, with the exception of Senator Specter, showed their strong tilt toward Bork. Senator Metzenbaum, almost as clearly, sided with Kennedy. Senator Leahy commented:

> Robert Bork is an intellectual of the first order. He is a thinker; he is a philosopher. And he comes before this committee with a more comprehensive and clearly expressed judicial philosophy than any nominee to the Supreme Court in recent history . . . . In article after article, in speech after speech, Judge Bork has criticized the constitutional decisions of the Supreme Court . . . . His targets have included the Court's major decisions in areas as important as free speech, the right of privacy and equal protection of the laws.

In opening statements, Senators Biden, Howell Heflin of Alabama, Robert Byrd of West Virginia and I, all Democrats, did not indicate how we would vote.

Bork's Testimony

Five volumes of hearings, more than 6,000 tightly printed pages, provide evidence of the thoroughness of the hearings. Bork's writing, much more than his testimony, showed why he had become a hero to many of the far-right and close-to-far-right. In his testimony he came across as a person of great ability as well as rigidity. My concerns about his attitudes on fundamental questions of civil rights and civil liberties, as well as sensitivity to the least fortunate, were not allayed.

We did not expect him to answer questions on how he might rule on *Roe v. Wade.* A potential Justice properly can decline to answer that direct question, though if the nominee has specific views, they could be disclosed with the cautionary word that a general attitude might not dictate how the nominee would vote on a specific case that would come before the Court. There are critics who say that what Bork said before the nomination and what he has written afterward suggest a clear course of evasion on his part in the hearings.

The question of privacy, however, is beyond dispute a legitimate area of inquiry. Bork's views on the privacy issue concerned some of us, what he called "the general and undefined 'right of privacy' invented in *Griswold v. Connecticut,*" the decision that said a state could not outlaw the use of contraceptives.[13]

While the Constitution does not speak directly of a general right of privacy in Amendments III and IV of the Bill of Rights, it does speak about specific examples of privacy: "No Soldier, shall, in time of peace be quartered in any house, without the consent of the Owner, nor in time of war, but in a manner prescribed by law" (Amendment III). And in the next amendment: "The right of the people to be secure in their persons, houses, papers, and effects, against unreasonable searches and seizures, shall not be violated, and no Warrants shall issue, but upon probable cause, supported by Oath or affirmation, and particularly describing the place to be searched, and the persons or things to be seized."

These two amendments speak about specific aspects of privacy. When these are combined with the little noticed but extremely important Ninth Amendment, the spirit of the Constitution is clear. Madison drafted the Ninth Amendment because Alexander Hamilton wrote to him that if he spelled out certain basic rights, there will be some who would claim that these are the only rights people have. So the Ninth Amendment became part of the Constitution: "The enumeration of certain rights shall not be construed to deny or disparage others retained by the people." Combine all three amendments, and there is a strong spirit for protecting the privacy of citizens.

The Supreme Court recognized the liberty clause of the Fourteenth Amendment as an additional source of protection for the fundamental right of privacy. The Court relied on the Fourteenth Amendment in *Roe v. Wade,* holding that the right to privacy includes the right of a woman to decide whether or not to have an abortion.

Bork's testimony made clear that the Ninth Amendment is not high on a list of Constitutional amendments that are significant to him. In a 1986 speech about abuses of the Constitution, he mentioned as one abuse that

> a few judges, and even more academics, flirt with the Ninth Amendment as yet another . . . source of substantive rights to be created by the federal judiciary.[14]

In other speeches he referred to the Ninth Amendment as an ink blot or a water blot on the Constitution, a meaningless smudge.[15] When Senator Thurmond asked him, "What do you believe the Ninth Amendment means?" the Judge responded:

> That is an extremely difficult question . . . . I have seen . .
> . some historical research appearing in the Virginia Law
> Review which suggests . . . that the enumeration of
> Federal rights in the Bill of Rights shall not be construed
> to deny or disparage the right retained by the people in
> their State constitutions. And that is the only explanation
> that has any plausibility to it that I have seen so far.[16]

That is a rigidly narrow interpretation of rights "retained by the people." When witnesses testified that Bork had a limited view of civil liberties and civil rights, the evidence was not only his numerous writings and court decisions, but also testimony before the Committee, particularly as it related to the Ninth Amendment. In response to Senator Kennedy, he also said that "a generalized, undefined right of privacy is not in the Bill of Rights."[17]

Up until this point, the mail on Bork, generated by both sides in an organized fashion, came into Senate offices about evenly on both sides. But the nominee's comments on privacy in nationally televised hearings caused the opposition mail to rise.

The *Roe v. Wade* abortion decision made these privacy questions particularly pertinent, but the concerns about the nominee's philosophy went much beyond that one issue. Former Secretary of Transportation William T. Coleman, a Republican who served under Presidents Ford and Nixon, told the Committee: "While Judge Bork is willing to read the Commerce Clause broadly, when it comes to the great clauses dealing with human rights, for some reason Judge Bork says such rights are not there."[18] Professor Barbara Jordan of the University of Texas, a former member of the House, made an eloquent plea against the nomination.

The White House staff tried to get Bork to appear less rigid, to lecture less to the Committee. They sensed that he had disdain for the whole process, both the White House part and the Senate part. They advised him to soften his approach by starting with the phrase, "That's a fascinating question." He partially followed their advice, but after using the phrase immediately moved into the lecture mode again. When a series of questions on the privacy issue seemed to be hurting him, the White House staff slipped a question to Senator Gordon Humphrey, Republican of New Hampshire, changing the subject. Bork answered in part by saying, "I haven't given that much thought." He then immediately got back into the previous dispute. Bork tended to want to score debate points, rather than appeal to the Committee for votes. "He's too professorial," Senator Heflin told a Justice Department staff member.[19]

All the witnesses praised his ability; that never came into question. But many respected witnesses said approving him would be too great a risk for the nation. Historian John Hope Franklin testified: "There is no indication in his writings, his teachings or his rulings that this nominee has any deeply held commitment to the eradication of the problem of race or even its mitigation. One searches his record in vain to find a civil rights advance that he supported from its inception."[20] Legal scholar John Frank observed:

> Bork is a judicial activist beyond anything Earl Warren ever dreamed of. The difference between Judge Bork and his predecessor, Justice Powell, is very dramatic; Justice Powell was a conservative judge who restricted his necessary lawmaking to new situations. Judge Bork . . . makes law as though precedent were meaningless and the Congress were in permanent recess.[21]

Yale Law School's Paul Gewirtz, well regarded by Senators who have had a chance to work with him, said that Bork's

> long-standing and forcefully espoused views critical of so much of constitutional law lead me to conclude that this nomination poses a serious risk to settled and fundamental constitutional values . . . . What is especially troubling about Judge Bork's positions about such landmark racial equality [matters] . . . such as the historic civil rights legislation in 1964 . . . is that Judge Bork stood against all of those legal developments when it counted, and no

latter day recantation or acceptance of prior precedent
can really erase that . . . . When it really counted in the
development of the law, Judge Bork repeatedly objected
to any 14th amendment coverage of sex equality matters.[22]

Harvard scholar Laurence Tribe testified against him. And
former President Jimmy Carter sent the committee a letter:

As a Southerner who has observed personally the long
and difficult years of the struggle for civil rights for black
and other minority peoples, I find Judge Bork's impres-
sively consistent opinions to be particularly obnoxious . .
. . Only recently, with the vision of a seat on the Supreme
Court providing some enlightenment, has Judge Bork
attempted to renounce some of his more radical writings
and rulings. It seems obvious that, once confirmed, those
lifelong attitudes that he has so frequently expressed
would once again assert themselves on the court and have
a deleterious effect on future decisions involving personal
freedom, justice for the deprived, and basic human
rights.[23]

But if he had an array of star witnesses opposing him, the
nominee also had an array of star supporters, including the
former Chief Justice, Warren Burger, describing him as "well
qualified."[24] Lloyd Cutler, Washington attorney and former
counsel to President Jimmy Carter, called him "a highly
qualified, conservative jurist, who is closer to the moderate
center than to the extreme right."[25] Governor James Thompson
of Illinois, a former U.S. Attorney, testified for him. Former
Attorney General Griffin Bell, who served under President
Carter, told the Committee, "I would vote to confirm Judge
Bork, and I do so on the view that he is sensitive and he has never
taken any right away from anyone."[26] Professor Thomas
Campbell of Stanford University's Law School (now a member
of the U.S. House) testified that the AFL-CIO's claim that
Bork's record had a strong anti-union bias to it was in error. "The
committee's hearings might be advanced," he said, "by remov-

ing from the debate the concept that Judge Bork is anti-union. That simply is not true."[27] He analyzed several cases to reach that conclusion.

Bork's pattern of coming out fairly consistently on the side of the financially powerful bothered some of us. Senator Leahy compounded that problem for Bork when he questioned whether he had done any *pro bono* work (free legal service) for those less fortunate, either while in private practice or while teaching at Yale. Bork said, "To tell you the truth, Senator, I was not asked, and I was busy working on other things and I didn't think about it."[28] The American Bar Association's Model Rules of Professional Conduct include this admonition: "A lawyer should render public interest legal service." When my turn came for questioning, I said:

> I was a little surprised to hear your response to Senator Leahy on pro bono work. One of the things that is important for a Justice on the Court . . . to have is some understanding of those less fortunate in our society. Are there other things that you have done with the less fortunate in your sixty years . . . helping or volunteering to work with the retarded or whatever it may be?

Bork responded, "No, Senator, I can't claim a record of that sort."[29]

Not a dominant consideration in the hearings, but a small factor, was the role Bork played as Nixon's Solicitor General during the Watergate trauma the nation experienced. A special prosecutor had been appointed to look into the matter, and when it became clear to the President that the appointed counsel, Archibald Cox, had every intention of being aggressive, the President ordered Attorney General Elliot Richardson to fire Cox. Richardson refused and resigned. Nixon then told Deputy Attorney General William Ruckelshaus to dismiss Cox and he refused and resigned. Nixon then told Bork, as Solicitor General and Acting Attorney General, to fire Cox, and he did. The firing and forced resignations became known as the Saturday Night

Massacre. One of those active in the House Judiciary hearings on the Watergate matter, Barbara Jordan, told the Senate Committee:

> On the day and at the time that Robert Bork fired Archibald Cox, there were rules and regulations in place . . . with the force and effect of law. They were violated, and to me that means the Solicitor General acted illegally.[30]

The majority of the Committee members felt Bork should not have complied with the President's request to fire Cox; but having done that, he conducted himself responsibly afterwards with the appointment of Leon Jaworski as the new Special Prosecutor, assuring Jaworski of complete independence as well as cooperation. After the Saturday Night Massacre, Bork sent a message to all of the employees of the Department of Justice:

> Until very recently, I was a professor at Yale Law School. I am not a politician in any sense of the word and I have no intention of becoming one . . . . The past week has not been easy for any of us . . . . I will try, as long as I am acting Attorney General, to meet the highest standards of professional responsibility and integrity. I have no doubt you will continue to do the same. Mr. Richardson, Mr. Ruckelshaus and the American people have a right to expect we will do no less.[31]

An examination of the records of the Judiciary Committee in the National Archives does not suggest any improper conduct after the initial firing, and Bork would argue that the firing itself was a proper action, one that helped prevent chaos from erupting in the federal government.[32]

The evaluation committee of the American Bar Association gave Bork a mixed review: Ten members found him well-qualified; one did not oppose him; and four found him not qualified. The American Bar Association's mixed reviews, extraordinary if not unique in the history of its evaluation of Supreme Court Justices, caused fury on the part of Bork supporters on the Committee. They accused the Bar Association of having a political litmus test.

The Judiciary Committee voted 9-5 not to confirm Judge Bork, all Democrats voting no, joined by Senator Specter. Although the hearings started with a majority for him, the vote gradually changed. This shifting of votes is difficult to pinpoint, but after some experience with a legislative body, members and observers develop a sense of what is happening. Two things were clear: Bork portrayed himself as both rigid and professorial–Senators were the students receiving the lectures–and the small signals in comments from the members, both private and public, did not signal a favorable omen. The two factors that tipped the decision for me were his restrictive views of civil liberties and a lack of any empathy for the less fortunate. Before the hearings started, most observers agreed with *Newsweek*: "Bork is likely to be confirmed."[33] What changed the Committee vote was not a mail or media campaign, nor even the testimony of other witnesses, but the testimony of the nominee himself. In its report to the full Senate, the Committee cited an exchange I had with Bork:

Simon: At a speech at Berkeley in 1985, you say, "When a court adds to one person's constitutional rights it subtracts from the rights of others." Do you believe that is always true?

Bork: Yes, Senator. I think it's a matter of plain arithmetic .
. . .

Simon: I have long thought it is kind of fundamental in our society, that when you expand the liberty of any of us, you expand the liberty of all of us.

Bork: I think, Senator, that is not correct.[34]

The report also quotes Senator Heflin of Alabama: "A lifetime position on the Supreme Court is too important a risk to a person who has continued to exhibit — and may still possess — a proclivity for extremism in spite of confirmation protestations."[35]

The minority on the Committee filed its dissent, praising Judge Bork's abilities — which no one questioned — and said he is "well within the judicial mainstream"–which many questioned.[36]

The Floor Debate

When the nomination reached the floor, debate was more solemn than usual. Members checked their speeches — often prepared by staff — with more care. There is a widely held belief among Senators that, next to a declaration of war, voting on a Supreme Court nominee is the most long-ranging decision a Senator can make.

A Senator who does not receive as much favorable attention as he merits, Harry Reid of Nevada, spoke on the floor the same day the Judiciary Committee issued its report, saying that as a conservative Democrat, he hoped for "a conservative Justice to fill that vacant seat. It has been my belief that in some areas the court has gone much too far . . . I hoped to see a restraining brake applied." But he concluded, "Raw intellect is not enough."[37]

Senators loaded the Congressional Record with editorials endorsing or faulting Bork, with more editorials supporting him. Senator Daniel Evans, Republican of Washington, told the Senate: "I have had . . . over 15,000 letters which probably, if you measure them for and against, give me little solace for they are split almost precisely evenly."[38] The National Conservative Political Action Committee mounted a national telephone drive in which President Reagan told the listener:

> Judge Bork . . . has been subjected to a constant litany of character assassination and intentional misrepresentation. Tell your Senators to resist the politicization of our court system. Tell them you support the appointment of Judge Robert Bork.[39]

People for the American Way and the American Civil Liberties Union ran anti-Bork advertisements and made appeals. A group called "We the People" ran pro-Bork, full-page advertisements in key states. Each side accused the other of misrepresentation and unethical conduct.

The formal debate on the floor started October 21, 1987, within a month of the two-hundredth anniversary of the Philadelphia agreement for a new Constitution. The debate appropriately became a discussion of what the Constitution means and what it does and does not say about privacy, civil rights and other liberties. Senators Biden and Thurmond, the leaders of their parties on the Judiciary Committee, launched the formal debate. Biden said the debate centered on what rights the government has and what rights are reserved to the people. Thurmond, on a point-by-point basis, refuted the charges made against Bork.

Most speeches were predictable, and most Senators had decided by this time how they would vote. But in a close contest, one vote might be crucial, so Senate oratory continued for the one or two or six Senators not yet decided. The President and the Cabinet were on the phone to Senators, to firm up votes, to switch votes, to convince those uncommitted. As the campaign intensified, the President made national appeals in five of his weekly radio broadcasts and a national television address in prime time. "His nomination is being opposed by some because he practices judicial restraint," Reagan said. "That means he won't put their opinions ahead of the law; he won't put his own opinions ahead of the law."[40] Wherever the President spoke, he made appeals for the nominee, whether to a meeting of presidential appointees, or to citizens gathered at North Platte, Nebraska, or at the signing of the proclamation for National Hispanic Heritage Week. He told a convention of law enforcement officials in Los Angeles:

> Robert Bork has demonstrated a genuine concern for the right of our citizens to live in safe communities and a clear understanding of the problems facing today's law enforcement officials.... It's time we reassert the fundamental principle of the purpose of criminal justice is to find the truth, not to coddle criminals.[41]

When it became clear that Bork had serious problems in the Senate, Reagan told a New Jersey audience: "If I have to appoint another one, I'll try to find one that they'll object to just as much as they did for this one."[42] As the campaign intensified, public interest increased, and polls showed the American people opposing the nomination. The first poll by *CBS-New York Times* showed 14 percent for Bork, 13 percent opposed, 63 percent undecided. Just prior to the hearings, a Gallup poll showed 31 percent for Bork, 25 percent opposed. After the hearings, opinion shifted dramatically: 32 percent for, 52 percent opposed.[43] An *Atlanta Constitution* poll of twelve southern states showed 51 percent against Bork's confirmation, and even whites opposed him 44 to 39 percent.[44]

National television had, once again, lifted interest and sharpened opinions. One national political observer said off-screen, "His beard doesn't help him. He looks like the radical some paint him to be." Bork had asked the White House staff whether he should shave it off. They advised against it, though one staff member had second thoughts when a Republican Senator told him, "He does look sort of weird." The beard should not have played a role, but it may have had a slight impact on public opinion and, through public opinion, on the Senate.

Senator William Proxmire, Democrat of Wisconsin, said he had yet to make up his mind, but he felt the administration dominated the decision-making far too much. He criticized the nominee visiting Senators in their offices and major players within the administration doing the same. "It is very easy to say, I like you. I'm going to vote for you," Proxmire told his colleagues.[45]

Senator Biden inserted into the *Record* the names of 1,925 law school faculty members who went on record against Bork, approximately forty percent of the law school faculty in the nation. That was countered by articles and letters from others supporting the nominee. A group calling itself "Citizens for Bork" placed a large advertisement in the *Birmingham* (Alabama) *News,* addressed to Senator Heflin, who voted against Bork in the Committee. Signed by hundreds of citizens, it had this message:

> Perhaps better than anyone else in our nation, you knew and understood the events which were being played out in your presence .... We know that every fiber of your being cried out against the lynch mob of the special interest and media blitz against the nomination of Judge Bork. And yet, in the end, you capitulated .... Your vote on Judge Bork will determine whether the Supreme Court is going to control America or whether we will remain a constitutional government .... Since no American wants the Supreme Court to run the country, please place principle above party and vote for Judge Bork .... Signed: Your fellow countrymen who bow our knees not to political expediency, but only to God.[46]

On October 23rd the Senate voted; all one hundred Senators were present. Judge Bork lost, 58-42, the largest vote against a Supreme Court nominee in history. In the words of Senator Specter, the Senate rejected him "because his views were so extreme."[47] Six Republicans voted with an almost solid group of Democrats. Two Democrats, Senator Ernest Hollings of South Carolina and Senator David Boren of Oklahoma, voted for Bork. The attempt to sell the nominee as a moderate, similar to the retiring Justice Powell, simply did not wash.

Less than two months later, Judge Bork resigned his seat on the Appellate Court to write and lecture and stimulate, perhaps an occupation he enjoys more. In a warm letter accepting his resignation, the President wished him well "on this new course in selfless service of the cause of truth and justice in the public arena." Reagan said he was "uniquely well suited to carry that debate forward."[48]

Bork lost in the Senate, yet even those of us who voted against confirmation came away with respect for him. Most Senators at least partially agree with the writer who commented:

> Few compare in the seriousness of their lifelong engage-
> ment with the fundamental questions of constitutional
> law . . . . It is a tragedy that the Republic should repay him
> for his decades of service by publicly humiliating him.[49]

I would vote against him again — as he would vote against
me — because of our differing political philosophies. But he will
contribute significantly to the continuing dialogue that is so
essential for a free people.

After the Bork vote, National Public Radio commentator Nina
Totenberg wrote:

> The Senate Judiciary Committee's job must be to inves-
> tigate the nominee thoroughly. Usually, it fails miserably,
> relying with great consistency on the press and even the
> Bar Association to do its work . . . . the Committee's
> hearings on the nomination of Judge Robert Bork were . .
> . the first time the process worked properly . . . . The
> Senate, for a change, gave itself enough time, and the
> Senators prepared themselves. They asked probing but,
> for the most part, respectful and proper questions, and
> they knew enough to follow up and find out what the
> nominee really meant in his answers.[50]

After the Bork defeat, Reagan nominated another Appellate
judge, Douglas H. Ginsburg, on October 29. The media soon
reported that some years earlier — in his post-student days as a
college professor — he had used marijuana. The problem was not
simply the use of the marijuana but that it had not been disclosed.
Nominees appear before the White House "Murder Board," an
informal grilling group of ten or twelve designed to make the
Judiciary Committee questioning easier. They ask the toughest
questions they can, and then critique the answers to improve
them. One of the questions routinely asked is, "What is the most
embarrassing thing in your past the Committee might ask you?"
Ginsburg did not mention the marijuana. Now all potential
nominees are routinely asked "the Ginsburg question," whether

they have used marijuana or any illegal drug. Before any hearings could be held, Ginsburg withdrew his name.

On November 11, the President nominated another Appellate Court Judge–Anthony Kennedy of California. Less outspoken and more diplomatic, Judge Kennedy did a good job of what the White House calls "schmoozing Senators." When he saw Senator Byrd, Kennedy mentioned his interest in history and his appreciation of the contributions Byrd had made to the study of Senate history. It pleased Byrd, who has spent a great deal of time on this project. The White House learned that Senator Hatch was mildly unhappy because when Kennedy visited a few key members on a fast trip to Washington, he had not visited Hatch who had been prominently mentioned as a possible nominee to the Court. The White House got word to Kennedy, and the nominee called Hatch from the airport. Kennedy told Hatch that he teaches part-time and then added: "I have a film of the Bork hearings, and your questions were superb. I use them in my class to illustrate questioning at its best." The next day Hatch told a White House staff member, "Kennedy will be OK." Kennedy gained easy Senate approval.

How had Bork become the nominee? Former Senator Howard Baker, highly esteemed on the Washington scene, served as President Reagan's chief-of-staff after Donald Regan had been fired, with a not-so-gentle nudge from Nancy Reagan and others. Baker and the President had their regular 9:00 a.m. meeting to talk over the day's events and other matters, a meeting not to be interrupted except for an emergency. A message came that the Chief Justice was on the phone for the President. Reagan asked Baker to take the call, and they learned that Justice Powell had submitted his resignation. The President asked for a list of possible nominees. Baker, Attorney General Edwin Meese and White House Counsel A. B. Culvahouse prepared a list of five names and gave it to the President. The four of them discussed the names, with Meese pushing Bork, and Baker having another choice. "Meese at no time strong-armed the President on this as some accounts have charged," Baker said. Baker went to the

Senate and talked to Senators Biden, Thurmond, Bob Dole of Kansas and Robert Byrd of West Virginia. He mentioned they were in the process of selecting a nominee but took great pains to be discreet so that names would not appear in the newspapers. He did drop the names of two or three possibilities. Baker's recollection is that Biden indicated storm signals for Bork.

Senator Biden, in Chicago in the midst of his campaign for the 1988 Democratic presidential nomination, received a phone call from the White House that the President wanted to see him. Biden had to be in Houston that evening for a televised debate. He flew to Washington to meet with Reagan, who showed him a list of five possible nominees, to get Biden's advice. Without committing himself, Biden gave an analysis of various possibilities. One name on the list, Robert Bork, caused Biden to tell the President, "If you nominate him, you'll have trouble on your hands." Biden flew immediately to Houston, and when he arrived, found himself surrounded by reporters who wanted to know what he thought of the Bork nomination. The President had "consulted," but obviously had determined his course before talking to Biden, hoping to appear to follow the "advice" part of the Constitution by talking to Biden.

When the President decided on Bork, the White House went all out for the nominee. Baker's analysis of what happened: "Bork was brilliant, but he turned off the Committee."

Having learned his lesson with Bork's loss, when the next vacancy occurred, the President genuinely consulted with Biden and showed him a list that included David Souter and Anthony Kennedy. Without committing himself, Biden indicated to the President that he felt Kennedy would be approved by the Senate, as he was.

When Bush became President, even a gesture toward consulting with the Senate ended.

Endnotes

1. "Transformative Appointments," by Bruce Ackerman, *Harvard Law Review,* April 1988.

2. Abraham, p. 340; and "Sandra Day O'Connor," by David Savage, in *Eight Men and A Lady* (Bethesda, MD: National Press Books, 1990), p. 214.

3. Quoted in Abraham, p. 340.

4. Vincent Michelot, memorandum to Paul Simon, undated.

5. "Scalia on Women," *Legal Times,* February 17, 1992.

6. *Public Papers of Ronald Reagan, 1987* (Washington: Government Printing Office, 1989), Book 1, p. 736.

7. "Senate to Anti-Bork Vote Would Fit U.S. Tradition," by Robert Drinan, *National Catholic Reporter,* July 31, 1987.

8. Unnamed person quoted in "Catching the Last Train to the Court," by Frank Trippett, *Time.* July 13, 1987.

9. "Judicial Selection and the Mask of Nonpartisanship, " by Carol Rose, *Northwestern University Law Review,* Spring/Summer 1990, Vol. 84, Nos. 3 and 4.

10. "The Confirmation and the Public," by Nina Totenberg, *Harvard Law Review,* April 1988.

11. *Nomination of Robert H. Bork to Be Associate Justice,* Hearings, Senate Judiciary Committee (Washington, Government Printing Office, 1989), Part 1, p. 10; hereafter referred to as *Bork Hearings.*

12. *Ibid., pp. 33-34.*

13. Robert Bork, *The Tempting of America* (New York: Free Press, 1990), p. 290.

14. Speech to the Attorney General's Conference, Washington, D.C. June 14, 1986, National Archives.

15. Quoted in *Battle for Justice,* by Ethan Bronner (New York: Norton, 1989), p. 269.

16. *Bork Hearings,* Part 1, p. 130.

17. *Ibid.,* p. 150.

18. *Ibid.,* p. 872.

19. Quoted in Bronner, p. 227.

20. *Bork Hearings,* Part 2, p. 2121.

21. *Ibid.,* pp. 2556-2557.

22. *Ibid.,* pp. 2556-2557.

23. Jimmy Carter to Joe Biden, September 29, 1987, *Ibid,* p.4249.

24. *Ibid,,* p. 2101.

25. *Ibid.,* p. 2158.

26. *Ibid.,* Part 3, p. 2807.

27. *Ibid.,* Part 2, p. 1368.

28. *Ibid.,* Part 1, p. 419.

29. *Ibid.,* Part 1, p. 438.

30. *Ibid.,* Part 1, p. 1006.

31. Robert Bork, Message to All Justice Department Employees, October 31, 1973, National Archives, 62-55047-1887.

32. National Archives, NNL-92-59; 36 and 39 of 43.

33. "Trying to Leave a Conservative Legacy," by Aric Press, *Newsweek,* July 13, 1987.

34. *Nomination of Robert H. Bork,* Report of the Senate Judiciary Committee (Washington: Government Printing Office, 1987), p. 11.

35. *Ibid.,* p.95.

36. *Ibid.,* p.215.

37. *Congressional Record,* Senate, October 13, 1987, p. 14087.

38. *Congressional Record,* Senate, October 15, 1987, p. 14363.

39. Quote in *Congressional Record,* Senate, October 20, 1987, p. 14572.

40. *Public Papers of Ronald Reagan, 1987* (Washington: Government Printing Office, 1989), Book 2, p. 943.

41. *Ibid.,* pp. 985, 986.

42. *Ibid.,* p. 1175.

43. "Publicity, Public Opinion, and the Court," by Walter F. Murphy and Joseph Tanenhaus, *Northwestern University Law Review,* 1990, Vol. 84, Nos. 3 and 4, Spring/Summer.

44. "Background Paper," by David M. O'Brien in *Judicial Roulette* (New York: Priority Press, 1988), p. 104.

45. *Congressional Record*, Senate, October 22, 1987, p. 14765.

46. *Birmingham News,* October 18, 1987, quoted in 47. *Congressional Record*, Senate, October 22, 1987, p. 14856-14857.

47. "On the Confirmation of a Supreme Court Justice," by Arlen Specter, *Northwestern University Law Review,* 1990, Vol. 84, Nos. 3 and 4, Spring/Summer.

48. *Public Papers of Ronald Reagan, 1987* (Washington: Government Printing Office, 1989), Book 1, pp. 39-40.

49. "Transformative Appointment," by Bruce Ackerman, *Harvard Law Review*, April 1988.

50. "The Confirmation Process and the Public," by Nina Totenberg, *Harvard Law Review,* April 1988.

4

Clarence Thomas: Round One

On July 20, 1990, Justice William Brennan announced his retirement. Popular with his colleagues on the Court, he had been a Rock of Gibraltar for civil liberties. Many of us viewed his retirement as a sad day for the Court. The issues that the Brennan resignation raised would reach full bloom soon in the resignation of Justice Thurgood Marshall and the nomination of Judge Clarence Thomas.

What intensified the sense of loss with the Brennan resignation was a widespread opinion that George Bush, who came to the presidency with a rich background of government experience and a great resume, lacked one thing: a sense of direction and purpose — conviction. He was not good, as he himself said, "on this vision thing." Unlike with Ronald Reagan, the conservative wing of the Republican Party never felt comfortable with Bush.

They didn't know where he was going. With Reagan, they understood that occasional diversions in direction were necessary, but they knew he was headed in the "right" direction. Bush went out of his way to provide comfort and assurance to these people. He spoke about being "born again," language an Episcopalian ordinarily does not use. But the hard core group in his party still did not trust him. They suspected that his acceptance of their causes was a marriage of convenience, not conviction. The Pat Buchanan vote of thirty-seven percent against Bush in the 1992 New Hampshire Republican primary later showed the depth of the mistrust.

Political observer E. J. Dionne Jr. has written accurately:

> The sparks that inflamed the Religious Right came from the judiciary—specifically the Supreme Court's decisions on issues such as school prayer, abortion, pornography, and government aid to religious schools.[1]

To keep that portion of his political base together, Bush made an often spoken but almost unwritten contract with them: He would appoint Supreme Court Justices to their liking. He gave the right wing of his party veto power over Supreme Court nominations. I said "almost unwritten contract," because the Republican Party in its platforms of 1980, 1984 and 1988 pledged to nominate Supreme Court Justices who would reverse the *Roe v. Wade* decision and carry on the conservative agenda. But political platforms are more often ignored than honored. Bush's primary interests lay elsewhere, especially in foreign affairs. This pact, not with the Devil but with the Religious Right, did not have the visibility of Bush's awkward moves from the pro-choice position on abortion to support of the pro-life position.

The conservative wing of the Republican party saw the great gains they were already making in judicial nominations, with appointees that pleased them. They were achieving their goals in the courts, while the President had no goals there. To keep—or gain—their faith, the key for the President and his operatives was to give those with an agenda for the Court, on his right, what they wanted without stirring up political storms, without inflaming the media. That is the basis for so many of progressive bent being concerned with Justice Brennan's departure from the Court.

To replace Brennan, Bush nominated Judge David Souter, a former Rhodes Scholar and a judge on the U.S. Court of Appeals for three months. He had one other major asset: a close friendship with Senator Warren Rudman of New Hampshire. Souter had written little and avoided controversy. He handled himself well before the Judiciary Committee, appeared thoughtful and, on the key *Roe v. Wade* decision, he did not respond. However, he had been on the board of a hospital that voted to permit abortions, so the nominee had at least reflected on the issue. Probably no Senator expects a nominee to say in specific terms how he or she would rule on a case pending before the Court. However, candidates who have expressed attitudes on controversial issues such as *Roe v. Wade* should tell us any general approach they might have, but could qualify that by saying, "I cannot tell you how I would rule on a specific case until I examine the merits of that case as well as the constitutional principles that may be involved." We would respect that. Souter had virtually nothing in his record that gave us any clues, other than his vote on a hospital board, and the views of the President who nominated him.

Conservatives found him acceptable, and liberals felt he was about as good as they would get from Bush. The Committee voted 13-1, Senator Kennedy voting no. The Senate confirmed Souter 90-9. I voted for Judge Souter both in the Committee and on the floor.

The vote did not show the considerable feeling of uneasiness that existed among many Senators. The question was not ability. Souter had the mental skills necessary. He was a Phi Beta Kappa graduate of Harvard, but he had shown little inclination to put ideas on paper. He stood in marked contrast to Bork, and a later nominee, Clarence Thomas, both of whom provided the Senate with an abundant paper trail. As a New Hampshire Supreme

Court Justice seven years, and then on the U.S. Court of Appeals, he had not defined himself clearly and had written remarkably few opinions. (On the U.S. Supreme Court he also writes surprisingly few opinions.) The only article he ever wrote was a tribute to another New Hampshire Supreme Court Justice. He probably represented as blank a slate as anyone ever offered by a President for a seat on the Court. That was his strength and his weakness, and Senators of all political philosophies felt some unease as we proceeded to vote.

Senator Rudman reduced the possible negative votes by coming around to each of us with the reassuring words, "Take my word for it. He'll be okay." And the Souter supporters in New Hampshire brought to Washington three of its bright young Democratic lawyers whom Joe Biden and I had come to know and respect in our ill-fated presidential campaigns of 1988. All three knew Souter well and gave us virtually the same words of assurance that Rudman had used. It is too early to make any definitive judgment on what the Souter legacy will be, but so far he has generally been voting a conservative line, occasionally shifting to the center, but casting the unfortunate decisive vote in *Rust v. Sullivan,* discussed elsewhere in this book.

The Nomination

Age crept up on Justice Thurgood Marshall, and on June 27, 1991, he announced his retirement from the Court. In a span of eleven months, two widely acknowledged giants on the Court — Brennan and Marshall — stepped down. I sat in my Chicago office, watching on television as the President announced on July 1, 1991, that he had selected forty-three-year-old Judge Clarence Thomas, an African-American, to succeed the eighty-three-year-old Marshall, also an African-American. Bush said race had nothing to do with the selection, that Thomas was the best person in the nation for the seat.

Within ten minutes Senator John Danforth of Missouri, a Republican Senator respected by solons of both political parties, called me and said the President could not have made a better selection, that he wanted to visit about the appointment at our first opportunity. Thomas had once worked for Danforth. The Missouri Senator had talked to me before about Thomas, when he appeared before Senate committees on two other occasions. I knew that Danforth genuinely liked Thomas and thought highly of him.

Bush's statement did not strike me so favorably. I want diversity on the Court, and the Thomas nomination is one representation of that. But I also agree with the statement of the retiring Justice Marshall that the most important consideration should be the views of the nominee, not his or her ethnic background. There was this immense feeling of sadness on the part of many of us that the Court had already shifted direction dramatically toward curtailing the rights of all Americans and that this nomination would be one more shove in the wrong direction.

The disappointment the Thomas nomination created in terms of sensitivity to civil liberties was compounded with the uneasy feeling that the President had not weighed the nomination carefully, that there is a huge chasm between a Thurgood Marshall and a Clarence Thomas not only in viewpoint, but also in terms of background for Supreme Court service. If you were to ask one hundred lawyers to name the top twenty attorneys in the nation, it is extremely doubtful that Thomas's name would be on the list of any of them. The nomination simply did not carry the stature of a Louis Brandeis, Oliver Wendell Holmes Jr., Benjamin Cardozo, Harlan Stone or Charles Evans Hughes, four of the five appointed by Republican presidents. As James Reston wrote:

> One mystery of this avoidable scandal is why President Bush ever nominated Clarence Thomas in the first place. He said he never even considered Judge Thomas's race but sent his name to the Senate because he regarded Judge Thomas as the best qualified person for the job, and nobody even laughed.[2]

The *Economist* of London observed:

> The system has been abused. Prime among the abusers is George Bush. The President said he nominated Mr. Thomas because he was the best man for the job. That is simply not true . . . . His sterling qualities were not his ability or his experience but the color of his skin combined with his right-wing views.[3]

What happened was not a careful search for the best in the nation. The President wanted a black conservative, someone far enough to the right to satisfy both his hard-core rightists and African-Americans, and apparently did it.

No stranger to the Senate Judiciary Committee, Thomas had twice been approved for the chairmanship of the Equal Employment Opportunity Commission (EEOC), once for Assistant Secretary of Education, and once for the U. S. Appellate Court. After Reagan's reelection, when the President reappointed him as chair of the EEOC, I joined several of my colleagues on the Committee in voting against his confirmation, though he carried the majority in the Committee. He had a good relationship with the employees at EEOC, and he had the ability to do the work, but he found himself caught in a squeeze between a law that required him to act against those who blatantly discriminated and the Reagan administration, which had no interest in enforcing the law. How much zeal Thomas himself had never has been clear. A 1988 study by the General Accounting Office found that more than forty percent of cases closed by the EEOC were not fully investigated. The backlog of cases rose from 20,000 in 1983 to 46,000 in 1989. It took longer to process cases, and the average settlement award dropped. Age discrimination cases were massively neglected. Thomas said he did not have adequate staff to carry out all of these responsibilities, yet he wrote for the Cato Institute:

> I am confident it can be shown, and some of my staff are now working on this question, that blacks at any level, especially white-collar employees, have simply not benefitted from affirmative action policies.[4]

What is key in that sentence: He had staff working on under-mining the basic mission of EEOC but said he did not have adequate staff to carry out the assignment given him by law. Overall, his record was not impressive.

After Bush nominated Judge Thomas to the Supreme Court, twelve House committee and subcommittee chairs who worked with him as Chief Administrator of the EEOC sent this letter to members of the Senate Judiciary Committee:

> In 1989, we wrote to President Bush urging him not to appoint Clarence Thomas to the U.S. Court of Appeals. We made this recommendation as chairpersons of con-gressional committees and subcommittees overseeing the Equal Employment Opportunity Commission (EEOC). We were troubled by his record as Chair of that agency—a record which we believed raised serious questions about his judgment, respect for the law and general suitability to serve as a member of the Federal judiciary. We now write to express our strong opposition to his nomination to the United States Supreme Court . . . . Our comments are confined to the nominee's conduct as a high-ranking federal official. The reports show a radical switch in his views on Supreme Court affirmative action decisions, including court-ordered affirmative action to remedy past discrimination. Judge Thomas supported a majority of these decisions in his early tenure at EEOC. But in 1985, he challenged the holding in *Griggs v. Duke Power* (barring employer use of discriminatory practices that are unre-lated to job performance). By 1987, he denounced *Bakke v. Regents of University of California* (permitting colleges and universities to consider race to insure diversity in admis-sions, but prohibiting rigid admission quotas). If a majority of the Court were to join Judge Thomas in reject-ing these fundamental principles it would greatly damage the hard-fought guarantee of equal opportunity embodied in our Constitution and federal civil rights laws . . . . Two years ago, we concluded Chairman Thomas "demonstrated an overall disdain for the rule of law." More recent, detailed reports reaffirm that conclusion. . .

. Judge Thomas should not be confirmed as Associate Justice of the United States Supreme Court. His confirmation would be harmful to that court and to the nation.[5]

Thomas's record on civil liberties also has been a cause of concern. At one point he wrote that the Ninth Amendment to the Bill of Rights, the added protection to basic freedoms that Madison wrote at the suggestion of Hamilton, is harmful: "Far from being a protection, the Ninth Amendment will likely become an additional weapon for the enemies of freedom."[6]

When he came before the Judiciary Committee for the Appellate Court nomination, only Senator Howard Metzenbaum voted against him. I supported him for this non-administrative job, believing he had the ability to handle the position, while policy would be set at the higher level, the Supreme Court. Because of rumors that he might be a future Supreme Court nominee, I stated at the time that I might not be able to vote for him if he should later be nominated to the Supreme Court. So prior to his Supreme Court nomination, I had voted once for him and once against him.

After Bush nominated Thomas to the high court, my staff put together 800 pages of articles he had written, speeches he had delivered, opinions handed down, as well as articles about him and analyses of his record. As chair of the Senate Subcommittee on Africa, I occasionally have long flights, and on one return trip from Africa I carefully read those 800 pages. The picture that came across was of an extremely conservative person. But how much of that extreme conservatism did Thomas simply design to please his bosses in the Reagan administration? What did Clarence Thomas really believe?

Before the actual hearings began, Senator Danforth came to my office with Judge Thomas, and we discussed some of my concerns. I told him that I wanted a Supreme Court Justice who would defend civil liberties and civil rights and be willing to do what may be temporarily unpopular. I also told him that I have observed two trends among those who have been markedly successful after an early struggle: Either they remember that past and help those continuing to struggle, or they assume that "if I can make it, so can they" and turn a cold shoulder to those who still struggle. Thomas assured me he would remember and help. I told him the general nature of the questions I would be asking: on privacy, on civil liberties, on separation of church and state, on his sensitivity to the powerless in our society. As they started to leave my office, Danforth leaned over to me and said, "You'll never get a better nominee from this administration." The meeting was cordial. In terms of personality and how he conducts himself, Thomas makes an excellent impression. Visiting with Judiciary Committee members in advance is a fairly standard procedure, but Danforth and Thomas went far beyond that. They visited a majority of the Senate. I encountered them one day in a Senate office building, and I said, "Still at it?" Danforth replied, "We just visited our fifty-ninth senator."

At 10:05 on the morning of September 10, 1991, Senator Biden pounded the gavel, opening the Clarence Thomas Judiciary Committee hearings, and stated: "In this time of change, fundamental constitutional rights which have been protected by the Supreme Court for decades are being called into question."[7] Biden, a former Democratic presidential candidate, handles such hearings with skill, treating both Republicans and Democrats fairly.

Gathered in the large and acoustically difficult Caucus Room in the Senate Russell Office Building were the fourteen members of the Committee, television cameras, more than 150 reporters, perhaps sixty members of the public who were rotated regularly, plus staff people. Outside in the hallway were more reporters and cameras and curious on-lookers, all ready to swarm around a witness or a Senator who might emerge. The marble floors and walls magnified an already noisy situation.

The ranking Republican on the Committee, Senator Strom Thurmond of South Carolina, has, in his thirty-seven years in the Senate, participated in hearings for more than one-fifth of those who have been seated in the history of the Supreme Court. In launching the Thomas hearing, he cautioned: "To reject a nominee based solely on ideology is inappropriate."[8] (During the Fortas hearings under Lyndon Johnson, he had taken precisely the opposite position.) Senator Kennedy, in his opening statement, decried the direction the Supreme Court has taken in recent years.

> It has increasingly abandoned its role as the guardian of the powerless in our society. It has repeatedly sought to turn back the clock on civil rights. It has relaxed the rules prohibiting the use of coerced confessions . . . . It has begun to retreat on the right to privacy. It has ruled that Government officials can prohibit doctors in publicly funded clinics from practicing their profession to the best of their ability in giving their patients full medical advice.[9]

Senator Orrin Hatch of Utah praised the appointment: "I don't think President Bush could have made a better decision or better judgment than to nominate [Thomas] for the Supreme Court."[10]

Each Senator had a brief opening statement, and the comments generally indicated where the Senators stood, though at least half the Committee had not revealed their positions before the hearing started. Republican Senators spent much time reviewing the hard road Thomas had traveled; Democratic Senators tended to question how rigid the nominee would be ideologically. The final Senator to speak because of seniority rules, Senator Herb Kohl of Wisconsin, said, addressing Thomas,

> If you cannot articulate a constitutional philosophy, one that includes full safeguards for individuals and minorities and that also squares with your past statements, then . . . you are not qualified to sit on the Supreme Court.[12]

What was — and is — impressive in the Clarence Thomas story is his rise from poverty in the then–segregated state of Georgia, to college, Yale Law School and finally positions of major responsibility.

Thomas's opening statement stressed his background:

> In 1955, my brother and I went to live with my mother in Savannah. We lived in one room in a tenement. We shared a kitchen with other tenants and we had a common bathroom in the backyard which was unworkable and unusable. It was hard . . . . Our mother only earned $20 every two weeks as a maid, not enough to take care of us. So she arranged for us to live with our grandparents . . . . Imagine, if you will, two little boys with all their belongings in two grocery bags.[13]

It was a moving story, and Thomas obviously had his heart in it. Seated behind him as he told it were his mother and sister. In his opening statement he mentioned Martin Luther King and Rosa Parks, the woman in Montgomery, Alabama, who had refused to move to the back of the bus because she was black and had, with that one small show of independence, launched Dr. King on his crusade.

I spotted Rosa Parks in the audience, and when she left, I went to greet her. Obviously unhappy, she told me, "With what he stands for, he shouldn't be permitted to use Martin Luther King's name that way!"

Following the opening statement the questioning began and Judge Thomas, from the first inquiry by Senator Biden, tried to distance himself from his past opinions and writings. Biden said to him:

> In the speech you gave in 1987 to the Pacific Research Institute you said, and I quote: "I find attractive the arguments of scholars such as Stephen Macedo who defend an activist Supreme Court that would"—not could, would—"strike down laws restricting property rights."

The implications of this for environmental laws, civil rights laws and many others are profound. Biden asked him what he found "attractive about the arguments of Professor Macedo and other scholars like him?"[14] Thomas replied:

> It has been quite some time since I have read Professor Macedo and others. That was, I believe, 1987 or 1988. My interest in the whole area was as a political philosophy . . . . I found Macedo interesting and his arguments interesting.

Thomas shifted from *attractive* to *interesting*. Then a similar discussion occurred on natural law, and Biden told him: "Quite frankly, I find it hard to square your speeches . . . with what you are telling me today."[15]

Questions from Republican Senators were substantial but generally regarded as "softballs," with the exception of some from Senators Specter and Hank Brown of Colorado. Representatives of the White House who had been briefing the nominee sat in the front row and occasionally slipped an "appropriate" question to a sympathetic Senator, behavior that is not unique to the Bush administration. That happens under all administrations.

Kennedy quoted from a speech of Thomas:

> In the socialist view, the new freedom was only another name for the old demand for an equal distribution of wealth. The new freedom meant freedom from necessity, and it was a short road to what we call today entitlements. Before a right meant the freedom to do something. Now a right has come to mean, at least in some unfortunately growing circles, the legal claim to receive and demand something.[16]

Kennedy then asked: "Which entitlements were you referring to as socialism — Social Security or Medicare or unemployment insurance?"[17] Thomas responded: "I don't think . . . I was looking at a specific governmental program . . . . I thought it was a vibrant debate, about what our rights and what our freedoms were . . . . I don't remember the full context of that."[18]

Kennedy turned to the issue of citizen's rights: "In a 1988 article you stated, 'Our current explosion of rights, welfare rights, animal rights, children's rights, and so on, goes on to the point of trivializing them.' Which children's rights do you object to?" Thomas: "I guess I don't object to rights . . . ."[19] And then he made a valid point that if the word "rights" is attached to too many things, it tends to trivialize them.

But Thomas continued to back away from things he had said and written. Kennedy asked him about a review he had written praising a book by Thomas Sowell, a conservative economist and author, and particularly Thomas's lauding a chapter about women, which suggested that the wage disparity between men and women was justified. Thomas replied that he praised the book and chapter, but "I did not indicate that . . . I agreed with his conclusions."[20]

Thomas stressed in his answers that as a Justice, his responsibility would be "to uphold the Constitution of the United States, not personal philosophy or political theories."[21]

Senator Metzenbaum began the second day of questioning with a statement that summed up the feeling of many:

> Instead of explaining your views [yesterday], you ran from them and disavowed them . . . . In 1987, in a speech to the ABA [American Bar Association], you said, "Economic rights are as protected as any other rights in the Constitution." But yesterday you said, "The Supreme Court cases that decided that economic rights have lesser protection were correctly decided." In 1987, in a speech at the Heritage Foundation, you said, "Lewis Lehrman's diatribe against the right to choose was a splendid example of applying natural law." But yesterday you said, "I disagree with the article, and I did not endorse it before." In 1987, you signed on to a White House working group report that criticized as "fatally flawed" a whole line of cases concerned with the right to privacy. But yesterday you said you never read the controversial and

highly publicized report, and that you believe the constitution protects the very right the report criticizes. In all
of your 150-plus speeches and dozens of articles, your
only reference to a right to privacy was to criticize a
constitutional argument in support of that right. Yesterday you said that there is a right to privacy . . . .

Senator Metzenbaum continued, "Your complete repudiation
of your past record makes our job very difficult. We don't know
if the Judge Thomas who has been speaking and writing
throughout his adult life is the same man up for confirmation
before us today."[22]

Thomas responded, in part, by saying what became a theme:
"I have no agenda . . . I don't have an ideology to take to the
Court."[23]

In Thomas's defense, Senator Simpson accused the anti-
Thomas crowd of getting hysterical, and cited examples of
statements that had been made. Simpson pointed out that
Thomas would be only one vote on the Court.

While some of Thomas's supporters and opponents were
making extreme statements — which happens on any major,
controversial nomination or issue — Democrats who had privately indicated to me they would probably vote for Thomas now
were less certain. Those doubts can be summarized in one
question: Is he telling us the truth?

Natural Law

The Lewis Lehrman article that Thomas had praised in a
speech raised a red flag for us on the matter of credibility. The
article stated that natural law prohibited abortion, even in the
case of risking the life of the mother. Thomas called it "a
splendid example of applying natural law."[24] The Lehrman
article had denounced both the Supreme Court and Congress on
Roe v. Wade for "a spurious right born exclusively of judicial
supremacy with not a single trace of lawful authority."[25]

Thomas had two explanations for his words of praise. First, he wanted to pay a "compliment to someone they [his audience] believed in."[24] He said he hoped to "get a conservative audience that was skeptical of a concept [applying natural law to civil rights] to be more receptive." He told them what they wanted to hear in one area to convince them in another.

His second explanation for the praise — the article "is a splendid example of applying natural law" — is that he really didn't know what it contained. Senator Leahy asked: "Had you read the article before you praised it?" Thomas: "I think I skimmed it." Leahy: "You have read the article, now, though, now that it has been brought up . . ."[27] Thomas: "I have not re-read it."

On the first point, we asked ourselves: If he was shaping what he had to say to please his immediate audience, was he also shaping what he had to say now to please fourteen Senators? Second, because the newspapers had called attention to the Lehrman matter, and because it had come up in the previous day's hearing, we found it difficult to believe that he had not read it, unless his White House handlers had told him not to read it as a way of avoiding specific answers to questions. The Lehrman matter deepened Committee skepticism.

Senator Specter, one of the abler members of the Committee, took Thomas to task for a wavering on a different matter:

> Your reconfirmation hearings [for chair of the EEOC] came and you agreed to abide by them [Court decisions] . . . . In your career in the early 1980s [you] stated that you favored [affirmative action], and then appeared to accept the Supreme Court decisions, and then later disagreed with those decisions, although you agreed to abide by them, and still later just absolutely plundered those decisions with the very strong hostile comments about Congress . . . . You take a case like Local 28 of the Sheet-metal Workers, where the New York City Human Relations Commission cited them for discriminatory practices in 1964, and EEOC finally brought a lawsuit in 1971, and there was a finding of discrimination in 1975, and there was a court order to correct that discrimination, [on]

which there was contempt in 1977 and again in 1982 and contempt again in 1983 . . . and you have this kind of outrageous conduct that spans a 20-year-period, and then EEOC [under your leadership] comes in at the latter stages of the litigation in the 1980s and takes a different position and argues against the court orders to stop the flagrant discriminatory practices . . . and you as Chairman of the EEOC come in and oppose [the Court], and then sharply criticize the decision of the Supreme Court of the United States in upholding that kind of remedy [against discrimination].[28]

Confirmation Conversion

Senator Heflin, former Chief Justice of the Alabama Supreme Court, noted the disparity between Thomas's articles and speeches and his testimony. Heflin said it had the "appearance of confirmation conversion."[29] He cautioned that such answers can cause questions "as to integrity." Senator Brown said he "would be interested to know if in your own mind you have come to a decision on the right to terminate a pregnancy."[30] Thomas faced a number of questions in this area. The nominee said he declined to answer how he might rule but that "I am open about that important case. I have no agenda."[31] This question arose in several ways. A significant exchange took place between Senator Leahy and Thomas.

Leahy: Judge, you were in law school at the time *Roe v. Wade* was decided . . . . You would accept . . . that in the last generation *Roe v. Wade* is certainly one of the more important cases to be decided by the U.S. Supreme Court?

Thomas: I would accept that it has certainly been one of the more important, as well as one that has been one of the more highly publicized and debated cases . . . .

Leahy: When that came down, you were in law school . . . *Roe v. Wade* would have been discussed in the law school while you were there?

Thomas: The case that I remember being discussed most during my early part of law school was I believe in my small group with Thomas Emerson may have been *Griswold* . . . and we may have touched on *Roe v. Wade* . . . . Because I was a married student and I worked, I did not spend a lot of time around the law school doing what the other students enjoyed so much, and that is debating all the current cases . . . .

Leahy: Judge Thomas, I was a married law student who also worked, but I also found at least between classes that we did discuss the law, and I am sure you are not suggesting that there wasn't any discussion at any time of *Roe v. Wade?*

Thomas: Senator, I cannot remember personally engaging in those discussions. The groups that I met with at that time during my years in law school were small study groups.

Leahy: Have you ever had discussion of *Roe v. Wade,* other than in this room, in the 17 or 18 years it has been there?

Thomas: Only . . . in the most general sense that other individuals express concerns one way or the other, and you listen and you try to be thoughtful. If you are asking me whether or not I have ever debated the contents of it, that answer to that is no, Senator.

Leahy: Have you ever [in] private gatherings or otherwise, stated whether you felt that it was properly decided or not?

Thomas: Senator, in trying to recall and reflect on that, I don't recollect commenting one way or the other. There were, again, debates about it in various places, but I generally did not participate. I don't remember or recall participating, Senator.

Leahy: So you don't ever recall stating whether you thought it was properly decided or not?

Thomas: I can't recall saying one way or the other, Senator . . . .

Leahy: Have you made any decision in your own mind whether you feel *Roe v. Wade* was properly decided or not, without stating what that decision is?

Thomas: I have not made, Senator, a decision one way or the other with respect to that important decision . . . .

Leahy: So you cannot recollect ever taking a position on whether it was properly decided or not properly decided, and you do not have one here that you would share with us today?

Thomas: I do not have a position to share with you here today on whether or not that case was properly decided . . . .

Leahy: Well, with all due respect, Judge, I have some difficulty with your answer that somehow this has been so far removed from your discussions or feelings during the years since it was decided while you were in law school. You have participated in a working group that criticized *Roe.* You cited *Roe* in a footnote to your article on the privileges or immunity clause. You have referred to Lewis Lehrman's article on the meaning of the right to life. You specifically referred to abortion in a column in the *Chicago Defender.* I cannot believe that all of this was done in a vacuum absent some very clear considerations of *Roe v. Wade,* and, in fact, twice specifically citing *Roe v. Wade.*

Thomas: Senator, your question to me was did I debate the contents of *Roe v. Wade,* the outcome in *Roe v. Wade,* do I have this day an opinion, a personal opinion on the outcome in *Roe v. Wade;* and my answer to you is that I do not.[32]

The next day, Senator Kohl commented:

> Yesterday, you told Senator Leahy . . . that you had no opinion, either personally or professionally about the legal issues raised in *Roe,* and that you have never had an opinion and never discussed it. That is a very strong statement to make to this Committee . . . . As Clarence Thomas the man, the human being, do you have a personal view on whether society ought to provide women with the option of having an abortion?

Thomas responded to Kohl: "I would essentially reply as I have yesterday."[33]

This added to the credibility problem. If he had no opinion on the decision, he almost certainly was the only person in that huge room in that category. If he had responded, "I have an opinion, but it would be unwise to state it, because it is an opinion not steeped in careful study," we would have understood. But to state he has no opinion and cannot recall discussing *Roe v. Wade* invited disbelief.

The nominee's preparation for the hearing came into questions. Senator Leahy referred to candidates as "packaged, coached and scripted," and it is an apt description.[34] At one point in the questioning, Senator Kohl asked Thomas:

> When you were holding practice sessions, did your advisors ever critique you about your responses to questions? . . . Did they say, for example, "You should soften that answer," or "Don't answer that question, just say that you can't prejudge an issue that may come before the Court"?

The nominee responded: "The answer to that is unequivocally no. I set down ground rules at the very beginning that they were there simply to ask me and to hear me respond to questions . . . . but not to tell me whether it was right or wrong or too little or too much."[35] At least some Senators, knowing how the process works, had a hard time believing that.

Also disturbing to some of us was Thomas's close friendship with James (Jay) Parker, an African-American who was paid large sums to lobby for the then-pro-apartheid, whites-only government of South Africa, but Thomas claimed he did not know that Parker worked for the South African government.

Senator Simpson rallied to the nominee's side, telling of a visit to the EEOC offices and of high praise from the employees there of Thomas's leadership and his relationship with his employees. One employee told Simpson, "He is the kind of person I would like to have decide if I ever go before a judge. He listens, keeps an open mind, and makes a decision based on reason."

Thomas vs. Holmes

One of the final exchanges of Thomas with the Senators was about a former Justice, Oliver Wendell Holmes Jr. In a speech,

Thomas had said: "The homage to natural right inscribed on the Justice Department building should be treated with more reverence than the many busts or paintings of Justice Oliver Wendell Holmes in the Department of Justice. You will recall Holmes as one who scoffed at natural law, that 'brooding omniprescence in the sky.' If anything united the jurisprudence of the left and the right today, it is the nihilism of Holmes. As Walter Berns put it . . . 'No man who ever sat on the Supreme Court was less inclined and so poorly equipped to be a statesman or to teach people what a people needs in order to govern itself well.' "

Senator Heflin commented:

> For you to attack with words like this . . . a Justice of the Supreme Court, as well as one who is generally regarded as one of the giants of the Supreme Court, raises some question in my mind.[37]

Thomas said he had since read more and now regarded Holmes as "a great Justice." I sit next to Heflin on the Committee, and I could tell that he found the response far from satisfactory.

Senator Specter, who ended up voting for Thomas, observed, "I am not so sure but what your roots are not more important in trying to predict what you will do, if confirmed, than your writings. Your writings and your answers are at loggerheads."[38]

The Media and the Organizations

Media reaction to his testimony varied. Joe Klein wrote in *New York* magazine: "The judge was worse than unconvincing; he was an embarrassment, frightened, hollow, running away from his writings of the past ten years."[39] Toward the beginning of the hearing, Senator Kohl said that it was essential for the nominee to indicate to the Committee his constitutional philosophy. Ronald Dworkin wrote in *New York Review:* "Thomas flunked that test in a spectacular way."[40] But Juan

Williams, reporter for the *Washington Post,* said in an interview: "Clarence Thomas has proven himself to be a fair-minded, open individual, which is what you want on the Supreme Court."[41]

Following Thomas, a parade of witnesses testified on both sides, representing groups such as the American Bar Association, which gave Thomas the lowest approval rating of any Supreme Court nominee it has ever endorsed, as well as academic associations and other groups and some distinguished former public servants.

Two groups deserve special mention. While witnesses from the African-American community were fairly evenly divided in their appearance before the Committee, the leadership of the black organizations overwhelmingly opposed Thomas. I emphasize the word leadership because in grass roots America, blacks were strongly supportive of Thomas. Polls showed approximately three-fourths of African-Americans favored the nominee. Their response was the same that I have seen in politics for Polish-Americans, Italian-Americans and other ethnic groups. The leaders can study and come to solid conclusions, but ethnic Americans — whether Greek-Americans, Polish-Americans or African-Americans — who still feel they have not received adequate opportunity in leadership, will overwhelmingly support someone from their group who appears to have a chance to move up. And so, despite the statement of the leaders, polls showed strong support for Thomas among black Americans.

William H. Brown III, an attorney, and Erwin H. Griswold, the former dean of Harvard Law School and Solicitor General, testified for the Lawyers Committee for Civil Rights, urging that Thomas be turned down. Brown charged the nominee with "rejecting much of the decisional framework on which our nation's protection of civil rights is based," and, Griswold added: "Compare his experience and demonstrated abilities with those of Charles Evans Hughes or Harlan Fiske Stone, with Robert H. Jackson or the second John M. Harlan, with Thurgood Marshall or Lewis H. Powell, for example. To say that Judge Thomas now has such qualifications is obviously unwarranted."[42] Brown indicated the vote of their group was 90-8 opposing Thomas.

While Benjamin Hooks, the national chief executive of the NAACP, opposed Thomas, Evelyn Bryant, president of the Liberty County, Georgia, NAACP testified for the nominee: "My comments reflect the opinion of the vast majority of black Americans . . . . Who is to tell all blacks that we are compelled to join in a lock-step mentality toward the best approaches to improve the life of blacks and other minorities? Who is to tell us that we cannot and should not exercise our right to demonstrate an ability for independent thinking? . . . Clarence Thomas has demonstrated that he is an independent thinker, maybe too independent for some self-appointed spokesmen against his confirmation."[43]

Five House members appeared on behalf of the Congressional Black Caucus: John Conyers of Michigan, Louis Stokes of Ohio, Major Owens of New York, Craig Washington of Texas and John Lewis of Georgia. All African-American Democratic members of the House (there is now one Republican) went on record in opposition to Thomas. Congressman Conyers made a point that several black leaders later reiterated: "If–contrary to the views of the Congressional Black Caucus, the progressive Baptist church organizations, the NAACP, state black caucuses of elected officials, the labor movement which includes many African-American leaders – if he were to go on the bench, he would preclude any administration from within our lifetime of having an opportunity of considering another African-American jurist to this high post."[44]

Because it is unlikely that two blacks will be named to the Court, he and others felt that the person on the Court should represent the thinking and concerns of a majority of blacks, as Justice Marshall did but Thomas does not. Congressman Owens said that after African-Americans

> get over the shock of understanding that a person of his education and his position could espouse those [anti-affirmative action] ideas, their reaction . . . I'll tell you what

one lady told me at church: "Let's take the Christian approach . . . . You, Congressman, go out there and fight as hard as you can to see that this man does not get a place on the Supreme Court. But since the President is powerful . . . you might lose and he might be placed on the Supreme Court. After you get through fighting and you lose, then we'll start praying that he will be born again and will act right when he gets on the Court. But we'll fight first, and then we'll pray later."[45]

Eighty-one-year-old Washington lawyer Joseph Rauh, one of the giants of the civil rights movement, testified in behalf of the Leadership Conference on Civil Rights:

> I had the honor to serve as the last law clerk to Justice Benjamin Cardozo and the first law clerk to Felix Frankfurter, the two great successors to the legendary Oliver Wendell Holmes. When Senator Kennedy read Clarence Thomas's trashing of Oliver Wendell Holmes last week, I was made ill . . . . Republican conservative President Calvin Coolidge appointed Justice Harlan Fiske Stone, a great Justice and ultimately the Chief Justice . . . . Conservative President Hoover appointed Justice Cardozo even though that meant two Jews and three New Yorkers on the Court and knowing how liberal he was . . . . How could the President . . . tell the people that this is the best person for the job when he can't get one of fifteen conservative lawyers [on the American Bar Association committee] to say he is well qualified? Even Carswell had a better record . . . . I can't see how the Senate can confirm somebody who has a worse record, a worse evaluation than Carswell . . . . You are the keeper now of the Bill of Rights. There is a majority of the Court which is very prone to having an erosion of the Bill of Rights. Don't add one more.[46]

Champions of Thomas went back again and again to his personal story, assuring the Committee that anyone who went through that experience would be a person on the Court who would seek justice for everyone. One of my Republican colleagues said to me: "He had a bad record under the Reagan administration because he knew that was the way to get ahead. Now he'll be free to follow his convictions." But we faced the unknown: What are his convictions?

Women's groups formed an almost solid phalanx against the nomination, centered on the uncertainties — at best — of the nominee on the abortion issue. Major leaders of the women's movement testified, with the most moving commentary coming from Kate Michelman, President of the National Abortion Rights Action League, who is respected both by those who agree with her and by those who differ. She told her personal story for the first time in a national forum:

> I thought very long and hard about the focus of my testimony today. During this process, we must remember a very simple truth: What is decided here will profoundly affect the lives of millions of Americans outside this hearing room—Americans who depend on you to protect their most cherished rights and liberties. Among them are the countless desperate women who, prior to *Roe v. Wade*, were deprived of their privacy, their dignity, and even their health and their lives. . . .
>
> Today I must tell you that I was one of those women. I was relatively lucky. I was able to avoid resorting to the back alleys. But I suffered the shame, degradation and humiliation of being deprived of my right to make one of the most important decisions of my life. Like most women in this nation, I never expected to need an abortion. Most women don't. But before *Roe*, I faced the trauma of a crisis pregnancy. I was raised a Catholic, married young, and as a young woman I had three wonderful daughters in three years. But in 1970, my husband suddenly announced that he was leaving me and the children. I was devastated. Without money, a job, or a car, I was even unable to get a charge account at the local five-and-dime beause I wasn't married any longer. I was also very ill at the time. My self-esteem was destroyed. My entire world was shattered, and my family was forced onto welfare. Almost immediately after my husband left me, I learned

that I was pregnant. With three children under the age of six, I alone had to meet their every need—financial, emotional and physical. The very survival of my family was at stake. Indeed, my family was at risk of being split apart. Because abortion was largely illegal at the time, I had to struggle with this decision all by myself, all alone. Deciding whether or not to have this abortion was probably one of the most difficult and complex decisions of my life. It challenged every religious, moral and ethical belief I had. But I looked into the eyes of my three daughters and made what I think was one of the most moral decisions I have ever made.

It was at this point that I became painfully aware that having another child would have made it absolutely impossible to cope with an already desperate situation. I am certain that my family would not have survived intact. But in 1970, the government did not allow me to make this decision for myself. I was forced to appear before a hospital-appointed panel of four men. These complete strangers cross-examined me about the most intimate and personal details of my life. It was humiliating. I was an adult woman, a mother of three, and yet I had to win their permission to make a decision about my family, my life and my future. And I alone would have to live with the consequences of their decision. But, finally, they granted me their permission. I was admitted to the hospital. Yet as I awaited the procedure, I was told by a nurse that they had forgotten one more legal requirement. I would not be able to have the abortion without written permission from the man who had just deserted me and my children. I literally had to leave the hospital and find the man who had rejected me and ask his permission. It was a degrading, dehumanizing experience, an assault to my integrity, my dignity and my very sense of self. At all times during this process, I carried with me the phone number of an illegal abortionist. And if at any juncture I was thwarted in my attempt to have a hospital abortion, I was prepared to break the law and risk my life because my family's survival depended on it. Mr. Chairman, Senators, perhaps now you can begin to understand the pain and anger I feel when I hear the right to choose dismissed as a mere single issue. This right is absolutely fundamental—fundamental to our dignity, to our power to shape our own lives, to our ability to act in the best interests of our families. No issue—none—has a greater impact on the lives and futures of American women and their families. The record shows that, if confirmed, Judge Thomas would indeed vote to take away this fundamental right—to take this nation back to the days when women had no alternative but the back alleys for health care . . . . I urge you to refuse to confirm Judge Thomas.[47]

The First Vote

Judge Thomas sat through five days of questioning and, while the witnesses that followed had some impact, overwhelmingly the nominee's own words and perceived attitude were the decisive factors in the Committee decision. Almost everyone expected Thomas to be approved by the Committee and then by a large Senate majority. Already, fifty-three senators had announced their support of the nominee, including thirteen Democrats.

As we approached the day for the Committee vote, all the Republicans except Brown and Specter had announced their support of Thomas. They were expected to support him, though there were Thomas opponents who hoped for Specter's vote. On the Democratic side, DeConcini had announced for Thomas. Kennedy and Metzenbaum opposed the nomination. I had taken no public stand, but the testimony of Judge Thomas resolved any doubts I had; I would vote against him, and I told that to my staff and others privately. As the hearings started, Kohl had said privately that he probably would vote for Thomas, and my reading is that Heflin and Biden were tilted favorably to Thomas, though not a strong tilt, and neither said that to me. Public opinion polls showed support for Thomas. Heflin had a particularly hard struggle because although politically he would have benefited in voting for Thomas, he had great respect for the Supreme Court — awe is not too strong a word — and in my brief discussions with him, I sensed an inner struggle.

Before the Committee met to vote, most members announced their decisions on the floor. To the surprise of many, Heflin and Kohl and Biden all stated they would vote against Thomas. Specter and Brown voted for him. The Committee voted 7-7. Then Thurmond made a motion to send the nomination to the floor without a recommendation. That carried 13-1. I voted against it, as I always do on that motion, whether it refers to a bill or a nominee. A committee should do its work, and if a committee cannot summon a majority that is favorable, a nominee or bill should stay in the committee.

With that vote, the nomination went to the Senate floor where I expected Thomas to win with relative ease. But I did not know what would take place in a few days to reshape the vote and to change the nation.

Endnotes

1. E. J. Dionne Jr., *Why Americans Hate Politics* (New York: Simon and Schuster, 1991), p. 224.
2. "More than Just Up or Down," by James Reston, *New York Times,* October 15, 1991.
3. "Unsupreme Court," editorial, *The Economist,* October 19, 1991.
4. "Civil Rights as a Principle Versus Civil Rights as an Interest," by Clarence Thomas in *Assessing the Reagan Years,* David Boaz, editor (Washington, Cato Institute, 1988), p. 397.
5. Signed by: Don Edwards, Edward Roybal, John Conyers, Matthew Martinez, William Clay, Tom Lantos, Patricia Schroeder, Barbara Boxer, Gerry Sikorski, Pat Williams, Cardiss Collins and Charles A. Hayes.
6. David Boaz, *supra,* p. 399.
7. *Clarence Thomas Hearings,* Senate Judiciary Committee, unpublished transcript, September 10, 1991, Morning Session, p. 2.
8. *Ibid.,* p. 18.
9. *Ibid.,* p. 22.
10. *Ibid.,* p. 26
11. *Ibid.,* p. 43.
12. *Ibid.,* p. 90.
13. *Ibid.,* September 10, 1991, Afternoon Session, p. 129.
14. *Ibid.,* p. 136.
15. *Ibid.,* p. 138.
16. *Ibid.,* p. 183.
17. *Ibid.,* p. 184.
18. *Ibid.,* p. 184-186.
19. *Ibid.,* p. 186.
20. *Ibid.,* p. 193.
21. *Ibid.,* p. 210.
22. *Ibid.,* September 11, 1991, Morning Session, pp. 3-4.
23. *Ibid.,* p. 8.

24. "Why Black Americans Should Look to Conservative Policies," by Clarence Thomas, Heritage Lecture, Heritage Foundation: Washington, June 18, 1987.

25. "The Declaration of Independence and the Right to Life," by Lewis Lehrman, *American Spectator*, April, 1987.

26. *Clarence Thomas Hearings*, September 11, 1991, Afternoon Session, p. 95.

27. *Ibid.*, pp. 97-98.

28. *Ibid.*, pp. 126-129.

29. *Ibid.*, p. 132.

30. *Ibid.*, p. 150.

31. *Ibid.*, p. 151.

32. *Ibid.*, September 11, 1991, Afternoon Session, pp. 102-106.

33. *Ibid.*, September 12, 1991, Morning Session, pp. 7-8.

34. *Congressional Record*, Senate, October 24, 1991, p. 15117.

35. *Clarence Thomas Hearings*, September 12, 1991, Morning Session, p. 5.

36. *Ibid.*, September 13, 1991, Afternoon Session, p. 77.

37. Ibid., September 13, 1991, Afternoon Session, pp. 122-123.

38. *Ibid.*, p. 175.

39. "Tabloid Government," by Joe Klein, *New York,* October 28, 1991.

40. "Justice for Clarence Thomas," by Ronald Dworkin, *New York Review,* November 7, 1991.

41. Transcript from "Inside Washington with Gordon Peterson," *Federal News Service,* September 21, 1991.

42. *Clarence Thomas Hearings*, September 17, 1991, Afternoon Session, pp. 137-138.

43. *Ibid.*, p. 262-263.

44. *Ibid.*, September 19, 1991, Afternoon Session, p. 168.

45. *Ibid.*, pp. 201-202.

46. *Ibid.*, pp. 336-339.

47. *Ibid.*, September 1991, Morning Session, pp. 9-12.

5

Round Two:

The Anita Hill Challenge

Late in the afternoon, two days before the Committee voted on Clarence Thomas, Ted Kennedy mentioned to me on the floor of the Senate that Joe Biden had an affidavit from a woman alleging sexual harassment by Thomas. But, he said, she wanted the statement and her name kept confidential. It took perhaps one minute of time as we rushed between votes or appointments, but because it had the potential to be significant I remember it distinctly.

The next day Biden asked Howell Heflin and me to step into the corridor in back of the Senate, where we were joined by Herb Kohl. Biden explained to the three of us that he had an affidavit from a woman charging Thomas with sexual harassment but that she wanted her name kept confidential, and that he had asked the FBI to check out the story. Since the person who signed the affidavit asked that her name be kept confidential, all three of us expressed the opinion that Biden had handled the situation in about the only way he could.

After my conversation with Kennedy, I told three of my Judiciary staff people who are lawyers — Susan Kaplan, who heads that staff, John Trasviña and Jayne Jerkins — that there was an allegation that they should be aware of, but it should be kept confidential; however, they should be alert to it in case any further information developed.

Within a matter of hours, Susan Kaplan called and said that the woman who made the allegation was Anita Hill and that she wanted to talk to me. The message came from a friend of hers in Washington, Sonia Jarvis, who had called and left Anita Hill's phone number. Jarvis also identified Hill as a law professor at the University of Oklahoma. As a Senator you simply do not have the time to personally return most phone calls; you leave that to your staff. But the stakes involved were so high that I felt I should make this one, primarily to get some sense of whether Anita Hill was a substantial person or "off the wall."

From our conversation, I quickly determined that she was a stable person, not some flake clamoring for publicity. In fact, the opposite was true. She asked if I had read her affidavit. I told her I had heard about it, but I had not read it. She expressed concern that I had not seen it, concern that it would not be considered by the Committee before the vote on Thomas. She asked if I would distribute it to all Senators, with the understanding that the statement and her name be kept confidential. I told her that would be impossible, that if I sent it to one hundred Senators, it would be in the newspapers and on television the next morning. I sensed she was troubled and caught in a dilemma: She genuinely wanted to stay out of the limelight, yet she felt Senators should have the information. I told her that she had to make an extremely difficult decision that could change her life, that I would not want to advise her one way or another on what to do. She could either make it public and undergo massive media attention, or she could withhold her name and the document but be troubled by her inaction. Neither course would be easy, I told her. At the conclusion of our conversation, I remember thinking: She makes a solid impression. Whether she attempted to contact any other members of the Committee I do not know. I know that I was the only member of the Committee to talk to her prior to the Thomas vote. Our conversation was brief, all business, but cordial.

Before the Committee vote, Jeff Peck, who headed Biden's Judiciary Committee staff, came to me with the FBI study. The FBI report could hardly be called in-depth, but in fairness to the FBI, they had little time in which to act. One other factor must be kept in mind that most people do not realize about the FBI: They regard the White House as their client. That does not mean that reports are twisted intentionally by the Bureau, but what questions are asked and who is interviewed sometimes can make a huge difference, and the White House can play a role in that. FBI reports draw no conclusions, and this one was no exception.

At the Committee meeting of Friday, September 27, where the 7-7 vote took place, no one hinted at the information the Committee held, nor did I hear any private discussions about it. Over the weekend Senators scattered to their states or their homes. When we returned, there was more discussion among Senators privately about the vote on Thomas scheduled for Tuesday of the following week and the general feeling was that Thomas would make it, but that that could change if Anita Hill went public. There was nothing in the newspapers about the potential bombshell, although all the Committee members and, presumably, their staffs were now privy to the allegations.

In the middle of that week, I received a call from a lobbyist working against the nomination to discuss a couple of key Thomas votes. I remember ending the conversation saying, "There is still one matter that has not been disclosed that could make a difference in the Senate vote if it became public." She startled me by responding, "Do you mean the statement of the woman from Oklahoma?" That was the first I had heard of anyone outside the Senate knowing about it. Obviously, it was getting around Washington.

That Friday, my wife, Jeanne, and I flew to Nebraska where I attended a Board of Regents meeting of a fine liberal arts school, Dana College, that I attended for two years. After renting a car in Omaha, we drove thirty miles north to Blair and checked in at a motel where a phone message said: "Call Nina Totenberg of National Public Radio." I called. She said she had the Anita Hill affidavit (not the FBI report) and had talked to the Oklahoma professor.

She asked me when I had seen the information about Anita Hill, and inaccurately, I said I had seen it after the Committee vote. When I checked the sequence afterwards with Susan Kaplan of my staff to refresh my memory, she told me I had seen the FBI report in advance of and the Anita Hill affidavit after the Committee vote. The timing had not meant that much to me, because prior to even hearing the report about Anita Hill I had determined to vote against Thomas. Totenberg also asked if I felt that once the information became public, the Senate should delay its vote on Thomas. I said it should. National Public Radio broadcast my comment on Sunday when they broke the story.

That Friday afternoon — before the story broke — while I attended the Dana College meeting, Senator Nancy Kassebaum, Republican of Kansas, called and said she had just heard about the Hill affidavit and wanted my judgment on the matter. She had not seen the affidavit. Because I was speaking in a hallway within hearing range of a number of people, my end of the telephone conversation was limited, but the call told me that the story was spreading.

The next day Tim Phelps of *Newsday*, a New York newspaper, called. I told him as well that I felt the Senate vote should be delayed and the charge investigated more fully. He asked about the FBI report and I had to tell him — repeatedly — that I could not disclose the FBI information. Phelps later said on ABC's "Nightline" that he had had the basic elements of the story for more than eight weeks. Both Nina Totenberg and Tim Phelps did a superb job of investigative journalism.

How they got the story has caused much speculation. White House officials, under all administrations, regularly leak "confidential" or "secret" information when it suits their purposes. While most speculation in this case has focused on two of my Democratic colleagues and me, the source could have been a Republican or a staff person from either side, or someone else altogether. On the John McLaughlin television program, the host indicated that "a White House source" told him I had leaked the story. When I heard about this, I called McLaughlin and told him I don't operate that way. I believe in what Gandhi said: "Bad means corrupt good ends."

The White House source charging me with the leak, I learned from newspaper reporters, was Boyden Gray, counsel to the President. He put together the fact that I cast the lone no vote on the 13-1 Committee tally against sending Thomas to the Senate without recommendation, and the fact that I had been confused about my interview with Nina Totenberg as to when I got the Anita Hill information. That the counsel to the President would in this way damage my — or anyone's — reputation so casually does not instill great confidence in that key White House person.

I am grateful to Senators DeConcini, Simpson and Hatch — all of whom supported Thomas — who told reporters they did not know who leaked it, but they knew Paul Simon didn't leak it. As I write this, an investigation is underway to determine who leaked the affidavit, a question that I hope can be–but doubt will be–answered. However that is resolved, the more significant question is not who leaked the affidavit, but whether the affidavit is true.

For a period of about twenty-four hours, I stood alone in asking for a delay, then Senators Leahy, Barbara Mikulski of Maryland, James Exon of Nebraska and Alan Dixon of Illinois joined me.

Initially, the leadership in the Senate said there would be no delay in the Thomas vote, that the Senate would proceed as scheduled on Tuesday. When the Senate leadership gave that signal, Senator Daniel P. Moynihan of New York stepped in and made a motion to adjourn the Senate for one week to give the

Senators time to consider the Anita Hill information. Such a delay, however, is a prerogative that traditionally is reserved to the leaders. Temporary chaos erupted. An angry Majority Leader, Senator George Mitchell of Maine, assured Moynihan and all of us that efforts were being made to work out a delay. When this cloud of uncertainty about a delay hovered over the Senate, women's groups around the nation erupted in outrage that the Senate might simply ignore the Hill assertions. Finally, a one-week delay was set. The Judiciary Committee would launch hearings once again, but only on the issue of sexual harassment.

The Committee agreed to have two chief questioners on the Democratic side and the Republican side, in addition to the chair. Democrats designated Leahy and Heflin, and Republicans Hatch and Specter. They and Biden would each get thirty minutes during questioning; the rest of us on the Committee would have five minutes each. We approved that procedure unanimously.

Everything intensified. The drama of the previous hearing heightened. Press coverage grew. Public interest did not just grow, it erupted. In the earlier hearings, we discussed with the nominee legal theories about privacy and separation of church and state, about whether precedent should be binding and about affirmative action. Most of the public finds all of this dull. But now, soap-opera time was filled with a real soap opera that people sensed would have an impact on their lives.

Judge Thomas, the first witness, bristling with emotion, spoke briefly and said that Anita Hill's charges "shocked, surprised, hurt and enormously saddened me . . . . For almost a decade my responsibilities included enforcing the rights of victims of sexual harassment."[1] When the FBI first approached him with the charges, "I categorically denied all of the allegations and denied that I ever attempted to date Anita Hill . . . . I strongly reaffirm that denial."[2] Then he added:

> Something has happened to me in the dark days that have followed since the FBI agents informed me about these allegations. And the days have grown darker, as these

very serious, very explosive, and very sensitive allegations were selectively leaked, in a distorted way to the
media over the past weekend . . . . This apparently calculated public disclosure has caused me, my family, and my
friends enormous pain and great harm. I have never, in
all my life, felt such hurt, such pain, such agony . . . . Anita
Hill is a person I considered a friend, whom I admired
and thought I had treated fairly and with the utmost
respect.[3]

Then he said:

I will not allow this Committee or anyone else to probe
into my private life. This is not what America is all about.
. . . I am proud of my life, proud of what I have done, and
what I have accomplished . . . . No job is worth what I have
been through, no job. No horror in my life has been so
debilitating. Confirm me if you want, don't confirm me if
you are so led, but let this process end.

Professor Hill entered the hearing room as the next witness,
accompanied by her large family. Thirty-five years old, poised,
low-key, she told the Committee and the millions watching:

I am the youngest of thirteen children . . . . I was reared in
a religious atmosphere in the Baptist faith, and I have
been a member of the Antioch Baptist Church in Tulsa,
Oklahoma, since 1983. It is a very warm part of my life at
the present time . . . .
After approximately three months of working [at the
Department of Education under Clarence Thomas], he
asked me to go out socially with him. What happened
next and telling the world about it are the two most
difficult . . . experiences of my life.
It is only after a great deal of agonizing consideration
and a number of sleepless nights that I am able to talk of
these unpleasant matters to anyone but my close friends.
I declined the invitation to go out socially with him, and
explained to him that I thought it would jeopardize . . . a
good working relationship. I had a normal social life with

other men outside of the office . . . . He pressed me to justify my reasons for saying no to him. These incidents took place in his office or mine. They were in the form of private conversations which would not have been overheard by anyone else.

My working relationship became even more strained when Judge Thomas began to use work situations to discuss sex. On these occasions, he would call me into his office for reports . . . . After a brief discussion of work, he would turn the conversation to a discussion of sexual matters. His conversations were very vivid.

He spoke about acts that he had seen in pornographic films involving such matters as women having sex with animals, and films showing group sex or rape scenes. He talked about pornographic materials depicting individuals with large penises or large breasts involved in various sex acts. On several occasions Thomas told me graphically of his own sexual prowess. Because I was extremely uncomfortable talking about sex with him at all, and particularly in such a graphic way, I told him that I did not want to talk about these subjects. I would also try to change the subject . . . . My efforts to change the subject were rarely successful . . . .

During the latter part of my time at the Department of Education, the social pressures and any conversation of his offensive behavior ended. I began to believe and hope that our working relationship could be a proper, cordial and professional one. When Judge Thomas was made chair of the EEOC . . . I was asked [to go there with him] and I did . . . . I also faced the realistic fact that I had no alternative job. While I might have gone back into private practice . . . I was dedicated to civil rights work and my first choice was to be in that field . . . . Moreover, at that time the Department of Education was a dubious venture. President Reagan was seeking to abolish the entire department.

For my first months at the EEOC . . . there were no sexual conversations or overtures. However, during the fall and winter of 1982 these began again . . . . He commented on what I was wearing in terms of whether it made me more or less sexually attractive . . . . One of the oddest episodes

I remember was an occasion in which Thomas was drinking a coke in his office, he got up from the table, at which we were working, went over to his desk to get the coke, looked at the can and asked, "Who has put pubic hair on my coke?" On other occasions he referred to the size of his own penis as being larger than normal and he also spoke on some occasions of the pleasures he had given to women with oral sex. At this point, late 1982, I began to feel severe stress on the job .... In January of 1983, I began looking for another job. I was handicapped because I feared that if he found out he might make it difficult for me to find other employment, and I might be dismissed from the job I had. Another factor that made my search more difficult was that this was during a period of a hiring freeze in the Government.

In February of 1983, I was hospitalized for five days on an emergency basis for acute stomach pain which I attributed to stress on the job.[4]

Anita Hill then secured a position teaching at Oral Roberts University. On her last day on the job, Thomas took her to dinner, she testified, at a restaurant near the office and told her that if she ever "told anyone of his behavior that it would ruin his career." Professor Hill added, "From 1983 until today I have seen Judge Thomas only twice," once to get a reference from him, and the second time when he spoke in Tulsa, where she taught.

The hearing room was deadly silent as she spoke, all of us sensing the drama and tragedy unfolding before us.

When Senator Specter began his questioning, he said, "I do not regard this as an adversary proceeding."[5] But he conducted himself as though it were, one newspaper noting his "tough questioning."[6] Political commentator William Schneider accurately described him as playing "the role of chief prosecutor against Hill."[7] He and Senator Hatch, the Republican questioners, were strong advocates for the man accused. On the Democratic side, Senators Leahy and Heflin were "seekers for the truth." So one side had advocates, the other side did not, and that skewed the final result. Schneider observed:

> Republicans seized on the leak as evidence that the Democrats would stop at nothing to discredit Thomas. Sen. Orrin Hatch called it 'indiscriminate, mean-spirited mud-slinging' perpetrated by 'slick lawyers' in league with 'liberal interest groups.' If that is true, then the liberal conspiracy to destroy Thomas was the worst organized conspiracy since the attempted coup in the Soviet Union. First, the Democrats fumbled the investigation. Then they were embarrassed by the leak. Then they failed to keep the hearings under control. The Democrats learned a lesson: If you're going to play hardball, you'd better have a game plan. The Republicans had a game plan: attack. Everyone, including Thomas, followed the script. The issue became her credibility, not his.[8]

None of us on the Democratic side looked good, but there was a lack of complete awareness of the dimensions of the problem we faced. There were several caucuses of the Democratic members of the Committee, but they generally involved procedural questions rather than "the big picture" questions. We did not sit back and ask ourselves what was happening, in terms of public perception, and how we might deal with that. I share the responsibility for this failure with my colleagues.

Harriett Woods, president of the National Women's Political Caucus, said: "The Democratic side fell over on their fannies. The White House and the Republican side knew what to do with the hearing and the Democrats acted like freelancers."[9] Maureen Dowd of the *New York Times* noted:

> While the vote on Tuesday is expected to be close, there was a strong sense among Professor Hill's backers that Judge Thomas came out of the hearings in better shape because of the difference in the parties' approaches. The Democrats made a pass at figuring out what had happened in the case. The Republicans tried to win. While the Democrats were pronouncing themselves flummoxed by

two diametrically opposed stories, the Republicans had already launched a scorched-earth strategy against Professor Hill.[10]

A magazine editorial observed: "Once the Republican Senators began their disgraceful attacks on Professor Hill, Senate Democrats and liberal media people fell into a deferential 'objective' mode of inquiry."[11] Kevin Phillips, a Republican commentator, said on National Public Radio: "The Republicans went for the jugular, the Democrats for the capillaries." One woman told me: "The television show *Designing Women* did more to defend Anita Hill than the United States Senate did." *Congressional Quarterly* reported: "The White House, which aggressively managed the process from the start, undertook a concerted effort to discredit Hill. Democrats who opposed Thomas never had an overall strategy . . . . They remained unorganized during the Hill-Thomas testimony."[12]

Still, aggressive questioning by Committee Republicans did not shake Hill's basic story. They pursued why she had followed him from one job to the next and why, over the next seven years, she had made eleven telephone calls to his office. She explained that three were made at the request of the Dean of her law school, who wanted Thomas to speak there. There were similar explanations for most of the others. She added, "I hoped to continue to maintain a professional relationship, for a variety of reasons. One was a sense that I could not afford to antagonize a person in such a high position."[13] She also made a social call, to congratulate him on his marriage.

The questioning also brought out how she made the gradual move to public disclosure. Gail Laster, a member of Senator Metzenbaum's staff, first contacted Hill. Laster asked if she knew anything about allegations of sexual harassment or tolerance of sexual harassment in the Clarence Thomas office. Hill replied that she had no comment. That brief "no comment" started to make history. Then Ricki Seidman of the Senate staff followed through with another call on the same subject, and Hill told the Committee: "I told Ms. Seidman that I would neither confirm nor deny any knowledge of that."[14]

Leahy questioned Hill about her feelings in retrospect, mentioning she had testified that the experiences depressed her at the time. "Today I feel more angry about the situation," she said. "It was very irresponsible for an individual in the position of that kind of authority to engage in that kind of conduct. It was not only irresponsible, in my opinion, it was in violation of the law."[15]

Then she replied to Senator Leahy's question about what she had to gain by testifying:

> I have nothing to gain. No one has promised me anything. I have nothing to gain here. This has been disruptive of my life and I have taken a number of personal risks. I have been threatened and I have not gained anything except knowing that I came forward and did what I felt that I had an obligation to do and that was to tell the truth.[16]

That Friday evening Judge Thomas returned. His statement early in the day had passion, but now he showed more than passion; he exhibited fury:

> I would like to start by saying unequivocally, uncategorically that I deny each and every single allegation against me today . . . . Today is a travesty. I think it is disgusting . . . . This hearing should never occur in America. This is a case where this sleaze, this dirt was searched for by staffers of members of this Committee, was then leaked to the media, and this Committee . . . displayed it in prime time over our entire Nation . . . .
> The Supreme Court is not worth it. No job is worth it. I am not here for that. I am here for my name, my family, my life and my integrity. I think something is dreadfully wrong with this country, when any person . . . in this free country would be subjected to this . . . . This is not an opportunity to talk about difficult matters privately or in a closed environment.

> This is a circus. It is a national disgrace. And from my standpoint, as a black American . . . it is a high-tech lynching for uppity blacks who in any way deign to think for themselves, to do for themselves, to have different ideas, and it is a message that, unless you kow-tow to an old order, this is what will happen to you, you will be lynched, destroyed, caricatured by a committee of the U. S. Senate, rather than hung from a tree.[17]

Thomas showed his statement to no one on the White House staff, only Senator Danforth. The Missouri Senator asked him whether he was sure he wanted to use "high-tech lynching," and he got a firm, "Yes."

His charge about being seen as "an uppity black" received no response from the Committee, in part because the Committee was obviously all white and all male. Diversity would be as good for the Committee as it is for the Court. My guess is that the presence of one woman or one African-American on the Committee would have changed the climate and some of the exchange, as well as the final vote. As to our resenting his being "an uppity black," it was the contrary. We regretted that on the EEOC he had become so completely subservient to those in the white community who had always fought opportunity for blacks. We wanted someone who would stand up for minorities and the less fortunate, as Thurgood Marshall had done.

Clarence Page, columnist for the *Chicago Tribune* and an African-American, wrote:

> As for Thomas's 'lynching' . . . it was interesting to see a man who has admonished his fellow African-Americans not to blame their troubles on racism suddenly blame his troubles on racism . . . . when caught in a pinch, Thomas whipped the race card out of his hip pocket adroitly.[18]

Rep. Eleanor Holmes Norton, the District of Columbia's non-voting House member, described Hill as a black woman who was too honest to use race and too believable to be denied. Thomas reached below the belt. That Anita Hill was also black did not count for much; she declined to use her race (or her gender, for that matter) to enhance her charges, while Thomas made race his central, indeed his only, defense. Though he had spent his entire career criticizing blacks for ascribing their conditions to race, Thomas reached for a racial rock and angrily hurled it at the monolith that comprised the Senate Judiciary Committee. To many blacks the Committee looked like nothing as much as an all-white jury.[19]

During Thomas's evening appearance, Specter took the opportunity to launch a broad-side against Anita Hill. "Professor Hill testified in the morning and demolished her testimony in the afternoon . . . . It is my legal judgment . . . that the testimony of Professor Hill in the morning was flat-out perjury."[20] By reading into the record the full statements at that point, Biden indicated strong, immediate disagreement with Specter. Democrats and some Republicans on the Committee felt Specter really went far afield on that point.

That night the Pennsylvania Senator and I appeared on the Larry King television show together, and I stated the obvious: There is not a prosecutor in the nation who would look at the testimony and say she had committed perjury. The *New York Times* editorialized: "Lawyers winced when Arlen Specter, a former prosecutor who knows better, sternly pronounced Anita Hill guilty of perjury for sparring with him over a side issue."[21] F. Lee Bailey, writing in the *American Bar Association Journal,* called Specter's questioning "mean-spirited" and added: "No lawyer reading the record of these proceedings would even consider, on any objective basis, that a case of perjury could be made against Hill."[22]

The questioning and dialogue grew more intense. At one point in a heated exchange, Thomas said to the Ohio Senator: "God is my judge, not you, Senator Metzenbaum."[23]

Senator Simpson, at the initial Thomas hearings, commented about himself, "I have a propensity to sometimes cross the line between good humor and smart aleck. And when I do, I certainly pay for it dearly, and should."[24] Popular with his colleagues and a moderate Republican on many issues (including the abortion issue), Simpson proceeded to get himself into trouble. In a preface to two questions, Simpson said: "I really am getting stuff over the transom about Professor Hill. I have got letters hanging out of my pockets. I have got faxes. I have got statements from her former law professors, statements from people that know her, statements from Tulsa, Oklahoma, saying, watch out for this woman. But nobody has got the guts to say that because it gets all tangled up in this sexual harassment crap."[25]

Before he left the witness chair, Thomas told the Committee with some bitterness: "There has never been one minute of joy in having been nominated to the Supreme Court of the United States of America."[26]

Thomas was not alone in having a difficult time. A University of Oklahoma law school student told *Newsweek:* "We went about the business of making Anita Hill's life a living hell."[27] A partner in the law firm at which Anita Hill worked issued a statement that she was fired for poor work, and that went out on national television. Another partner, Donald H. Green, sent the Committee a letter saying that Anita Hill never worked with the man who sent the letter or under his supervision and that he did not serve on the firm's associate development committee. He said that "her performance had not been unsatisfactory, that she was not asked to leave the firm and that she left of her own volition."[28] He checked with two others who supervised associates with him and they all agreed the statement about Hill was unwarranted and inaccurate. He said another African-American woman did work with the partner who made the first statement and that her work did not satisfy the firm, and she was asked to leave. The implication: The person making the charge confused the two people.

Four witnesses testified that years earlier Anita Hill had told them of being sexually harassed on the job by her supervisor and being deeply bothered by it. All four were substantial witnesses, including an administrative law judge and a law school professor. Three of the four came forward voluntarily, after hearing about the challenge to Hill's veracity and remembering her. In the fourth instance, Hill had recalled mentioning the sexual harassment and the witness came at the request of the Committee. Hill did not provide details of the harassment to them.

Then another group testified that they had worked with Thomas and had never heard of any sexual harassment charge against him by anyone. A man who testified against Hill caused many viewers to write us: "How could you let that egomaniac go unchallenged?" My impression was that he had serious emotional problems and I hoped that would be apparent to most viewers. He needed help, not hostile questions. Witnesses ordinarily are screened, but occasionally someone like that slips through.

From time to time the Judiciary Committee recessed to determine what procedures to follow. We were faced with a deadline of Monday afternoon to get the report to the Senate for a vote on Tuesday. Biden stretched himself to be fair to both sides. With one minor exception, all members of the Judiciary Committee agreed unanimously on the procedures.

Because the hearing was going well past midnight on Sunday into early Monday morning, one of the agreements reached was to offer Angela Wright, another former EEOC employee who had charged sexual harassment, the chance to testify, but she would have to testify at approximately 1:00 in the morning. Pro-Thomas senators were not eager to have her testify for obvious reasons, and those of us opposed to the Thomas nomination were not that eager to hear her because she had been fired by Thomas and her motivation for testifying could be brought into question. In retrospect we made a mistake in not hearing her. Had I read her testimony — as well as that of a corroborating witness — in advance, I would have favored hearing her, even at 1:00 in the morning. Democratic and Republican staff members jointly questioned Angela Wright, an assistant metro editor of the *Charlotte Observer,* and that was placed into the printed record, but it received little attention, because she did not appear before the Committee, and did not reach the television audience.

She said: "I want it on the record that the information that I am about to give is not information that I approached anyone on Capitol Hill or on the Senate Judiciary staff with, but it is something that I have struggled with since I have seen Anita Hill on television . . . and once I got a call from the Senate Judiciary Committee, that decision became quite obvious as to what I should do."[29]

Under questioning, she said:

> During the course of the year that I worked for Clarence Thomas . . . [he] did consistently pressure me to date him. At one point, Clarence Thomas made comments about my anatomy. Clarence Thomas made comments about women's anatomy quite often. At one point, Clarence Thomas came by my apartment at night, unannounced and uninvited and talked in general terms, but . . . he would try to move the conversation over to the prospect of my dating him.

She said that was the only time he stopped by her apartment. She reported his conduct to a supervisor at EEOC. She said she did not know Anita Hill, but "that the Clarence Thomas I know is quite capable of doing just what Anita Hill alleges."[30] A sworn affidavit was entered into the printed record by another employee regarding Angela Wright:

> When Ms. Wright first came in, she was very enthusiastic about her job. She was very happy to be there. As time went on, she became increasingly—she confided to me increasingly that she was a little uneasy and grew more uneasy with the Chairman, because of comments she told me that he was making concerning her figure, her body, her breasts, her legs, how she looked in certain suits and dresses . . . . One time she came into my office in tears, said she had bought a new suit that I thought was quite attractive . . . and he had evidently quite a bit of comment to make about it and how sexy she looked in it . . . and it unnerved her a great deal . . . .

> He asked her to have a one-on-one meeting, which
> would not be unusual . . . with the head of the public
> relations department, and these were scheduled in the
> evening, at the end of the workday, and she was increas-
> ingly uneasy about being there, and would say, why don't
> you wait for me . . . asking me to remain in the building
> until she would be able to leave.[31]

The difficulty with Angela Wright's testimony is the question of motivation. Thomas testified, when her name came up,

> I summarily dismissed her . . . . She was hired to rein-
> vigorate the public affairs operation at EEOC. I felt her
> performance was ineffective . . . . And the straw that broke
> the camel's back was a report to me from one of the
> members of my staff that she referred to another male
> member of my staff as a faggot.[32]

It is of interest that when the *Charlotte Observer* contacted Thomas to check on Angela Wright's work performance, he described her as "an excellent employee" who had done "a fine job" but left because of a realignment in their public relations operation.[33]

At some point my staff relayed a question from Anita Hill's lawyers, whether I thought she should come back to testify the next morning. I said that I felt she should, that she made a strong impression and that final impressions often are lasting impressions. What happened on her end of things I do not know, but Anita Hill and her attorneys, who could have returned on Monday morning, decided against it. Thomas also had that opportunity and also declined.

Later, on NBC's "Meet the Press," Andrea Mitchell asked me why Democrats had not used the issue of pornography and mentioned a specific allegation and the name of the person making the allegation. We had some additional charges that came to us along that line. Even if we found them to be completely true, and we did not investigate them, I am not sure there is a direct tie-in between watching pornographic films and sexual harassment, at least I have not seen evidence of that. *Newsweek* reported: "At one major daily newspaper, editors uneasily debated over whether to print the title of X-rated movies rented by Judge Thomas. An enterprising reporter had dug up the records. The paper decided to hold off."[34] In my opinion the newspaper made the correct decision. It is true that Anita Hill mentioned his conversations about pornographic films, but even if we had evidence that he saw them, that provides no clear link to conversations at the workplace. I felt uneasy getting into that field and I learned some time ago if you don't feel comfortable doing something, don't do it. Some believe this is what Thomas had in mind when he earlier told us, "I will not let this committee or anyone else probe into my private life." But that may well be an inaccurate assumption.

An Eruption of Public Concern

Three things happened while the hearings were going on.

First, telephone lines into the Capitol and Senate offices around the nation were swamped. Illinois Bell, for example, said that on one day, 58,780 callers tried to get through on the phone lines Senator Alan Dixon and I have to our Chicago offices. Even the possibility of launching a war in the Middle East did not evoke that kind of response.

Second, an avalanche of mail descended on the Senate. It had a markedly different tone from the mail before Anita Hill's public charges. The difference was substantially more than quantity, which multiplied. Earlier, people had urged me to vote for or against Thomas, but they did so with a touch of civility. Now, whichever side they were on, the letters screamed. Citizens all over the nation reflected strong feelings . . . on sexual harassment, psychology, the Supreme Court or whatever else they wrote about.

The certitude of their positions on both sides was greater than anything I recall. One letter-writer commented: "Your behavior during the Anita hill hearings and subsequent vote reminded me of a man who watches a brutal gang rape of a woman and does nothing, but afterwards eloquently talks about how horrible and terrible the rape was." Another observed: "You were deferential to Anita Hill to the point of nausea." The Iraq-Kuwait war issue evoked strong opinion because it involved life and death but it was nowhere near the passion of the Clarence Thomas/Anita Hill matter. During the decision-making on the Iraq-Kuwait war, my office received about 15,700 letters, compared to 19,600 letters on this. But the emotional zeal of those who wrote on the Thomas/Hill clash was measurably stronger.

Third, public opinion polls showed the majority of Americans favored Thomas. The *USA Today* poll, for example, showed 47 percent believing Thomas and 24 percent Hill, with 55 percent favoring confirmation of Thomas. Other polls showed higher numbers favoring confirmation. The Gallup poll showed 54 percent believing Thomas and 27 percent Hill. The higher the education level, the greater the likelihood of supporting Hill, according to Gallup. It also showed 71 percent of blacks supporting the Thomas nomination.[35] This became important to some of my colleagues who tend to vote the polls rather than their convictions.

As late as six months after the hearing, a poll taken in Illinois — which usually shows a remarkably close reflection of national opinion — by Southern Illinois University political scientists showed the public believing the Senate did the right thing to confirm Clarence Thomas, 53 percent to 23 percent, the balance with no opinion or undecided.

A Cultural Earthquake

Out of the Clarence Thomas/Anita Hill confrontation came a totally unplanned and unexpected cultural earthquake on sexual harassment. Like all earthquakes, it shook everything. How much lasting damage or improvement it will bring about is not yet certain, but after every serious earthquake, things never are completely the same again–and this one was serious.

Many thought approval of Thomas not only would result in his harsh-on-the-less-fortunate votes on the Court, but would also discourage women from standing up when abused because Hill's testimony met such a cool response from some Senators. Newspaper columnist Carol Ashkinaze voiced the sentiments of many when she wrote: "Thomas may yet be confirmed, at the expense of every woman who has ever tried to have such a charge taken seriously."[36] With that outcome, it appeared this six-word summation accurately portrayed what had happened: "He was promoted. She was repudiated."[37]

But the non-Court results turned out differently than many expected. Gloria Steinem, champion of the cause of women, reported, "Sexual harassment complaints are up 500 percent since the hearings."[38] Five months after the hearings, the *Chicago Tribune* carried this main headline on the front page: "Sex Harassment Complaints on Rise," and the two-column sub-heading read: "More Women Come Forth After Allegations by Hill."[39] Five days later the *Washington Post* had a six-column banner on an inside page: "Hill-Thomas Legacy May Be Challenge to Old Workplace Patterns."[40] The full impact of the televised hearings was starting to become clear.

On the David Brinkley television show, Senator Barbara Mikulski of Maryland called the hearings a national "teach-in on sexual harassment."[41] The big heading in the business section of a Sunday newspaper: "Businesses Take Another Look at Sexual Harassment." An *Associated Press* story distributed to newspapers across the nation said that businesses are reviewing their policies as a result of the hearings. It noted: "At American Telephone and Telegraph, for instance, management warns its 279,000 employees that they can be fired for making repeated unwelcome sexual advances, using sexually degrading words to describe someone, or displaying sexually offensive pictures or objects at work. But the company says in light of the issues raised in Thomas's hearings, it is considering expanding the number of voluntary training courses on sexual harassment."[42]

Many men were stunned to learn what women regard as sexual harassment. "He didn't even touch her!" one of my Senate colleagues commented to me about Thomas when the issue first arose. While many men would regard such conversation over the phone as an obscene phone call and deplorable, they did not make the connection between that and similar face-to-face conversation. Men who are not mean-spirited learned for the first time the problems that women face. All of us learned more about the dimensions of the problem. Women who had felt isolated, powerless, guilty and frustrated suddenly talked more openly, even to their families for the first time. This sharing has been good for the women involved and for all of us who have been at least partially unaware of the problems women face. (While statistically the problem is overwhelmingly women being harassed by men, there is also a lesser problem — but serious for those involved — of women harassing men and of same-sex harassment, none of this dealt with specifically here.)

Immediately after the hearings, but before the vote, Senator Mikulski said, "What disturbs me as much as the allegations themselves is that the Senate appears not to take the charge of sexual harassment seriously."[43]

Not everyone is welcoming the new sensitivity. One writer commented: "If unsubstantiated charges of sexual harassment make life for the American male as embarrassing as they recently made life for Justice Thomas, I suggest one vast all-male exodus to a freer society. The New Russia comes to mind." He also condemned "the explosion of prudery over indelicate language."[44]

Another writer charged: "The noise surrounding the [sexual harassment] issue is drowning out all rational conversation."[45]

Parade magazine did "a week's worth of random calls" in Washington and discovered "that the communications gap between the sexes is miles wide on this serious issue."[46] It found 70 percent of the women polled who serve in the military said they had been sexually harassed; 50 percent of the women who work in congressional offices; and 40 percent of the women who work for federal agencies. Women included "vulgar language, suggestive jokes, comments about one's body" as sexual harassment, while men thought it meant "touching, fondling, something physical." Significantly, the survey and the article grew out of the Hill/Thomas hearings.

My first insight into what the televised Hill/Thomas hearings were producing came in a note from someone I have known a long time. I have changed details to avoid identification: "Dave and I have been married forty years, and were watching Anita Hill testify when I suddenly burst into sobs. He asked me what was wrong. For the first time I told him that prior to meeting him I worked at a mental hospital, and I had a supervisor who kept making advances, both physical and verbal. I finally complained to the head of the hospital, a psychiatrist, and he laughed about it, basically saying, 'Boys will be boys.' I was young, desperate to hold onto my job, and didn't know where to turn. Shortly after I reported this, the hospital held its annual Christmas party for employees, and I was the only one not invited. I finally got another job, but what I lived through will never leave me. I had never told anyone until the televised hearings, and now you and my husband know about it."

The Ratings and the Polls

The numbers of people who watched the Thomas hearings astounded all of us. More people watched the hearings than the National Football League games. *The New York Times* reported that "in many of the nation's largest cities, including Chicago, Washington and Boston, the ratings Sunday night for the hearings on PBS dwarfed the ratings CBS received for the National League play-off game between the Atlanta Braves and the Pittsburgh Pirates."[47]

While television brought the drama into our living rooms, several byproducts helped Thomas in the polls. One was timing. Both Thomas and Hill were credible witnesses. Those who saw only Anita Hill tended to believe her, and those who saw only Clarence Thomas tended to believe him. But she appeared on national television on Friday, during the day, when the audience was smaller. He appeared on Friday night and Saturday with a significantly larger audience.

A second advantage he had was that he appeared last. He offered the first testimony, and then after Anita Hill appeared, he came on again. Any debater knows that the person who appears last has the best opportunity to convince people.

Finally, whether it was from passion or acting ability or a sense of drama, Thomas spoke with a vehemence that convinced many people. Hill, the academician, testified in much more subdued, low-key fashion. Many people who wrote to me thought that if she had really experienced what she said she went through, Hill would have shown more emotion. If she could have shed a few tears, shouted a little, more television viewers would have been convinced. But that is not her style.

On the Senate Floor

Newspapers predicted that Thomas would be confirmed, but as we approached the vote on the floor, no one knew that with certainty.

The weakest argument made on the Senate floor by the pro-Thomas forces was that "the benefit of the doubt goes to the accused." If this were a trial to determine the innocence or guilt of someone, to determine whether someone's rights should be taken away, then that would apply. But no one has a "right" to sit on the Supreme Court. We were not talking about a trial, but of the heavy responsibility of deciding who will sit on the Supreme Court for forty years, if he remains until the age of his predecessor, Justice Marshall. The benefit of the doubt must go to the people of the nation. If there is doubt, that person should not be seated on the Supreme Court.

The two most powerful speeches were by Senator Robert Byrd of West Virginia, white-haired President Pro Tempore, and Senator John Danforth, Thomas's mentor. It is of significance that the sexual harassment charges had so mesmerized the Senate and the nation that the two most significant speeches were centered on that rather than the usual considerations for a Supreme Court nominee.

Danforth concluded his eloquent speech: "It cannot be true that in the process of trying to defeat a nominee absolutely anything goes. It cannot be true that the sky is the limit. It cannot be true that we are going to tolerate a situation where anybody who wants to throw the mud gets to throw the mud and, if it sticks, that is just wonderful. It cannot be the case. I believe that our confirmation process is at issue, as is Clarence Thomas himself. I believe that the character of the Senate is at issue, as well as the character of Clarence Thomas. I believe that the eyes of the country are focused on us as well as on him, and I believe that the time has come for us as a body to stand up and say 'No' to what we have seen this weekend."[48]

Byrd inserted into the Record the speech he intended to give supporting Thomas. It indicated "reservation about the nomination" but a favorable vote. Then Byrd told the Senate about watching "every minute of the hearings with the exception of fifteen minutes" on television. He taped Anita Hill's and Clarence Thomas's testimony and replayed them. Speaking with passion and not reading from a text, he said he had switched his vote:

> I believe Anita Hill . . . . I watched her on that screen intensely and I replayed, as I have already said, her appearance and her statement. I did not see on that face the knotted brow of satanic revenge. I did not see a face that was contorted with hate. I did not hear a voice that was tremulous with passion. I saw the face of a woman, one of thirteen in a family of southern blacks who grew up on a farm and who early in her life belonged to the church, who belongs to the church today, and who was evidently reared by religious parents . . . . Some thought there were inconsistencies, but a careful reading of the exact language of the questions that were put to her can . . . explain away the appearance of an inconsistency.

Then with obvious reference to Specter, he denounced "loose talk . . . made about possible perjury." Byrd said he found her

> thoughtful, reflective and truthful . . . . She was testifying under oath.

He professed nothing more than to clear his name. Yet he could not be bothered to even listen to the allegations from the person making the allegations [Thomas had said he did not watch her testimony] . . . . He not only effectively stonewalled the committee; he just, in the main, made speeches before the committee; he managed his own defense by charging that the committee proceeded to "high-tech lynching of uppity blacks." . . . That was an attempt to shift ground. That was an attempt to fire the prejudices of race hatred, and shift the debate to a matter involving race . . . . Judge Thomas sought to blame his troubles on the process, but his problem was of his own making . . . . He is not running for the U. S. Senate, when there would be another chance in six years to pass judgment on him . . . . He has been nominated to the Supreme Court of the United States, and if he is not rejected—I believe he will not be rejected; too many people have made up their mind . . . too many have been swayed with this argument about the benefit of the doubt— . . . the country will live with this decision for the next thirty years.

Byrd then demolished the argument about "doubt going to the accused," pointing out this was not a trial. "As far as I am concerned the benefit of the doubt will go to the Court and to my children and to my grandchildren and to my country."[49]

Senate attendance is usually sparse, with members attending committee meetings and appointments with constituents and other activities. When Byrd spoke, there were probably not more than eight Senators on the floor. When Byrd is at his best, he is powerful. On this occasion he showed power and conviction. My instinct is that if all Senators had been there, this is one instance where votes would have been changed and Thomas would have lost.

Indeed, three Senators who had announced for Thomas did switch their votes: Joseph Lieberman of Connecticut and Harry Reid and Richard Bryan of Nevada. Bryan received a phone call from President Bush; he received 6,000 other phone calls from the public, the majority in favor of Thomas; he consulted his children on the issue and they were divided; he talked to his staff, and they were unanimously opposed to Thomas. What helped determine Bryan's vote in the end were the assertion by Thomas that he did not watch Anita Hill's testimony and the use of "racism to divert attention from the sexual harassment story."[50]

Before Anita Hill's testimony, Senator Danforth had predicted a vote for Thomas in the sixties. However, the Hill testimony created a different atmosphere. Most members thought Thomas would be approved, but the unprecedented hearings, the publicity and the spectacle haunted us with uncertainty.

Thomas won 52-48, the closest vote for a Supreme Court nominee in more than a century. Eleven Democrats voted for him: David Boren of Oklahoma, John Breaux of Louisiana, Dennis DeConcini of Arizona, Alan Dixon of Illinois, James Exon of Nebraska, Wyche Fowler of Georgia, "Fritz" Hollings of South Carolina, Bennett Johnston of Louisiana, Sam Nunn of Georgia, Charles Robb of Virginia and Richard Shelby of Alabama. Two Republicans voted against him: James Jeffords of Vermont and Robert Packwood of Oregon. Of more than minor interest, every one of the thirty senators still in the Senate in 1991 who voted against the Civil Rights Bill of 1990, voted for Clarence Thomas. Charles Bowser, a distinguished Philadelphia lawyer who is an African-American, commented: "I'd be willing to bet . . . that not one of the Senators who voted to confirm Clarence Thomas would hire him as their lawyer."[51]

The Aftermath

After the Senate vote, the retired Chief Judge of the Court of Appeals of the Philadelphia area, Leon Higginbotham Jr., an African-American, wrote an eloquent — and historically unique — open letter to Justice Thomas, saying that Thomas now had "the option to preserve or dilute the gains this country has made in the struggle for equality."

Higginbotham recited the battles for equality that had preceded Thomas's assent to the Court, including the right to vote. Because of the enfranchisement of black voters, no longer

> could a United States Senator say what Senator Benjamin Tillman of South Carolina said in anger when President Theodore Roosevelt invited a moderate Negro, Booker T. Washington, to lunch at the White House: "Now that Roosevelt has eaten with that nigger Washington, we shall have to kill a thousand niggers to get them back in their place."

Higginbotham pointed out that Thomas could not reside where he does, because of the legal racial housing barriers in Virginia, but for the courage of those who tore down those legal barriers. He noted that Virginia also banned interracial marriages, which the Virginia Supreme Court ruled constitutional as late as 1966. "If the Virginia courts had been sustained by the United States Supreme Court in 1966, and if you and your wife had defied the Virginia statute by continuing to live in your present residence, you could have been in the penitentiary today rather than serving as an Associate Justice of the United States Supreme Court."

He concluded:

> You were born into injustice, tempered by the hard reality of what it means to be poor and black in America, and especially to be poor because you were black. You have found a door newly cracked open and you have escaped. I trust you shall not forget that many . . . have found, and will find, the door of equal opportunity slammed in their faces through no fault of their own.[52]

From my perspective, Clarence Thomas's finest moment did not come during his testimony, but after the bitter and acrimonious debate that had divided the nation. Meeting television reporters outside his home after the vote, he commented: "No matter how difficult or painful, this is a time for healing in our country. We have to put these things behind us.

We have to go forward. We have to look for ways to solve problems."[53]

Thomas won, but in a real sense, in part, so did Anita Hill and the women of America. The issue of sexual harassment exploded across the television screens and reached the heart of the nation. Men understood the issue much more clearly than they ever had. Women talked about it more openly than they ever had. Months after the hearings, national television news still carried feature stories on the problems of sexual harassment. Most American men had no idea of the extent of the problem, and many American women thought they were in isolation facing a disheartening difficulty. Clarence Thomas will change the nation through the Court. Anita Hill has already changed the nation through her courage.

After the emotionally draining Thomas confirmation, another positive change occurred: The administration, which had been doing everything possible to bury the civil rights bill, found itself indebted to the chief Senate sponsor, John Danforth, and found many Senators who had voted against Thomas wanting to improve their social sensitivity records; the previously moribund civil rights bill passed, and the President signed it. As with the 1990 civil rights proposal, all those in the Senate who voted against the Civil Rights Act of 1991 voted for Clarence Thomas's confirmation.

On October 23, 1991, "at a hastily arranged private swearing-in ceremony," Clarence Thomas became the 106th Supreme Court Justice.[54]

Endnotes

1. *Nomination of Judge Clarence Thomas,* Senate Judiciary Committee Hearings (Washington: Government Printing Office, 1991), October 11, 12 and 13, p. 5.

2. *Ibid.,* p. 5.

3. *Ibid.,* p. 7.

4. *Ibid.,* p. 35-37.

5. *Ibid.*

6. *Roll Call,* February 10, 1992, "Woman Enters Dems' April Primary Race to Unseat Sen. Specter."

7. "The Politics of the Court," by William Schneider, *Los Angeles Times* syndicate, October 20, 1991.

8. *Ibid.*

9. Quoted in "Getting Nasty Early Helps GOP Gain Edge on Thomas," by Maureen Dowd, *New York Times,* October 15, 1991.

10. *Ibid.*

11. "Free Associations," editorial note, *Tikkun,* November-December 1991.

12. "Thomas's Victory Puts Icing on Reagan-Bush Court," by Joan Biskupic, *Congressional Quarterly,* October 19, 1991.

13. Nominations of Judge Clarence Thomas, Senate Judiciary Committee Hearings (Washington: Government Printing Office, 1991), October 11, 12 and 13, p. 97.

14. *Ibid.,* p. 100.

15. *Ibid.,* p. 107.

16. *Ibid.,* p. 107.

17. *Ibid.,* p. 147.

18. "Clarence Thomas Feeds Blacks' Conspiracy Fears," by Clarence Page, *Chicago Tribune,* October 16, 1991.

19. "And the Language is Race," by Eleanor Holmes Norton, *Ms.,* January/February 1992.

20. *Nomination of Judge Clarence Thomas,* pp. 212-214.

21. "Against Clarence Thomas," editorial, *New York Times,* October 15, 1991.

22. "Where Was the Crucible? The Cross-Examination That Wasn't," by F. Lee Bailey, *American Bar Association Journal*, January 1992.
23. *Nomination of Judge Clarence Thomas,* p. 220.
24. *Clarence Thomas Hearings,* Senate Judiciary Committee, Unpublished Transcript, Morning Session, September 11, 1991, p. 24.
25. *Nomination of Judge Clarence Thomas,* p. 235.
26. *Ibid.,* p. 238.
27. Chris Wilson in "Perspectives," *Newsweek,* February 10, 1992.
28. *Congressional Record,* Senate, October 31, 1991, letter from Donald H. Green to Joseph R. Biden.
29. *Ibid.,* p. 415.
30. *Ibid.,* p. 444.
31. Rose Jourdain, *Ibid.,* pp. 487-489.
32. *Ibid.,* p. 236.
33. "Thomas Testimony on Wright Contested," *St. Louis Journalism Review,* November 1991.
34. "There is Always Something," by Evan Thomas, *Newsweek,* October 21, 1991.
35. "On Night Before Vote, Support for Thomas Remains Strong," by Larry Hugick, *Gallup Poll News Service,* October 15, 1991.
36. "Confirmation would be slap in face for sexual harassment victims," Carol Ashkinaze, *Chicago Sun-Times,* October 11, 1991.
37. "Becoming the Third Wave," by Rebecca Walker, *Ms.,* January/February 1992.
38. "Deconstructing Gloria," by Leslie Bennetts, *Vanity Fair,* January 1992.
39. *Chicago Tribune,* March 7, 1992, story by Carol Kleiman.
40. *Washington Post,* March 12, 1992, story by Dana Priest.
41. Quoted in "Hill v. Thomas," by Thomas H. Stahel, *America,* November 2, 1991.

42. "Businesses Take Another Look at Sexual Harassment," by David Kalish, Associated Press, *Chicago Tribune,* December 29, 1991.

43. Quoted in "Thomas Drama Engulfs Nation," by Joan Biskupic, *Congressional Quarterly,* October 12, 1991.

44. "Fading Fear of Feminists," by R. Emmett Tyrrell Jr., *Washington Times,* October 27, 1991.

45. "The Thinking Man's Guide to Working With Women," by Denis Boyles, *Playboy,* February 1992.

46. "Sexual Harassment: Gender Gap on Capitol Hill," *Parade,* November 17, 1991.

47. "Hearings Remain a Champion in Ratings," by Bill Carter, *New York Times,* October 15, 1991.

48. *Congressional Record,* Senate, October 7, 1991, p. 14455.

49. *Ibid.,* pp. 14629-14634.

50. "Behind the Decisions," by Alissa Rubin, *Congressional Quarterly,* October 19, 1991.

51. "Bowser Is an Old Hand at Playing the Political Game in Philadelphia, by Peter Binzer, *Philadelphia Inquirer,* November 13, 1991.

52. "An Open Letter to Justice Clarence Thomas from a Federal Judicial Colleague," by Leon Higginbotham Jr., *University of Pennsylvania Law Review,* January 1992.

53. "New Justice Calls for Healing, Not Anger, After Senate Ordeal," Associated Press, October 15, 1991.

54. "Thomas Sworn in As 106th Justice," by Linda Greenhouse, *New York Times,* October 24, 1991.

6

Who Told The Truth?

When two persons are alone in a room, as Anita Hill and Clarence Thomas were, no one else can know precisely what their conversation holds, what words are used, what gestures are made. That was the quandary of the United States Senate. But distance from the passion of those hearings and a careful analysis in cold print of the charges and counter-charges do shed some light on the question of who told the truth.

Let me give you my assessment of the factors on both sides and what that assessment, if correct, ultimately means.

Factors for the Clarence Thomas Side

☐ *She followed him from one job to the next.*

The Committee did not hear from experts on sexual harassment (discussed briefly in chapter eighteen), but those who are knowledgeable in this field say this is typical. More significant, she said his sexual talk and advances ceased for a period. As she testified, "I began to believe and hope that our working relationship could be a proper, cordial, and professional one."[1] But when she got to the new position, she charges that the harassment began again.

☐ *She could have stayed at the job she had.*

As an assistant to a political appointee, she had every reason to believe a new political appointee would select his or her own assistant. While in theory covered by Civil Service, she was twenty-five years old and knew that President Reagan had publicly spoken about abolishing the Department of Education, where she worked.

☐ *She did not take notes about his conduct.*

She responded:

> It might have been a good choice to make the notes. I did not do it, though.... I was not interested in any litigation .... If I had been dismissed, very likely I would have just gone out and tried to find another job. I was not interested in filing a claim against him, and perhaps that is why it did not occur to me to make notes about it .... One of the things I did do at that time was to document my work. I went through very meticulously with every assignment that I was given .... This really was in response to concerns that I had about being fired.[2]

☐ *She gave the Committee more details than she gave the* FBI.

There is no inconsistency between the two. As time went on, she recalled additional details. The FBI report came from a one-time, brief visit. A former investigator for the Navy told me that if the FBI had regarded this as important, there would have been a follow-up interview, since they know that all people recall additional details after an initial questioning.

☐ *"If it were true, she would have shown more emotion."*

If I were scripting a television drama, she would have shown more emotion. But this was real life, not a soap opera. Some people are openly emotional, some are not. She is a person who generally keeps the display of emotion under tight control.

☐ *She made phone calls to him after leaving his employ.*

Eleven phone calls over a period of seven years are recorded. She did not reach Thomas in all of these calls. Three of those were made at the request of the dean of the law school where she taught. She also made clear that she wanted to maintain a cordial but professional relationship with him because of the high position he held and because she might need him as a reference for a future position. Again, experts in sexual harassment say this conduct is typical.

☐ *When Thomas spoke at Oral Roberts University, she took Thomas to the airport.*

The dean had requested her to do it and she did. Hill at no time expressed fear of physical harm by Thomas.

☐ *"The whole thing is a fantasy in her mind."*

She did not strike me as a person who fantasizes, nor was there any evidence produced to suggest this weakness. Her friends who testified that she told them some years earlier about the harassment all said she is a very down-to-earth person who does not fantasize. NBC interviewed psychiatrist Robert Spitzer on "NBC Nightly News," who voiced "extreme skepticism" about the fantasy theory. He said that Hill showed no signs of it.[3] Another psychiatrist wrote in the *Washington Post:* "By declaring someone mentally ill for political purposes, a group of Senators . . . had a dangerous lapse."[4]

☐ *"Some group got her to do this."*

Not only did she testify under oath that this was not the case, there is not one shred of evidence to support that theory.

☐ *"This is part of her political agenda."*

It is interesting that the two principle witnesses against Thomas on sexual harassment, one heard and one unheard, have conservative ties. Anita Hill strongly backed Robert Bork for the Supreme Court. Angela Wright met Clarence Thomas at the Black Republican Congressional Staff Association, of which she was a founder. Hill had some differences with Thomas, but her conservative ties were strong enough to help get her on the faculty of Oral Roberts University, one of the most conservative schools in the nation.

☐ *"She should have filed a complaint."*

Perhaps she should have, but the complaint at EEOC would ultimately go to the person in charge of enforcing sexual harassment charges in the federal government: Clarence Thomas. In addition, most people in this situation are not eager for legal action. They simply want the conduct to stop. They want their jobs. And frequently, except for the sexual conduct, they respect the person for whom they work.

The case would be clearer if Hill had not followed Thomas from one job to another, if there had been no phone calls, or if she had taken notes. The reality is that, however explainable, they did raise questions about her credibility and had some impact on the Senate and on the public.

There are other components, however, that also should be weighed as the truth is pursued.

Factors for the Anita Hill Side

☐ *Motivation.*

Clarence Thomas's motivation is apparent: to clear his name and to secure a seat on the Supreme Court. It is difficult to find any motivation for her, other than a sense of public duty. Unless you construct a complicated and unlikely scenario, she had much to lose and nothing to gain by coming forward.

☐ *Her reluctance to testify.*

I learned from that first telephone conversation with her that she did not want to surface publicly, much less testify on such a personal matter before fourteen Senators and the world. All the evidence points to her reluctance. If this were some planned scheme, there would not have been a reluctance to testify.

☐ *She could have invented a better story.*

If she were creating a story, she could have had him fondling her. She could have had him explicitly asking her to go to bed with him. The fact that she did not tell these things as part of her story lends it credibility. As *Time* magazine reported: "Given the detail and consistency of her testimony, it was almost inconceivable that Hill . . . was fabricating the portrait of a sexual-harassment victim."[5]

☐ *The hospital stay.*

In her statement, she said: "In February 1983 I was hospitalized for five days on an emergency basis for an acute stomach pain which I attributed to stress on the job."[6] She said they could find no cause for the stomach pain and her physician said it could be stress-related. Something caused the stress. A hospital stay is not the figment of someone's imagination. This occurred during the period when the sexual harassment is alleged to have taken place.

☐ *She voluntarily took a polygraph (lie detector) test.*

I am not a great believer in polygraph test use because it can be so easily abused. But when the FBI interviewed her, the agents asked: Would you be willing to take a polygraph test?

Anita Hill agreed to do it. My experience is that people who are lying do not volunteer to take polygraph tests. The irony of her taking it after the FBI asked the question for its client, the White House, is that she was then attacked by the White House and the Republicans for taking the test. NBC asked me why I had not asked Thomas about taking a polygraph test. I did not because it would be unhealthy to develop a situation where candidates and nominees are expected to do that. But once suggested by the FBI, the fact that Anita Hill voluntarily took it–and passed–adds to her credibility.

☐ *"If he were guilty, there would be a pattern of sexual harassment."*

Not necessarily. The president of a Washington-area university left under a cloud because he made obscene phone calls to one woman. No pattern was established; he confessed and underwent psychiatric treatment. In the Thomas case, the Angela Wright affidavit, corroborated by another witness, showed precisely the same behavior pattern Hill charged against Thomas. One magazine article notes that Angela Wright's "account to the committee of Thomas's sexual advances would seem to establish a pattern."[7] Two people coming forward may not establish a pattern, but it is stronger than one person alone.

☐ *The credible witnesses.*

Anita Hill recalled telling only one person about her difficulties. As a result of the publicity, three others came forward who said she had told them of having great stress because of her supervisor's sexual advances. All four witnesses were substantial and credible.

☐ *Thomas had a credibility problem with the Committee before the Anita Hill matter.*

Whether it was his expressed assertion that he had no opinion on the *Roe v. Wade* decision, or his claim that the White House advisers did not shape his answers in any way, or his dramatic shifts in position on everything from natural law to Oliver Wendell Holmes, some of us on the Committee came away with the feeling that he had not been straight with us. He had shaped his answers to please us, rather than telling us the truth.

☐ *Thomas's attempt—to some extent successful—to switch the focus from the harassment charges to race.*

If the person making the charge had been white, the nominee's attempt to shift the issue would have been easier. But Thomas had an "all-white jury" facing him in the Committee that did not counter the race charge. Shifting the issue is one factor in determining who told the truth.

☐ *Thomas did not watch her charges on television.*

Senators Heflin and Specter both expressed surprise that the nominee did not watch the television charges in order to refute them. Trial lawyers say that in a criminal trial, if the defendant does not listen to the witnesses describing the offense, ordinarily that is an indication of guilt.

No one of these factors by itself is decisive, but cumulatively, they make a powerful case for the veracity of the Oklahoma professor.

One other item of interest: The *National Law Journal* did a survey of state and federal trial judges, asking them whose testimony they found more credible. 41 percent said Hill, while 22 percent said Thomas, almost a two-to-one margin. 37 percent were not sure.[8] The same survey found 54 percent of those surveyed felt the Bush administration had suffered damage in the process, and 85 percent thought the credibility of Congress had been harmed. The trial judges probably caught bits and pieces of the televised hearings, as the rest of the public did, but people schooled by experience in evaluating testimony reached the opposite conclusion from the general public. If the polls are accurate, by roughly a two-to-one majority the public believed Thomas, and by roughly a two-to-one majority the trial judges believed Hill.

After the Senate vote, columnist Garry Wills wrote: "Now we have a perjurer on the bench." Speaking specifically about his abortion statements, Wills wrote: "There is a remarkably bipartisan consensus that Clarence Thomas was not telling the truth under oath."[9]

The Impeachment Alternative

What if additional evidence should emerge making it more obvious that Thomas lied to the Committee? First, it is not likely to happen. If it did happen, it probably would be in connection with his earlier testimony, not on the sexual harassment charges. It is possible that witnesses could come forward, for example, stating that he took a strong abortion stand. While the Episcopal Church generally takes a pro-choice position, Thomas and his wife joined the Episcopal Church in the Washington area that makes a crusade of its anti-choice position. By itself that proves nothing. But suppose several witnesses came forward stating that he said that is why he joined their church. Other examples of his strong position could emerge. What would happen then?

In all likelihood, nothing.

People are impeached under the Constitution for "high crimes and misdemeanors," but the Constitution does not define the terms. No federal judge has ever been removed for conduct prior to becoming a judge. Judges at the federal level have been removed for action after becoming jurists. However, there are state precedents. Voters in New York elected Joseph P. Pfingst as a justice of the Supreme Court in 1968. In 1972, he was convicted of fraud for actions taken in 1966 and New York's Court on the Judiciary removed him from office.[10] In two Pennsylvania cases, judges were removed for action taken prior to becoming judges. These are the only instances I have been able to find where that has happened. In a significantly larger number of cases, judges have been censured for action taken prior to becoming judges, often for violating election spending or election conduct limits. Several states have laws specifically permitting the removal of judges for conduct prior to assuming office. Wyoming limits it to conduct or action six years before becoming a judge. Arkansas law is an example of broader language, "conduct of a judge or justice occurring prior to or during service in judicial office."[11]

On Thomas, proof of perjury is unlikely to occur, and even if it did occur, it is not probable that a federal judge, at whatever level, would be removed for action taken prior to holding office. When the Senate confirmed Hugo Black, he immediately took his oath of office because of fear of what the opposition might do. "After I had taken the oath," he wrote afterwards, "my enemies would have to impeach me for something I had done *since* [emphasis in the original] taking the oath of office."[12]

That means the decision to seat the present Justice Thomas is final. What can be hoped is that out of this experience, he can grow; that the Clarence Thomas who appeared before our Committee and seemed sensitive to those least fortunate, can emerge, rather than the Clarence Thomas whose writings do not show that sensitivity. The initial votes by Justice Thomas on the Court are not encouraging. One of his first decisions involved a Louisiana prisoner, Keith Hudson, who while shackled was badly beaten by two guards after a supervisor told them not to have "too much fun" with him. Among other things, the two guards beat him badly enough to cause a broken dental plate, loosened teeth, facial swelling and general bruises. Seven members of the Court said that such conduct violated the Eighth Amendment ban on "cruel and unusual punishment." Justices Thomas and Scalia said it did not. The majority said of the Thomas/Scalia dissent: "To deny, as the dissent does, the difference between punching a prisoner in the face and serving him unappetizing food is to ignore the concepts of dignity, civilized standards, humanity, and decency that animate the Eighth Amendment." Thomas wrote the dissent. An editorial in the *New York Times* had the heading: "The Youngest Cruelest Justice," (February 17, 1992).

Some of our finest public officials achieved greatness despite scars in their past. Justice Cardozo's father was forced to resign from the bench for action that was at least unethical, a source of substantial embarrassment to the future Supreme Court Justice, but he did not let it stop him from great public service. And some of our best Justices had bruising battles before being confirmed; Brandeis is a prime example. Senator Kennedy, who sits on the Judiciary Committee, has his scars, but any Senator — Republican or Democrat — will tell you that he remains one of the most influential members of the Senate because of his hard work and strong convictions.

I do not condone lying to Congress, but Justice Fortas apparently did and served the Court well for approximately one year after that. Supreme Court Justices are not saints any more than Senators or those who read these words. That should cause some comfort to Justice Thomas.

After the final vote, Michael Gartner, president of NBC News, wrote: "You've been eloquent and moving, Judge Thomas. . . . You fought with dignity for dignity. You won. Now . . . please don't forget there are others fighting for their dignity. They are not all as articulate as you, as intelligent as you . . . . The poor, the black, the unlucky, the uneducated, the young and the old deserve dignity too. They have been wronged . . . in the workplace. Or in the schools. Or in the courts. Or in the streets. Fight for them, Judge Thomas, as passionately as you fought for yourself."[13]

If the entire Anita Hill episode had taken place in Europe, it would not have caused a great stir. Most Europeans are amazed at what they call our "morality plays." We have a different cultural climate and in some ways higher standards. A *New York Times* article from Paris noted that European media coverage of the controversy "seems to underline the cultural gap separating the United States from other Western countries where sexual harassment is not punishable and where the sexual behavior of public figures is considered off-limits to the press."[14]

I hope that after watching this "morality play," we Americans will do more than examine the process and look at the conduct and attitude of one nominee toward another human being. Our morality should also demand that we look at a nominee's attitude toward the millions whose lives will be affected by the decisions of a Supreme Court Justice. If personal morality is exemplary, yet there is indifference to those in this nation yearning for opportunity, then a greater wrong is permitted.

We should not have to choose between the two.

Endnotes

1. *Nomination of Judge Clarence Thomas,* Senate Judiciary Committee Hearings (Washington: Government Printing Office, 1991), October 11-13, p. 36.

2. *Ibid.,* p. 74.

3. October 13, 1991, quoted in "The Clarence Thomas Hearings," by William Boot, *Columbia Journalism Review,* February 1992.

4. Stanley Greenspan and Nancy Thorndike Greenspan, "Lies, Delusions, and Truths," *Washington Post,* October 29, 1991.

5. "She Said, He Said," by Jill Smolowe, *Time,* October 21, 1991.

6. *Nomination of Judge Clarence Thomas,* Senate Judiciary Committee Hearings (Washington: Government Printing Office, 1991), October 11-13.

7. "The Higher Hustle," by Sidney Blumenthal, *The New Republic,* November 11, 1991.

8. "Hearings Turn Off Judges," *National Law Journal,* October 28, 1991.

9. "Congress: The National Lie-In," by Garry Wills, Universal Press Syndicate, October 16, 1991.

10. Gerald Stern, New York Commission on Judicial, letter to Paul Simon, January 22, 1992.

11. Cindy L. Brown, Senior Historian, Wyoming, letter to Paul Simon, January 16, 1992; James A. Badami, Executive Director, Judicial Discipline and Disability Commission of Arkansas, letter to Paul Simon, January 17, 1992.

12. Hugo Black and Elizabeth Black, *Mr. Justice and Mrs. Black* (New York: Random House, 1986), p. 69.

13. "The Hearings: Silver Lining?" by Michael Gartner, *Des Moines Register,* October 20, 1991.

14. "Foreign Press Shrugs at Latest U.S. Morality Play," by Alan Riding, *New York Times,* October 14, 1991.

Part III

Judicial Roots

7

The Supreme Court Is Created

When the men who wrote the nation's Constitution gathered in Philadelphia in 1787, they devoted little time to the judicial branch of government. "The judiciary is beyond comparison the weakest of the three departments of power," Alexander Hamilton wrote in one of the Federalist Papers after the Constitution had been written.[1] None of those involved in writing the document had the remotest idea that the Supreme Court would eventually play a major role in moving the nation toward a civil war in the *Dred Scott* decision, nor, almost a century after that war, in protecting basic liberties.

Necessity brought the men together to write a new framework for the former colonies. Things were not going well. The Articles of Confederation, which held the young nation together loosely, gave so much authority to the states that a central government almost did not exist. The inability of the states to act coopera-tively, as well as resolve problems that arose between them, became obvious to those who led the colonies to independence from Great Britain. The states were in danger of becoming independent nations themselves, and both the dreamers and the activists among the early leaders saw that as undesirable.

In the one-chamber Congress that the Articles of Confedera-tion created, each state had one vote. That parliamentary body chose one of its number as a presider—from which we get the term "president"—but the "president" had no authority beyond presiding over the body. Along with many other deficiencies, the Articles had one additional major weakness: no federal judiciary. Congress did create a three-man "Court of Appeals in Cases of Capture" to deal with admiralty law, but it soon withered and died. The Articles of Confederation did, however, give to Congress the authority to settle disputes between states, and six such disputes were referred to Congress. While its judicial provisions were lengthy and complicated as well as anemic in almost every respect, that early document did set a precedent for having a mechanism to resolve matters that could not be adjudicated within one state.

The ineffectiveness of the Articles of Confederation, how-ever, became more and more obvious. George Washington wrote to Thomas Jefferson:

> The situation of the general government, if it can be called a government, is shaken to its foundation, and liable to be overturned by every blast. In a word, it is at an end; and, unless a remedy is soon applied, anarchy and confusion will inevitably ensue.[2]

The weaknesses of the system were so clear that more and more people were calling for a convention to draft a new constitution or at least make major changes in the Articles of Confederation. Alexander Hamilton was the first major leader to make this suggestion, and soon calls were coming from others in Massachusetts, New York, South Carolina and Virginia.

Gradually the idea gathered momentum, and the Congress officially joined the movement for a convention in February 1787, setting the convention in Philadelphia in May.

The Constitutional Convention

The convention opened on May 25th in Independence Hall. Twelve of the thirteen states sent representatives. Rhode Island, whose leaders did not want a national government meddling in their internal matters, was the exception.

The delegates unanimously elected George Washington presiding officer. Washington made only one speech to all the delegates during the entire proceedings, on the size of the future House of Representatives. But Washington had designated evenings when he would visit with delegates, either singly or in small groups. Regarded by some as cool and aloof, he nevertheless enjoyed enormous respect and in those informal meetings helped to shape the final result. The cast of characters in Philadelphia became familiar to those who watched the politics of the emerging nation: Hamilton, James Madison, 82-year-old Benjamin Franklin—always called Dr. Franklin—and others who were to be dominant figures for the early years of the nation.

Most of the debate centered on the formation of the executive and legislative branches of government. They spent more time on what the pay should be for those two branches than was spent in toto discussing the judicial branch. (Franklin at one point wanted to pay the President nothing, to discourage those who would seek the office for personal gain, and one delegate wanted to tie the salary of legislators to the price of wheat, a novel suggestion farmers might find appealing today.)

The convention agreed that its discussions and work would be kept secret until they completed the final product, a guideline that delegates (some were called "Commissioner") followed with surprising faithfulness, perhaps in part because the press had no great interest in an event that many felt was doomed to failure. Delegates adhered to that secrecy agreement even in correspondence with their families. The secretary of the convention, Major William Jackson, had little sense of history and destroyed "all the loose scraps of paper" that delegates left at their desks, feeling they were unimportant.[3]

Fortunately, James Madison took careful notes on what the delegates agreed to and summarized the comments of many of the speakers. Others had less extensive notes or wrote letters after the convention. In addition, there is the official *Journal* of the convention which records only formal actions and, as one historian notes accurately, "Journal entries are not the juiciest grapes from which to press wine."[4] We know with accuracy the final result of the Constitutional Convention, but with somewhat less accuracy, we know how they reached the result. Thirty-one years after the convention, John Quincy Adams, then Secretary of State to President James Monroe, pulled together what records he could and came to the conclusion that "a correct and tolerably clear view of the proceedings of the Convention" could be formed.[5]

An Uncharted Course

What is striking to the reader of Madison's notes and the other delegates' writings is how they faced an almost totally uncharted course. Ideas of every description were discussed. French essayist De Montesquieu, in a widely read work that influenced Jefferson and Franklin, wrote: "There is no liberty if the judiciary power be not separated from the legislative and executive."[6] That is reflected in the final result. Unlike newly independent nations of today that have a large number of government structures to consider, those who wrote our constitution had limited experience with what they regarded as a largely unsuccessful British form of government and limited contact with government leaders in a few other nations, primarily the French.

Successful governments that guaranteed their people basic freedoms were non-existent. It is small wonder that many who knew of the Philadelphia convention had scant hope that anything meaningful would result from it. After the convention concluded, the *Pennsylvania Packet* of Philadelphia had a brief news statement on page three, indicating neither great hope for nor great interest in the convention's activities.

The reality that the delegates had little of democratic tradition to guide them resulted in proposals that look unusual today. For example, any direct election of members of the national legislature was opposed by Roger Sherman of Connecticut. "The people should have as little to do as may be [possible] about the [national] Government," he told the delegates. "They lack information and are certainly liable to be misled."[7] At one point James Wilson of Pennsylvania suggested the constitution should stipulate one senator for each 100,000 people, an idea that might have worked in 1787 but today would mean 2,400 senators. Discussing how to select the new executive, Gouverneur Morris of Pennsylvania favored a direct election. "If people should elect," he told the delegates, "they will never fail to prefer some man of distinguished character or services."[8] Unfortunately, history has shown occasional flaws in that prophecy.

Fear of resting too much power in the executive branch dominated much of the discussion. In notes he made for a speech, delegate George Mason of Virginia wrote:

> If strong and extensive Powers are vested in the Executive, and that Executive consists of only one Person; the Government will of course degenerate . . . into a Monarchy.[9]

Because of this fear of executive domination, the widely accepted need to have a federal judiciary had to mesh with a much less widely accepted method of appointing judges. Delegates knew with clarity — reflected also in the Articles of Confederation — that they did not want a repetition of the British experience: a judiciary dominated by the executive branch. "In early times," historian Joseph Story wrote in 1833, "the kings of England often in person heard and decided causes."[10] As the numbers of cases grew, the kings appointed the judges, but they could also remove them or direct their verdicts. The delegates to the constitutional convention hoped to avoid judges dominated by the nation's chief executive. Most delegates wanted a major role for the legislative branch in the appointment process, but they differed on how to provide that.

On the third day of the convention, Edmund Randolph of Virginia introduced a 15-point program, the ninth of which read: "Resolved that a National Judiciary be established to consist of one or more supreme tribunals and of inferior tribunals, to be chosen by the National Legislature . . ."[11] His suggestions formed a temporary loose agenda for the convention, and soon Gouverneur Morris of Pennsylvania suggested creating a "*national* government consisting of a *supreme* Legislative, Executive and Judiciary" (emphasis in original). Vote was by state, one vote per state, and this proposal carried 6-1, Connecticut voting no and New York not counted because of delegation division on this issue.

On June 5th, Madison told the delegates he

> disliked the election of the Judges by the Legislature or any numerous body. . . . On the other hand, he was not satisfied with referring the appointment to the Executive. He rather inclined to give it to the Senatorial branch, as numerous eno' to be confided in—[yet] not so numerous as . . . the other branch; and as being sufficiently stable [at this point, Madison crossed out "and cool" in his notes] and independent to follow their deliberative judgments.[12]

He moved that Randolph's phrase "appointment by the Legislature" be struck and that a blank be left temporarily. His motion carried 9-2, with Connecticut and South Carolina voting no. Eight days later, there appears to have been an agreement on a Randolph recommendation from "the Committee of the Whole" to have one supreme tribunal.

Advice and Consent

By the middle of July, the delegates had decided to let the Senate — not yet named — appoint the federal judges. But

Nathaniel Gorham of Massachusetts suggested that the executive (still no agreement on title or details) appoint those judges "with the advice and consent of the second [legislative] branch."[13] In his remarks, Gorham stressed that the executive could "trust to information from the members about possible judicial nominees."[14] A substitute to have the judges simply "appointed by the National Executive" failed on a 6-2 vote, and then the Gorham proposal for executive appointment with approval of what would be later called the Senate failed on a 4-4 vote. That left the Senate making the judicial appointments.

Madison expressed concern that if the appointment was left to the Senate, judges "might be appointed by a minority of the people, tho' by a majority of the states."[15]

Then at some point in the convention — the date is not clear — as matters moved toward finalization, a committee instructed to polish up the results for the convention recommended the creation of "one Supreme Tribunal, the Judges of which shall be appointed by the second Branch of the national Legislature."[16] The committee also suggested the use of the term "Senate" to describe the second legislative body. Other refinements from the committee followed, describing the new top judicial body as the Supreme Court. By the ninth revision the executive had been designated as President; an earlier version gave him the title of Governor. The sixth revision called the nation the "United People and States of America," but that was later changed to the "United States of America."

In addition to the formal sessions of the convention, delegates gathered at "Mr. Carroll's lodgings" or in Franklin's secluded garden and in other settings for informal discussions where they perfected some of the final language. When decisions about some portion of the constitution needed further refinement and compromise, they were referred to ad hoc committees, unimaginatively given titles such as the Committee of Five or the Committee of Eleven.

Issues that would weigh heavily on the Supreme Court in decades to come surfaced occasionally in these discussions.

Slavery was one of those, dealt with primarily through silence. Wrote Maryland Delegate Luther Martin:

> Slaves ought never to be considered in Representation, because they are Property . . . . A Gentleman in Debate very pertinently observed that he would as soon enter into Compacts with Asses, Mules or Horses of the Ancient Dominion as with their slaves.[17]

A man ahead of his time, Elbridge Gerry of Massachusetts "moved for a Committee to prepare a Bill of Rights." Roger Sherman of Connecticut argued persuasively that the legislative body created could be relied upon to protect the basic rights of people, and the delegates defeated the proposal 10-0, a vote that haunted the Constitution's proponents later and caused Madison to work with others in preparing the first ten amendments to the Constitution, now known as the Bill of Rights.[18] By a 6-5 vote, the delegates defeated a proposal to insert: "The Liberty of the Press shall be inviolably preserved."[19]

The religious liberty issue crept up occasionally. At one point Madison and Charles Pinckney of South Carolina called for a provision "to establish an University, in which no preferences or distinctions should be allowed on account of religion."[20] The proposal lost 6-5. Pinckney introduced an amendment that there should be no religious test for holding public office; it carried 8-1, only North Carolina voting in the negative.

Gouverneur Morris of Pennsylvania gave a warning that fiscally prudent legislators of almost two centuries ago did not need but that sounds all too appropriate for the United States of the 1990s, with our huge deficits and indebtedness. Morris "dwelt on the importance of public Credit, and the difficulty of supporting it without some strong barrier against the instability of legislative Assemblies."[21] He warned against the temptation to simply print money to solve fiscal problems "with all the distressing effects of such measures." Nine years later, Thomas Jefferson wrote that if he could add one amendment to the Constitution, it would be to require a balanced budget.[22]

The discussion of the federal judiciary continued to focus primarily on jurisdiction, to the extent that this third branch of government entered the discussions at all. They agreed that the Supreme Court would settle disputes between states, and sometimes between citizens of two states. They also operated with the understanding — not spelled out in the Constitution — that Supreme Court Justices would "ride circuits," would have a designated territory to cover to hold trials when the Supreme Court was not sitting as a body. But how to select members of the high court perplexed the delegates until the concluding days. In the final version of the Constitution on September 12, 1787, the responsibility for nomination to the federal judiciary shifted to the President, "with the advice and consent of the Senate." This last-minute change seems to have been lost in the much more abundant discussion of the legislative and executive branch details. The shift was so little noticed that between the adoption of the Constitution at the convention and its acceptance by the states, at least two of the delegates continued to speak and write about the Senate naming the federal judges.

Precisely what did those who wrote the Constitution mean by "advice and consent"? Like many political compromises, it offered less than complete clarity. Complicating matters, some delegates viewed the Senate as a sort of informal advisory council to the President, in addition to being the second legislative body of Congress. In one of his Federalist Papers, Hamilton — who favored a strong executive — wrote that the provision requires cooperation between the President and the Senate. But what does "cooperation" mean? Hamilton explained only that the advice and consent provision "would be an excellent check upon a spirit of favoritism in the President . . . . It would be an efficacious source of stability."[23] One of this century's major political scientists has written:

> It is reasonable to suppose that if the framers had intended to limit the Senate to something less than full participation in the political process of choosing men for public office, they would have put language in the Con-

stitution to make that intention clear. If they had wanted such a procedure they might, for instance, have provided that the President should submit to the Senate the name of the person whom he preferred . . . and that the Senate should approve or reject the nomination by formal vote.[24]

That is a reasonable conclusion. Clearly the delegates wanted to avoid the government they had as colonists in which the executive could dominate the judiciary. The delegates wanted the Senate to have a significant role in the process, but as in many other matters, they did not spell it out with precision. Certainly, they had not the remotest idea of how important the Supreme Court would become, or what great controversies would be stirred through the simple "advice and consent" language of the Constitution.

Endnotes

1. Alexander Hamilton, *The Federalist Papers* (New York: New American Library, 1961), pp. 465-466, Paper No. 78.

2. *Records of the Federal Convention of 1787*, Max Ferrand, ed. New Haven: Yale University Press, 1911),–hereafter referred to simply as *Records*–Vol. III, p. 31, Letter of May 30, 1787.

3. *Records,* Vol. I, p. xi.

4. Julius Goebel, Jr., *History of the Supreme Court of the United States* (New York: MacMillan, 1971), Vol. I, p. 240.

5. *Records*, Vol. I, p. xii.

6. C.L. Montesquieu, 1748, *The Spirit of the Laws.*

7. *Records,* Vol. I, p. 48, Madison's notes.

8. *Records,* Vol. II, p. 29, Madison's notes.

9. *Records,* Vol. IV, p. 19.

10. Joseph Story, *Commentaries on the Constitution of the United States* (Boston: Hilliard, Gray, 1833), p. 464, reprinted by DaCapo Press, 1970.

11. *Records,* Vol. I, pp. 21-22, Madison's notes.

12. *Records,* Vol. I, p. 120, Madison's notes.

13. *Records*, Vol. II, p. 41, Madison's notes.

14. *Records,* Vol. II, p. 43, Madison's notes.

15. *Records,* Vol. II, p. 81, Madison's notes.

16. *Records,* Vol. II, p. 132, Wilson's notes.

17. *Records*, Vol. III, p. 156.

18. *Records,* Vol. II, p. 588, Madison's notes.

19. *Records,* Vol. II, p. 611, Journal. Also McHenry's notes. Madison's notes strangely do not mention this.

20. *Records,* Vol. II, p. 616. Madison's notes.

21. *Records,* Vol II, p. 299, Madison's notes.

22. Thomas Jefferson to John Taylor, November 26, 1798, *The Writings of Thomas Jefferson,* ed. Pal L. Ford (New York: Putnam's), Vol. 7, p. 310 (1896).

23. Alexander Hamilton, *Federalist Papers,* Clinton Rossiter, ed., (New York: New American Library, 1961), Paper No. 76, p. 457.

24. Charles S. Hyneman, *Bureaucracy in a Democracy* (New York: Harper and Brothers, 1950), p. 179.

8

Early Court Battles

As he put the pieces of a fledgling government together, George Washington had huge problems but two great assets, in addition to unquestioned integrity. Those two assets were the great respect — almost awe — people held for him, and the ability to select the leaders of our first government from among the most talented in the new nation, almost all of whom he knew.

Washington chose his Supreme Court carefully, calling upon men who believed in the new Constitution and in the need for a national government. With emotional divisions still running deep over state versus federal powers, he had to consider even something as basic as loyalty to the national government in his determinations. A member of the Cabinet wrote to Madison that he heard reports "that the President expects applications from those who are willing to become servants of the U.S. It is too outrageous to be believed, and even when believed, cannot be submitted to by men of real merit."[1]

Washington also played a role in shaping the Senate's advice and consent procedure. In August 1789, a resolution was introduced in the Senate to conduct advice-and-consent business "in the presence of the President." The Senate appointed a committee to discuss with Washington his wishes on this. He met with them three days after the resolution had been introduced, and his instincts proved to be both precedent-setting and sound. Washington recorded in his diary:

> It could be no pleasing thing I conceive, for the President, on the one hand to be present and hear the propriety of his nominations questioned; nor for the Senate on the other hand to be under the smallest restraint from his presence for the fullest and freest inquiry into the Character of the Person nominated. The President in a situation like this would be reduced to one of two things: either to be a silent witness of the decision by ballot, if there are objections to the nomination; or in justification thereof (if he should think it right) to support it by argument. Neither of which might be agreeable; and the latter improper; for as the President has a right to nominate without assigning his reasons, so has the Senate a right to dissent without giving theirs.[2]

The Senate acceded to the wishes of the President and established a precedent that is followed to this day.

Although not a lawyer, Washington had significant legal experience: seventeen years as a state legislator, seven years as a justice of the peace and judge of a county court, and experience as the administrator of at least nine estates. He respected the law. It is not surprising that his appointees to the Supreme Court were highly regarded and, with one exception, had served in a judicial capacity. (The one exception, James Wilson, had extensive legal experience but ended up being the Supreme Court Justice who spent more time in prison than any other. *The Documentary History of the Supreme Court* has this biographical footnote:

Beginning in the fall of 1796, James Wilson lived in constant fear of arrest because of angry creditors. After attending the February, 1797 term of the Supreme Court, he went into hiding in Bethlehem, Pennsylvania . . . . He was not present at the August 1797 term and [Justice] James Iredell . . . commented [in a letter to his wife] that Wilson was "absconding from his creditors." By September a creditor had caught up with Wilson, and Wilson had been imprisoned in Burlington, New Jersey . . . . After Wilson extricated himself from jail [he went south] . . . . However, one of Wilson's creditors caught up with him. Wilson again was arrested and spent two months in jail in Edenton, North Carolina.[3])

The President, aware of the controversies in the various states in approving the Constitution, showed great sensitivity for geography in selecting the first Supreme Court Justices. The Supreme Court (then six members) came from New York, Virginia, Massachusetts, Maryland, South Carolina and Pennsylvania. Not everyone Washington asked to serve expressed a willingness to do so. The Senate confirmed two who then declined their positions.

The Court first met in New York City on February 2, 1790, wearing black and red robes but discarding the British tradition of wearing wigs. New York's John Jay became the first Chief Justice and served until 1795, when he resigned to become Governor of New York. Jay thought it more important to be the chief executive of New York than Chief Justice, illustrating the less significant role the Court had then.

The Rutledge Controversy

To succeed Jay, Washington selected John Rutledge who had served as Governor of South Carolina and held other public offices. Earlier Washington had named Rutledge an Associate Justice, and he had been confirmed by the Senate, but before he could take an active role on the Court, he accepted the chief justiceship of the South Carolina court. Six years later, when Jay stepped down to become Governor of New York, Rutledge's situation had changed. Because Congress was not in session when Jay resigned, the President made a recess appointment, permitting Rutledge to serve as Chief Justice until confirmed by the Senate. (There have been fifteen Supreme Court recess appointments in our history.)

The Rutledge nomination sparked the nation's first controversy over a Supreme Court appointment.

On July 1, 1795, Secretary of State Edmund Randolph sent a letter to John Rutledge in South Carolina, officially notifying him that Washington would name him Chief Justice. Prior to that notification, the Senate had received and ratified what became known as the Jay Treaty, an agreement with Great Britain that set forth the final withdrawal of all British troops, defined borders and established certain trade provisions with West Indian territories. The treaty had been negotiated by Chief Justice John Jay. The Constitution has no requirement that Supreme Court Justices may not engage in other appropriate activities. Jay not only served on a diplomatic mission for the President that took him away from the Court for one year, he twice ran for Governor of New York while sitting as Chief Justice. Later Justice John McLean, a Jackson appointee, ran for President four times while on the Court.[4]

Obviously the practices of the Justices have changed over the decades. But there has been a sensitivity to this question even from earliest days. When Washington asked Senate approval to send Jay as Special Ambassador to England to negotiate the treaty, it caused three days of debate before the Senate went along with the President. At one point, a Senator introduced a resolution that "to permit Judges of the Supreme Court to hold at the same time any other office of employment emanating from and holden at the pleasure of the Executive is contrary to the spirit of the Constitution, and as tending to expose them to the influence of the Executive, is mischievous and impolitic."

Some parts of the nation reacted strongly to the Jay Treaty. At a public meeting in New York City, people threw stones at Alexander Hamilton for defending it. Residents of Charleston,

South Carolina burned Jay in effigy and dragged the British flag through the streets, burning it in front of the British Consulate. A large segment of the population felt that the Jay Treaty yielded too many concessions to the British.

At a protest meeting in St. Michael's Episcopal Church in Charleston, Rutledge gave an impassioned speech that denounced the treaty in inflammatory language, which even those who agreed with Rutledge called intemperate. The *South Carolina State-Gazette,* reporting his speech the next day, quoted Rutledge as saying that he would sooner see the President dead "than he should sign that treaty."[5] The Charleston meeting took place on July 16th — 16 days after a letter was sent to Rutledge notifying him of his appointment as Chief Justice, and three weeks after the Senate ratified the treaty by voice vote.

Whether Rutledge knew Washington had given him the appointment when he made his speech is not certain, but a Rutledge biographer writes that "the news of his new appointment had just appeared" in the local newspaper, but newspapers of that day often came out late.[6] At least one Charleston newspaper, the *Angus,* did not have the item about Rutledge's appointment until July 27th. But Rutledge had written Washington asking for the appointment upon hearing of the resignation of Jay. He sent his slave to deliver the letter to Washington. The President immediately decided to name Rutledge, whom he had considered naming when he selected Jay initially, and the slave brought back the favorable, informal Washington response to Rutledge. Secretary Randolph's formal notification went to him on July 1st. It is probable that Rutledge received Washington's response before the July 16th Charleston meeting.

Secretary of State Randolph wrote Washington on July 29th:

> The conduct of the intended Chief Justice is so extraordinary that Mr. Wolcott and Col. Pickering conceive it to be proof of the imputation of insanity. By calculating dates, it would seem to have taken place after my letter tendering the office was received, tho he has not acknowledged it.[7]

It is also possible that Rutledge thought a speech in Charleston would not reach the ears of government leaders in Philadelphia, then the seat of the federal government. Somewhere in this time span, he accepted Washington's offer to become Chief Justice and proceeded to Philadelphia where the President gave him a recess appointment, subject to the approval of the Senate.

But Washington and the Senators had heard about the speech. Newspapers in all of the states printed reports of the Charleston meeting, and the Federalist-leaning press urged the Senate to reject Rutledge. Several members of the Senate suggested that the Charleston speech did not reflect the balance a Chief Justice should have. In a letter to Hamilton, Attorney General William Bradford wrote about "the crazy speech of Mr. Rutledge" and added: "If he is disordered in mind and in the manner that I am informed he is — there can be but one course of prudence."[8] Some close to Washington advised him not to send the Rutledge nomination to the Senate, particularly in view of Rutledge's strong disagreement with the Administration's foreign policy, but Washington stayed with his nomination.

Some connected his odd behavior to other troubles in his life. His wife had died and he had financial problems. One of his supporters wrote Senator Jacob Read of South Carolina:

> No man could be more afflicted than I was at the part Mr. Rutledge took in opposition to the Treaty. I am sure he is now very sorry for it himself. After the death of his Wife, his mind was frequently so much deranged, as to be in great measure deprived of his senses; & I am persuaded he was in that situation when the Treaty was under consideration. I have frequently been in company with him since his return, & find him totally altered. I am of [the] opinion that no Man in the United States would execute the Office of Chief Justice with more ability & integrity than he would.[9]

Hamilton wrote to Senator Rufus King of New York that Rutledge should be turned down "if it be really true that he is sottish or that his mind is otherwise deranged."[10] In a letter to his wife Abigail, John Adams refers to Rutledge's "eccentricities." One observer wrote: "That crazy speech of Mr. Rutledge joined to certain information that he is daily sinking into debility of mind and body, will probably prevent him [from] receiving the appointment."[11] A letter from one Senator suggests that the principal opposition to Rutledge came from his commentaries at the Charleston meeting. Rutledge should not be punished for expressing ideas that "would in a very little time if pursued totally destroy all government and defeat our representative system entirely."[12] But he should not be rewarded with "the first Seat of Justice in the Union."

Rutledge had the support of the President, of most of the southern members of the Senate who did not want New York to dominate the Supreme Court, and of some non-southern newspapers. A Boston journal editorialized: "Our rights and liberties will be safe in such hands."[13]

When the matter finally came before the Senate in late 1795, it voted 14-10 to reject Washington's nomination of Rutledge. Washington wrote of the Senate action: "It had been expected."[14]

Twelve days later, Rutledge unsuccessfully tried to commit suicide by drowning. A physician wrote:

> He left his house by stealth early in the morning, and went down to Gibbes's Bridge [in Charleston]. There, with his clothes on he went deliberately into the water. It was just daylight. A negro child was near, and struck with the uncommonness of the sight she called to some negroes on the deck of a vessel. He had now gone beyond his depth and had sunk, but struggling sometimes rose. The fellows had the presence of mind to run with a boat hook and catch hold of his arm. He made violent opposition to them but they dragged him out and detained him by force.[15]

The next day he sent a letter to Washington resigning as Chief Justice because of poor health, without mentioning the Senate action. One touch of irony: At the Constitutional Convention, John Rutledge strongly resisted the suggestion by James Wilson of Pennsylvania that the President should be given the authority to name Supreme Court Justices without Senate advice and consent.

Wild Sam Chase

Washington had used great care in nominating his original Supreme Court, taking more time than some thought wise. In later appointments he used less care. In 1796, the day after Justice John Blair resigned, the President named Samuel Chase, strongly favored by Chase's fellow Marylander, James McHenry, Washington's Secretary of War.

Tart-tongued Samuel Chase, a signer of the Declaration of Independence and a former Chief Justice of the Maryland courts, became the only member of the Supreme Court ever tried by the Senate for impeachment. One historian has described Chase as "the most turbulent soul ever to serve on the nation's highest bench."[16] After Washington nominated Chase, John Adams wrote to his wife that Chase's "character has a mist about it of suspicion and impurity."[17] Supreme Court historian Charles Warren wrote: "Of all the Judges, no one was more hated than Chase."[18]

Earlier in his career he participated in activities that caused the Annapolis mayor to denounce him as a "busy restless Incindiary . . . a foul mouth'd and inflaming son of Discord and Faction." Chase responded, accusing the mayor and board of aldermen of Annapolis of being "despicable Pimps, and Tools of Power."[19] It did not augur well for a judicial career.

Chase had a history of controversy, as well as public service. While serving in the Continental Congress, he and a few others attempted to corner the flour market, using information they had received in Congress. Newspapers exposed it, and an article appeared in the *New York Journal,* probably written by Alexander Hamilton, describing Chase as having "the peculiar privilege of being universally despised."[20] As a Maryland judge, his conduct caused the Maryland legislature to consider a resolution to remove him from office. On top of everything else, he had substantial personal financial problems.

Once on the Court, Chase assumed the then-required duties of holding trials in an assigned circuit, in addition to meeting with his colleagues on the Supreme Court. Presiding at trials he soon found himself severely criticized. The lawyers of Philadelphia, for example, agreed that they would not practice before him. Criticism flowed, not simply for his Court conduct, but for his extreme, highly partisan speeches in behalf of John Adams and attacking Thomas Jefferson. He openly pressed for passage of the Alien and Sedition Acts, legislation that posed basic threats to free speech.

All of this occurred in an atmosphere not friendly toward the Court. Because of a lack of tradition, with no code of ethics for judges, the highest court members frequently involved themselves in controversies that others felt they should avoid. In the midst of this anti-Court sentiment, Chief Justice John Marshall and a unanimous Supreme Court brought hostility to the Court into greater focus in 1803 with the *Marbury v. Madison* decision that assumed the right of the Supreme Court to declare an Act of Congress unconstitutional. That authority had not been spelled out in the Constitution, and among the strongest critics of the *Marbury v. Madison* decision was Thomas Jefferson. Chase's judicial escapades occurred in the midst of an anti-Supreme Court mood among many government leaders, including members of the Senate and House.

The attitude toward Chase is illustrated by a letter from Speaker of the House Nathaniel Macon:

> Have you seen Judge Chase's charge to the grand jury at Baltimore? If you have not, it is worth reading if only for its novelty; it has made some noise with us, indeed all are dissatisfied with it, such men as he, no matter what party they may pretend to belong, are a real injury to the country. Their imprudence and ungovernable temper have no limits.[21]

A district judge wrote of him:

> Of all others, I like least to be coupled with him. I never sat with him without pain, as he was forever getting into some intemperate and unnecessary squabble. If I am to be immolated, let it be with some other victim or for my own sins.[22]

Impeachment

On January 5, 1804, the House voted 81-40 to investigate whether or not to adopt articles of impeachment against Chase on a variety of charges. The House later approved eight articles of impeachment, by margins of 72-45 to 84-34. The charges included:

☐ In Pennsylvania, he refused to let a defendant, John Fries, or his counsel defend himself by using "his constitutional privilege of addressing the jury . . . . the said John Fries was deprived of the right, secured to him by the . . . constitution, and was condemned to death without having been heard by counsel, in his defense, to the disgrace of the character of the American bench."[23] (President John Adams set aside the death sentence.)

☐ In Richmond, he failed to give rights to the defendant and used "unusual, rude, and contemptuous expressions toward the prisoner's counsel . . . induced them to abandon their cause and their client, who was thereupon convicted and condemned to fine and imprisonment."[24]

☐ In Newcastle, Delaware, he refused to let a grand jury go that would not indict a newspaper publisher, at which point Chase said "that a highly seditious temper had manifested itself in the state of Delaware, among a certain class of people, particularly in Newcastle County, and more especially in the town of Wilmington, where lived a seditious printer, unrestrained by any principle of virtue." He enjoined the district attorney to get the files of the newspaper "to find some passage which might furnish the ground-work of a trial against the printer of said paper."[25]

The other charges were similar.

Many of Chase's responses were feeble. In the Fries Pennsylvania case, part of his defense was that many cases were pending, and he had to expedite them. "Many of those causes had already been subjected to great delay," Chase told the Senate, "and it was the peculiar duty of this respondent, as presiding judge, to take care, that as little time as possible should be unnecessarily consumed, and that every convenient and proper dispatch should be given to the business of the citizens. He did believe, that an early communication of the court's opinion, might tend to the saving of time, and consequently to the dispatch of business."[26] He said he refused to let the counsel for Fries cite cases "because they could not inform but might deceive and mislead the jury."[27]

Rep. John Randolph of Virginia, serving as a prosecutor in behalf of the House, said that "a distinction [exists] between a judge zealous to punish and repress crimes generally, and a judge anxious only to enforce a particular law whereby he may recommend himself to power, or to his party."[28]

Under the procedures still followed in the Senate, when there are Articles of Impeachment, Senators remain in their chairs, and a roll call is held on each Article of Impeachment. Senators stand and vote as each name is called declaring, "Guilty" or "Not Guilty." It is a solemn moment in the life of the Senate, for members understand what is at stake, both for the individual and for the nation. Adding to the color if not the solemnity of Chase's impeachment, the Senate's gray walls were covered with new crimson wallpaper and the seats were reupholstered with crimson, but whether this occurred because of the intense national interest in the Chase trial or was only routine redecorating is not clear.

The vote count in that colorful chamber on six Articles was "Not Guilty," three by narrow margins, and on two Articles was "Guilty," 18-16. But since the Constitution requires a two-thirds vote for conviction on a charge of impeachment, Chase remained in office. Some Senators felt impeachment too harsh a penalty for the offenses. John Quincy Adams expressed the fear that reasons would be developed for emptying the entire bench of the Supreme Court, that impeachment would bring instability to the judicial system.

While Chase's conduct cannot be defended, the judiciary needed some other means short of impeachment to handle this type of conduct. Procedures have gradually emerged, but in 1804, there were no precedents and no traditions for the Senate or the judiciary. However, the trial of Chase had a wholesome effect on the Court. Members became less openly partisan, as Chase had been, and watched their conduct on the bench with greater care.

Chase became a better Justice, chastened by the congressional action and slowed by gout, and in the immensely important case of *Marbury v. Madison,* he backed Chief Justice John Marshall.

Marshall

No great Senate controversies arose from John Adams's nominations to the Supreme Court, but he made a huge contribution to the nation when he selected his Secretary of State, John Marshall, for Chief Justice in 1801. Marshall tops everyone's list as the greatest Chief Justice. The Senate would have preferred Associate Justice William Paterson, but time has shown the wisdom of the Adams choice.

While Marshall is primarily cited for the decisions of the Supreme Court under his guidance and for his strong leadership there, one procedural change during his tenure should be noted. Until Marshall became the Chief Justice, the Supreme Court followed the English system of having each Justice read his opinion. Marshall started the practice of having one opinion for the Court, which is followed to this day. Justices may issue a dissenting opinion or agree in part, but there is one dominant opinion to which future Supreme Courts, the lower courts, the bar and the public can ordinarily look.

The Wolcott Rejection

The next battle between the President and the Senate occurred during James Madison's presidency, when he "amazed the country," as historian Charles Warren states, by nominating Alexander Wolcott of Connecticut, who had served as U.S. Collector of Customs but was better known for his extreme partisan activities on behalf of the anti-Federalists. Today he would be labeled a political "boss."

Madison's party controlled the Senate 28-6, but while Wolcott could pass the political philosophy test in the Senate, he did not measure up to the emerging standards for the high court. Negative press reaction to the Wolcott appointment erupted at once. In his Customs position he had made enemies by strict enforcement of the unpopular Embargo and Non-Intercourse Acts, although that did not cause his Senate failure. One observer wrote to a friend: "It has excited the astonishment of even Democrats."[29] His defendants damned him with faint praise, one saying that "an industrious application to professional studies and official duties will soon place him on a level" with the other members of the Court.[30] The Senate took little time to reject Wolcott by a 24-9 vote.

Trimble and a Lame Duck Defeat

During John Quincy Adams's term as President, he had one successful and one unsuccessful battle with the Senate over a Court nominee. A District Court judge from Kentucky, Robert Trimble, appeared to have everything going for him: judicial experience, geography and a Democratic-Republican (anti-Federalist) political label, even though his views were thought to be acceptable to the Federalists. But his court decisions upholding the federal government's authority over state authority precipitated a bitter struggle in the Senate that lasted almost a month. The Senate finally approved Trimble 27-5.

While serving his final months as President after the election of Andrew Jackson, Adams in December 1828 nominated a former Kentucky Senator, John J. Crittenden. This appointment followed the death of Justice Trimble, who lived only two years after being confirmed to the Court. The Jackson forces were irate that Adams would make an appointment before the new President's term started, particularly of someone who, while well-qualified, held Whig (anti-Jackson) views. Crittenden had close ties to Henry Clay, one of the Senate giants of that era, but Clay and Jackson were in different political camps. Clay wrote to Crittenden: "Should your nomination be rejected, the decision will be entirely on party ground; and ought, therefore, to occasion you no mortification."[31] The combination of party and philosophical differences and simply the understandable desire of a new administration to make the significant appointments, killed Crittenden's chance to be on the Court. The Senate postponed action on the nomination 23-17, avoiding a direct vote on the nomination but in effect defeating it.

Chief Justice Taney

During his two terms, rough-and-tumble Andrew Jackson might have been expected to have serious troubles with the Senate on his Supreme Court nominees, but on only two of the six vacancies to the Court were there difficulties. Two of the other appointees were men with whom Jackson differed on political philosophy, and both went through the Senate with relative ease.

Jackson's big battle with the Senate came over his most important nominee: Roger Brooke Taney. The cigar-smoking Taney served as Jackson's Attorney General and when Jackson prepared for his second term, he reorganized the Cabinet and named Taney Secretary of the Treasury.

The President and the Senate were deeply divided over "the Bank issue." Jackson had ordered his previous Secretary of the Treasury, William J. Duane, to withdraw all federal government funds from the Bank of the United States, which had close and corrupt ties to some members of Congress. Duane refused; Jackson fired him and named Taney. As the Acting Secretary of the Treasury — before the Senate convened to confirm him — Taney carried out Jackson's wishes and removed all federal government deposits from the Bank of the United States, which Jackson hated, an action that precipitated a storm of opposition. The Senate then refused to confirm Taney as Secretary of the Treasury, though no one questioned Taney's abilities.

Taney became the first cabinet appointment ever rejected by the Senate. The furious Jackson wrote in a letter: "Nicholas Biddle [the head of the Bank] now rules the Senate, as a show-man does his puppets."[32] In revenge, when 82-year-old Associate Justice Gabriel Duval of Maryland resigned from the Court in January 1835 "in consequence of extreme deafness," Jackson nominated Taney.[33] Chief Justice Marshall, no friend of Jackson, nevertheless regarded Taney highly and sent a note favorable to Taney to a Virginia Senator.[34] "The President has no expectation that the Senate will approve," commented the Whig *Boston Courier.*[35]

The still-infuriated Senate not only refused to confirm Taney by postponing action (24-21) on the nomination on the last day of the session, they also passed a bill changing the structure of the Supreme Court, and making it impossible for Jackson to nominate Taney. But the House did not pass the measure. Even if both houses had, Jackson would have vetoed the bill, and there would not have been enough votes to override the veto. Relations between the President and the Senate were "sticky." In the President's room of the Capitol, when he received word that the Senate postponed action on Taney, Jackson immediately left and said he "would receive no more messages from the damned scoundrels."[36]

Jackson responded to the Senate's inaction by simply not filling the vacancy until mid-1835, when Chief Justice Marshall died. There were now two vacancies. Jackson proposed a geographically attractive package: Taney of Maryland to replace Marshall of Virginia as Chief Justice, and Philip Barbour of Virginia to succeed Duval of Maryland as Associate Justice. Barbour was a popular choice; a former Speaker of the U.S. House, he worked well with all political elements and observers viewed him as qualified. But because of the dual nomination, even Barbour's confirmation could not be viewed as a certainty. The Senate did not move quickly, but it eventually did confirm Barbour, 30-11, the eleven negative votes caused by the circumstances of the nomination rather than any reflection on Barbour.

The Senate battle over Taney's nomination was more intense, and more heated, with the giants of the Senate — Clay, Calhoun and Webster — lined up against Taney and the President. A New York newspaper called Taney "unworthy of public confidence, a supple, cringing tool of power."[37] One newspaper attacked Taney as a "political hack," but the prevailing sentiment, even among opponents, was one of respect, and that ultimately carried over to the Senate vote.[38] But it was a battle. The epic struggle turned out to be an easier victory for the Jackson-Taney forces than most thought possible; the Senate confirmed Taney 29-15.

Whether the Senate bruisings played even a subconscious role in Taney's 1857 *Dred Scott* decision, which headed us toward civil war, students of the mind can explore. Henry Clay, a bitter Taney opponent, authored the Missouri Compromise, which the *Dred Scott* decision killed, though it had earlier been reduced in effect by the passage of the Kansas-Nebraska Act. Clay, however, told a friend that he had reconciled with Taney and told the Chief Justice: "In the Senate . . . I said many harsh things of you . . . . But now I know you better . . . . I am now convinced that a better appointment could not have been made."[39]

Taney became the first Roman Catholic to serve on the Court. He married an Episcopalian and worked out an unusual agreement with his wife that all their sons would be reared as Catholics, and all their daughters as Episcopalians. They had six daughters.

In quiet ways, Taney made the Court more egalitarian, from the shift to trousers from knee breeches for court attire, to greater respect for community rights in opposition to property rights.

Taney turned out to be one of the giants in the history of the Court, a record marred by the tragic *Dred Scott* decision that had the effect of closing all doors to the non-violent solution of the slavery question. Taney proved to be a force for reconciliation on the Court and, through the Court for the country.

Taney's record as Chief Justice would bear a striking similarity to the later presidency of Lyndon Johnson. "He was a great President but for Vietnam," is the general opinion of historians. "He was a great Chief Justice but for *Dred Scott*," the same historians note of Taney. The *Dred Scott* decision significantly dimmed the luster of the Taney record.

The Taney appointment started a new era in the history of the Court. Taney presided as Chief Justice during the next major battle between the President and Senate, under the presidency of John Tyler.

Endnotes

1. Edmund Randolph to James Madison, July 23, 1789, *Documentary History of the Supreme Court* (New York: Columbia University Press, 1985), Vol. I, Part 2, p. 639.

2. *The Writings of George Washington,* edited by John C. Fitzpatrick (Washington: Government Printing Office, 1931-1944), Vol XXX, pp. 373-374.

3. *Ibid.,* p. 859.

4. Quoted by Charles Warren, *The Supreme Court in United States History* (Boston: Little, Brown, 1922) (reprinted by Fred B. Rothman, Littleton, Colorado, 1987), Vol. I, p. 119.

5. *South Carolina State-Gazette* of Charleston, July 17, 1795. *Documentary History of the Supreme Court,* Vol. I, Part 2, p. 767.

6. Richard Hayes Barry, *Mr. Rutledge of South Carolina* (Freeport, New York: Books for Libraries Press, 1971), p. 355.

7. Edmund Randolph to George Washington, July 29, 1795, quoted in Warren, Vol. I., p. 130.

8. William Bradford to Alexander Hamilton, August 4, 1795, quoted in Warren, Vol. I., p. 131.

9. Ralph Izard to Jacob Read, November 17, 1795, *Documentary History of the Supreme Court,* Vol. I, part 2, pp. 807-808.

10. Alexander Hamilton to Rufus King, December 14, 1795, *Documentary History of the Supreme Court,* Vol. I, Part 2, pp. 811-812

11. John Adams to Abigail Adams, December 17, 1795, *Ibid.,* pp. 813-814.

12. Jacob Read to Ralph Izard, December 19, 1795, *Ibid.,* pp. 814-815.

13. *Independent Chronicle,* Boston, August 10, 1795, Ibid., pp. 811-812.

14. George Washington to Edward Carrington, December, 23, 1795, *Ibid.,* p. 817.

15. William Read to Jacob Read, December 29, 1795, *Documentary History of the Supreme Court,* Vol I., Part 2, pp. 820.

16. "Samuel Chase," by Irving Dilliard, *Justices of the United States Supreme Court,* Leon Friedman and Fred Israel, editors, (New York: Chelsea House, 1969), Vol 1, p. 185.

17. John Adams to Abigail Adams, Feb. 6, 1796, *Documentary History of the Supreme Court,* Vol I., part 2, p. 835.

18. Warren, Vol. I, p. 273.

19. *Documentary History of the Supreme Court,* Vol I., part 1, p. 105.

20. "Samuel Chase," by Irving Dilliard, *Justices of the United States Supreme Court,* Leon Friedman and Fred Israel, editors, (New York: Chelsea House, 1969), Vol 1, p. 187.

21. Nathaniel Macon for J. Steele, August 7, 1803, quoted in *History of the Supreme Court,* (New York: MacMillan, 1981), Vol. II, by George Lee Haskins and Herbert A. Johnson, p. 221.

22. Letter of Judge Richard Peters, 1804, quoted in Warren, Vol. I., P. 281.

23. *Trial of Samuel Chase,* taken in shorthand by Samuel H. Smith and Thomas Lloyd, (Washington City: Printed for Samuel H. Smith), 1805, p. 5.

24. *Ibid.,* p. 6.

25. *Ibid.,* pp. 7-8.

26. *Ibid.,* pp. 33-34.

27. *Ibid.,* p. 114.

28. *Ibid.,* 125.

29. James Hillhouse to Timothy Pickering, February 17, 1811, Warren, Vol. I., p. 411.

30. Levi Lincoln to James Madison, February 15, 1811, Warren. Vol. I, p. 413.

31. Henry Clay to John Crittenden, January 27, 1829, Warren, Vol. I, p. 704.

32. Harris, p. 62.

33. *History of the Supreme Court,* by Hampton Carson (New York: Burt Franklin, 1902), reprinted in 1971, Vol. I, p. 296.

34. Justice Marshall to Senator Leigh, undated. Quoted in *Memoir of Roger B. Taney,* by Samuel Taylor, (Baltimore:

John Murphy, 1872, reprinted by Da Capo Press, 1970), p. 240.

35. *Boston Courier,* January 22, 1835.

36. Quoted in Harris, p. 63.

37. *New York Courier,* January 23, 1836, Warren, Vol. II, p. 11.

38. Quoted in Bernard Schwartz, *A Basic History of the U.S. Supreme Court,* (Princeton, N.J.: Van Nostrand, 1968), p. 29.

39. Henry Clay to Reverdy Johnson, quoted in *Roger B. Taney: Jacksonian Trust,* (Raleigh: University of North Carolina Press, 1936), p. 15.

9

Leading Up to the Civil War

The political phrase "Tippecanoe and Tyler Too" captured the imagination of the U.S. public in the 1840 election long before Madison Avenue slicksters were paid big sums to produce catchy slogans. That presidential election brought to office General William Henry Harrison, the hero of the Battle of Tippecanoe, and his Vice President, John Tyler.

The campaign focused on the presidential candidate, as all election efforts do. But Harrison caught pneumonia at his inauguration. On that day of both solemnity and celebration, Harrison delivered a two-hour inaugural address, the longest on record, as the snow and rain came down. He died thirty-one days later.

Vice President Tyler, the son of a Virginia governor, had also served as governor and in the U.S. House and Senate. Although a Whig, he joined the Democrats in opposing the U.S. Bank. When the Virginia legislature instructed him to vote for the Bank (in the days when the legislature chose Senators), Tyler resigned from the Senate rather than violate his convictions.

After Harrison's death, the little-known Tyler became the first Vice President ever to succeed to the presidency because of the death of a chief executive. He also amassed a record-breaking Senate rejection of five nominees to the United States Supreme Court.

When Justice Smith Thompson of New York died, Tyler nominated John C. Spencer of New York, who had been his Secretary of War and Secretary of the Treasury. Spencer had substantial legal ability and became one of the better Secretaries of the Treasury, but Spencer, like Tyler's later nominees, got trapped in the political warfare that Tyler had created.

Tyler, a Democrat, broke with the Democrats in order to become the vice presidential candidate with Harrison, a Whig. By that combination of maneuvers, he managed to alienate both political parties and found himself an unelected President, without a public base and without a base of support in Congress.

Spencer got caught in all of this. As a Whig he had accepted cabinet positions from Tyler, alienating the Whigs. Clay wrote: "If Spencer be confirmed he will have run a career of more profligate conduct and good luck than any man I recollect."[1] Democrats were not enthusiastic because of his Whig ties, and their lack of sentiment for the President did not help. Nevertheless, Spencer's qualities were substantial enough that the rejection vote was close. Spencer, who probably would have made a good Justice, failed to get Senate confirmation by a vote of 26-21. Tyler recorded that Spencer lost because of "the politics of the times."[2] The date of the vote became significant: January 31, 1844. That year, 1844, a presidential election would be held.

Within three months of Spencer's failed nomination, Justice Henry Baldwin died, leaving two vacancies on the Court. Tyler nominated both Chancellor Reuben H. Walworth of New York, who ranked high in legal ability but had offended many of the Whigs in the Senate; and James Buchanan of Pennsylvania, Baldwin's state. Buchanan, the future President, withdrew his name before the Senate could act, and then Tyler nominated

Judge Edward King, a highly regarded Philadelphia lawyer. The influential Thurlow Weed of New York wrote to a Senator about the New York nominee, Walworth: "He is recommended by many distinguished Members of the Bar of the State merely because they are anxious to get rid of a querulous, disagreeable, unpopular Chancellor."[3] But the months were going by, and an election approached in which the Whigs thought they would win the presidency. The Senate voted 27-20 and 29-18 to postpone action on the two nominees, in effect gracefully but firmly killing the nominations.

The election of 1844 produced an upset. Democrat James K. Polk defeated the much better-known Whig candidate, Henry Clay. Tyler thought that gave him one last chance as a lame duck President to get two nominations approved by the Senate. Tyler resubmitted King's name, but the Senate took no action. He then submitted the names of Samuel Nelson, Chief Justice of the Supreme Court of New York, and author and former U.S. Attorney in Philadelphia, John Meredith Read, whose legal credentials were not as strong as Nelson's. The Senate quickly approved Nelson, Tyler's lone victory on the Court, but did not act on the Read nomination, giving Tyler the distinction of being the only President to have five Supreme Court nominations rejected by the Senate.

Neither President Tyler nor the Senate look good in retrospect. The President created many of his own problems through his awkward political maneuvering. There is little evidence that he tried to work with the Senate in finding acceptable nominees. On the other hand, most of his nominees were people of superior qualifications, and the Senate rejection of them, largely for partisan reasons, reflected poorly on the Senate. And the Tyler nominations were better than those of his successor, James Polk.

The Polk Presidency

Historians regard Polk as a much better President than Tyler, but his Supreme Court nominations do not account for that esteem. For the vacant Baldwin seat, Secretary of State James

Buchanan, who had turned it down when Tyler offered him the seat, changed his mind and told President Polk he would like the nomination. Polk recorded in his diary: "He [Buchanan] said he would not conceal the fact that the appointment of Judge of the Supreme Court was one which he had for many years preferred to any under the Government."[4] Polk submitted his name, but then Buchanan asked for time to think it over and finally, changing his mind once again, decided against it, probably because he had his eye on the presidency.

In the meantime, another seat on the Court became vacant with the resignation of Justice Joseph Story of Massachusetts. Polk filled that seat by naming Senator Levi Woodbury of New Hampshire. His colleagues in the Senate quickly confirmed him.

Still trying to fill the Baldwin seat, Polk nominated a Pennsylvania judge, George W. Woodward, a Democrat but one with outspoken views that many regarded as extreme. Particularly irksome to some in a nation with many immigrants were his stands supporting severe limitations on immigration, and some anti-Irish-American comments. Perhaps more critical, Polk—who had been more generous to Buchanan than he should have been—did not consult with Buchanan before naming someone to "the Pennsylvania seat," Buchanan's state. Polk recorded in his diary:

> The information given me . . . left the painful impression that Mr. Buchanan has been willing to see my nomination of Mr. Woodward rejected by the Senate in order to obtain the office himself . . . . If Mr. Buchanan did not interfere with [Senators] to have Mr. Woodward rejected, he at least took no interest in his confirmation, and was willing to see him rejected.[5]

Among those who opposed the Woodward nomination was Democratic Senator Simon Cameron of Pennsylvania, whom Woodward had once opposed for the Senate. Cameron had at one point told the President he would support Woodward, but apparently Buchanan dissuaded him. After the vote Cameron, a Democrat, talked to the President and Polk wrote in his diary:

> I then told him that the public understood that there was a Democratic majority of six in the Senate, and that the effect of rejecting my principal nominations at the commencement of my administration . . . was calculated to weaken my administration, and destroy or impair my power and influence in carrying out the measures of my administration.[6]

Polk had not been consulting with the Senate on this, perhaps assuming the nomination of a Democratic Pennsylvania judge would go through easily since the Democrats had a Senate majority and since he had pleased the Senate by nominating one of its members with the Woodbury appointment. But five Democrats joined the Whigs in voting against Woodward, and he lost 29-20.

Polk let the Baldwin seat go vacant for another six months after this experience and again asked his indecisive Secretary of State, James Buchanan, to take the position. Buchanan agreed — and two months later changed his mind again. For the third time! There is more than a little evidence that Buchanan's repeat nominations were not actually a tribute to him but a way for Polk to get rid of him tactfully. Polk told a cabinet member, "He cares nothing for the success or glory of my administration further than he can make it subservient to his own political aspirations."[7] When Buchanan again turned him down, Polk nominated Robert Grier, presiding judge of the courts in the Pittsburgh area, whom the Senate confirmed. The Baldwin seat had been vacant twenty-eight months.

Millard Fillmore

The next President to do battle with the Senate over a Supreme Court nomination was Millard Fillmore, who succeeded to the presidency after Mexican-American War hero Zachary Taylor's death in the White House. Fillmore's first appointment to the Court, Benjamin Curtis of Massachusetts, widely respected and strongly backed by Daniel Webster, not only secured Senate approval but also turned out to be a clearly superior Justice, one of the two dissenting members of the Court in the *Dred Scott* decision. (One of the ironies of Supreme Court history is how often weak Presidents have appointed capable Justices and how often strong Presidents have appointed mediocre Justices.)

Fillmore had the opportunity to fill a second seat on the Court when Justice John McKinley died, shortly before the Senate was about to adjourn. Fillmore, anxious to strengthen his prospects both for the presidential nomination and for the general election, hastily suggested Edward A. Bradford, a respected attorney from Louisiana. The Senate adjourned without considering Bradford.

Fillmore did not get the presidential nomination. The Whigs chose General Winfield Scott rather than Fillmore, and Scott lost to Franklin Pierce. Fillmore, acting before Pierce's inauguration, tried an almost certain way to get Senate approval: He nominated a Senator, George Badger of North Carolina. Badger had been Secretary of the Navy for Harrison and Tyler. But the Democratic majority in the Senate (36-20) decided against approving a Whig, even though a Senator, on the eve of the assumption of the presidency by a Democratic President. Democrats considered Badger too extreme and too partisan a Whig. Even the *New York Tribune*, in urging confirmation, praised his virtues but admitted that he

> is an iron-heeled old fogy . . . wrong-headed, crabbed, intolerant, dogmatical, inveterate in his prejudices, dictatorial and unmannerly in his deportment . . . . He lacks breadth and comprehensiveness of view.[8]

Not a ringing endorsement! The Senate postponed consideration of Badger's nomination — in effect killing it — by the narrowest of margins, 26-25, with all twenty-six votes against him coming from Democrats. Of the twenty-five in the minority, twenty were Whigs, three were Free Soilers and two were Democrats.

Twenty-one days after the vote, Pierce would become President. Fillmore tried a last effort to fill the Court, offering the vacant seat to Senator-elect Judah P. Benjamin of Louisiana. Benjamin would have become the first Jew on the Supreme Court had he accepted and the Senate approved him. But Benjamin declined. Fillmore nominated his law partner, William C. Micou, but the Senate ignored that nomination.

President Pierce

Pierce turned out to be another weak President, but he filled one vacancy with John Campbell of Alabama, a superior member of the Court until he felt obligated to resign at the start of the Civil War, even though he opposed secession.

One weak presidency followed another, as John Buchanan came after Pierce, but Buchanan had less good fortune than Pierce in dealing with the Senate on Supreme Court nominees.

The Tragic Buchanan Years

When the nation needed a strong President to detour a country headed toward civil war, the United States had one of its weakest, James Buchanan. One Senator described his presidency as "petrified by fear, or vacillating between determination and doubt."[9] His on-again-off-again pursuit of a Supreme Court seat should have been an indication to political decision-makers of his leadership skills, or lack of them. But he seemed a non-threatening choice, both to the leaders and to the majority of voters. And he had long been eager for the presidency.

Buchanan took office in 1857, four years before the start of the Civil War, and only two possible barriers seemed capable of stopping the nation's drift toward that war: 1) A decision on the *Dred Scott* case upholding the already-weakened Missouri Compromise, which could mean that the plague of slavery gradually would disappear from the nation's landscape; and 2) a President able to act decisively, to bring together widely diverse and passionately held opinions in the nation enough for people to work with one another. Unfortunately, neither occurred.

In his inaugural address, Buchanan said that slavery "is a judicial question, which legitimately belongs to the Supreme Court of the United States, before whom it is now pending, and will, it is understood, be speedily and finally settled."[10] Not many days later in 1857, the Supreme Court handed down the *Dred Scott* decision. Buchanan sent a message to Congress indicating that the slavery question had now been permanently settled.

The historic *Dred Scott* case went to the heart of the slavery question. The case developed because a slave by the name of Dred Scott was owned by Dr. John Emerson, an Army physician who lived in the state of Missouri. The Army transferred Dr. Emerson to a military post at Rock Island, Illinois, a free state. Scott sued for freedom in a federal court on behalf of his wife, his two children and himself. Did ownership cease when Dred Scott reached a free state? If the Court affirmed his freedom, then not only would Scott and his family be free, but slaves who used the "underground railroad" through states like Illinois to escape to Canada could be in those states openly. There would be a great magnet to escape to free states. On the other hand, if the owner of someone in a slave state could take that person to a free state, and that person would continue to be his or her slave, the spread of slavery throughout the nation would be the inevitable consequence. The stakes in the Supreme Court decision were extremely high.

To get into federal court, there had to be a dispute between citizens of two states. Dred Scott had been purchased from Emerson by John Sanford of New York. But could Scott, a slave, claim to be a citizen of Missouri?

In the *Dred Scott v. Sandford* decision (the Court misspelled Mr. Sanford's name) Chief Justice Taney, speaking for the Court, said:

> The question is simply this: Can a negro, whose ancestors were imported into this country, and sold as slaves, become a member of the political community formed and brought into existence by the Constitution of the United

States? . . . [Does he have] the privilege of suing in a court of the United States? . . . The plaintiff could not be a citizen of the State of Missouri, within the meaning of the Constitution of the United States, and, consequently, was not entitled to sue in its courts . . . . Neither the class of persons who had been imported as slaves, nor their descendants . . . were [at the time of the Declaration of Independence] acknowledged as a part of the people, nor intended to be included in the general words used in that memorable instrument . . . . They had for more than a century before been regarded as beings of an inferior order, and altogether unfit to associate with the white race, either in social or political relations; and so far inferior, that they had no rights which the white man was bound to respect; and that the negro might justly and lawfully be reduced to slavery for his benefit . . . . The slaves were more or less numerous in the different colonies, as slave labor was found more or less profitable. But no one seems to have doubted the correctness of the prevailing opinion of the times. The legislation of the different colonies furnishes positive and indisputable proof of this fact . . . [These laws] show that a perpetual and impassable barrier was intended to be erected between the white race and the one which they had reduced to slavery . . . .

The unhappy black race were separated from the white by indelible marks and laws long before established . . . . When we look to the condition of this race in the several States at the time, it is impossible to believe that these [constitutional] rights and privileges were intended to be extended to them . . . Dred Scott was not a citizen of Missouri within the meaning of the Constitution of the United States, and not entitled as such to sue in its courts; and . . . the [U.S.] Circuit Court had no jurisdiction of the case . . . .

Then Taney — who came from the slave state of Maryland and had freed his slaves thirty years before the decision–dealt with the Missouri Compromise of 1820, which called for the prohibition of slavery north of Missouri and in the territory acquired through the Louisiana Purchase from France. He concluded for the Court that Congress did not have the right under the Constitution to take people's property away:

> The right of property in a slave is distinctly and expressly affirmed in the Constitution . . . . And the Government in express terms is pledged to protect it in all future time, if the slave escapes from his owner . . . . As Scott was a slave when taken into the State of Illinois by his owner, and was there held as such . . . his status, as free or slave, depended on the laws of Missouri, and not of Illinois.

Taney, eighty years old when he spoke for the Court, may have been persuaded by Buchanan that this would "solve" the whole slavery issue and keep the Union together. Buchanan clearly had such hopes. Instead, by overturning the Missouri Compromise, it made civil war inevitable.

Two Justices dissented from the *Dred Scott* decision — John McLean, appointed by Jackson, and Benjamin Curtis, appointed by Fillmore. Curtis wrote in the dissent:

> The question is whether any person of African descent . . . can be a citizen of the United States . . . . No cause is shown by the plea why he is not so, except his descent and the slavery of his ancestors . . . . Among the powers unquestionably possessed by the several States, was that of determining what persons should and what persons should not be citizens. It was practicable to confer on the Government of the Union this entire power . . . . It has been further objected, that if free colored persons, born within a particular State, and made citizens of that State by its Constitution and laws, are thereby made citizens of the United States, then . . . colored persons could vote, and be eligible to not only hold Federal offices, but offices even in those States whose Constitutions and laws disqualify colored persons from voting or being elected to office. But this position rests upon an assumption which I deem untenable. Its basis is, that no one can be deemed a citizen of the United States who is not entitled to enjoy all the privileges and franchises which are conferred on

any citizen. That this is not true, under the Constitution of the United States, seems to me clear.

A naturalized citizen cannot be President of the United States, nor a Senator till after the lapse of nine years, nor a Representative til after the lapse of seven years, from his naturalization. Yet, as soon as naturalized, he is certainly a citizen of the United States . . . . One may confine the right of suffrage to white male citizens . . . . I apprehend no one will deny that [females] are citizens of the United States . . . .

Nor, in my judgment, will the position that a prohibition to bring slaves into a Territory deprives any one of his property without due process of law, bear examination . . . . A citizen of the United States owns slaves in Cuba, and brings them to the United States, where they are set free by the legislation of Congress. Does this legislation deprive him of his property without due process of law? If so, what becomes of the laws prohibiting the slave trade? If not, how can a similar regulation respecting a Territory violate the fifth amendment . . . . For these reasons, I am of [the] opinion that so much of the several acts of Congress as prohibited slavery within that part of the Territory . . . north . . . and west of the river Mississippi were constitutional and valid laws.

The *Dred Scott* decision had added impact because the Court had held for only the second time in the nation's history that an act of Congress, signed by the President, was unconstitutional and invalid. The *Dred Scott* decision and the issue of slavery were major factors for the Senate in considering Buchanan's Supreme Court nomination when Justice Curtis resigned abruptly. Buchanan chose Nathan Clifford of Maine, Attorney General in Polk's cabinet when Buchanan served as Secretary of State.

The Curtis resignation focused more than usual attention on the Court vacancy. Coming immediately after the dramatic *Dred Scott* decision that had such a huge impact on the nation, the Senate and the press and the public looked to this nomination with unusual care, particularly in how it might affect slavery. The Clifford nomination divided the nation deeply. Some questioned his legal credentials, but more focused on his views on slavery that can best be described as being somewhere between pro-slavery and fuzzy.

As Attorney General under Polk, Clifford had defended the legality of the institution of slavery in terms that did not indicate any personal disagreement with the practice. This infuriated the Abolitionists and other anti-slavery forces. One anti-slavery newspaper observed:

> On the principle which seems to have governed the selection of Mr. Clifford, that the proper business of the Northern minority on the Bench is merely to fall in with and say yes to any extravagances which the Southern majority may choose to promulgate, Mr. Clifford is admirably fitted for the place in which he has been put.[11]

Clifford has been described by one biographer as having "a major sense of inferiority."[12] In addition to his cabinet service, Polk had designated him to work out final details with Mexico on peace arrangements following the War with Mexico. For a short period, he served as Minister to Mexico where he provided less than enlightened service. That he did not measure up to expectations for a Supreme Court Justice is suggested by the fact that while the Justices sometimes informally told Senators their favorable opinions about nominees, — a practice continued to this day — Clifford's nomination resulted in "troubled silence" from the Court.[13]

Party pressure on Democrats, plus the absence of two prominent foes of Clifford, Senator Charles Sumner and Senator Simon Cameron, enabled Clifford to be approved by the Senate 26-23.

Buchanan had less good fortune with his next nominee.

On May 30, 1860, Justice Peter Daniel died, leaving the Court with four Southerners and four Northerners on the eve of the Civil War. Buchanan typically moved slowly, amazingly slowly in this case because 1860 was an election year, and Buchanan had to know that after the election any nominee would have difficulty with the Senate.

A biographer of Jeremiah Black, the man Buchanan eventually did select, believes Buchanan hesitated because there were reports that Chief Justice Taney, then eighty-three years old and not in good physical health, though alert mentally, would resign.[14] Buchanan reportedly wanted to nominate Black for Chief Justice. What started the rumors about Taney stepping down is not clear, but they were widely held.

Taney did not step down, however, and finally, on February 5, 1861 — eight months after the vacancy occurred and one month before Lincoln's inauguration — Buchanan sent Black's name to the Senate.

By this time Lincoln had been elected President the previous November and Buchanan was a lame duck. Under the provisions of the Constitution then in effect, the new President did not take office until March of 1861. Black, Buchanan's Secretary of State, had an impressive resume. He had also been Attorney General of the United States and Chief Justice of the Pennsylvania Supreme Court. Black had been considered for the Court by Polk. But he did not favor immediate abolition of slavery. That, combined with Black's reputation for having a hot temper, and the political reality of a new President coming in, doomed his chances.[15]

Black's nomination had one other problem: Twelve Senators from the South who might be expected to support him had withdrawn as part of the first step in secession. After the election, with the soon-to-be-effected change from the Democratic Buchanan to the Republican Lincoln, Buchanan had difficulty with the Senate on all appointments. But his difficulty became magnified for the Supreme Court because of the *Dred Scott* decision.

The national press did not help. Horace Greeley's powerful *New York Tribune* commented:

> There is a decided majority against the confirmation . . . if pressed to a vote he must be rejected. The President was

informed of this fact after a careful canvass of the Senate
last week, and much surprise is excited that he should
expose a friend to unnecessary mortification.[16]

A few days later, the same newspaper told its readers: "Mr.
Buchanan has never hit upon a single nomination more eminent-
ly unfit to be made than this one."

The Senate defeated Black by one vote — 26-25; the twenty-
six killing the nomination were all Republicans. Of the twenty-
five supporting Black, twenty-four were Democrats and one was
a member of the short-lived American Party. The vote came
eleven days before Lincoln became President.

Buchanan's unfortunate presidency marked the end of the pre-
Civil War period. After Buchanan, relations between Presidents
and the Senate on Supreme Court nominations improved. Yet
tensions remained, and some major battles between the President and the Senate were yet to come.

Between the Jackson presidency and the Lincoln presidency,
the Senate rejected ten of eighteen nominations to the Supreme
Court. When the nominations were of people with extreme views
or lacking superior legal skills, their rejection is proper, but
generally that was not the case. While Presidents do not look
good in this process, the Senate record is worse.

Endnotes

1. Henry Clay to John Crittenden, January 24, 1844, Warren, Vol. II, p. 111.

2. John Tyler in *The Letters and Times of the Tylers,* by Lyon G. Tyler (New York: Da Capo Press, 1970, reprint of Whittet and Shepperson, 1885), Vol. II, p. 398.

3. Thurlow Weed to John Cittenden, March 17, 1844, Warren, Vol. II, p. 115.

4. *The Diary of James K. Polk,* (Chicago: McClurg, 1910), Vol I, p. 46.

5. *Ibid.*

6. *Ibid.,* Vol. I, pp. 216-217.

7. James Polk to Nathan Clifford, quoted in *The Presidency of James K. Polk,* by Nathan H. Bergeron, (Manhattan: University of Kansas Press, 1987), p. 34.

8. *New York Tribune,* Jan. 8, 1853, Warren, Vol II, pp. 243-244.

9. Senator Roscoe Conkling, quoted in *Congressional Globe,* January 30, 1861, p. 649, in *Roscoe Conkling of New York,* (Ithaca, N.Y.: Cornell University Press, 1971), p. 31.

10. Quoted in *A Basic History of the U.S. Supreme Court,* by Bernard Schwartz, (Princeton: Van Nostrand, 1968), p. 35.

11. *New York Tribune,* quoted in Warren, Vol. II, p. 324.

12. "Nathan Clifford," by William Gillette, *Justices of the United States Supreme Court,* Vol II, edited by Leon Friedman and Fred Israel, (New York, R. R. Bowker, 1969), p. 965.

13. *Ibid., p. 967.*

14. William Brigance, *Jeremiah Sullivan Black,* (New York: Da Capo Press: 1971; Reprint of University of Pennsylvania Press, 1934,) pp. 113-115.

15. *New York Tribune,* January 29, 1861. Warren, Vol. II, p. 364.

16. *New York Tribune,* February 7, 1861 quoted in William Brigance, *Jeremiah Sullivan Black,* (New York: Da Capo

Press: 1971; Reprint of University of Pennsylvania Press, 1934,) p. 115.

10

Legacies of the Civil War

Many historians rank Abraham Lincoln as our greatest President for holding the Union together, and some put George Washington first, for his important role in its formation. But in one respect, there can be no disagreement: Lincoln embodied a special spirit, a special sensitivity that is unique among our Presidents.

It is sometimes illustrated by his Gettysburg Address, a short and powerful speech that embodies much of what we as a nation try to be. But his greatest speech was his Second Inaugural Address, toward the end of the Civil War, when there was hatred toward "the enemy" like nothing this nation had ever known. Perhaps citizens expected the leader of the Union forces to boast and lift the morale of the wounded nation with words such as, "We're whipping them, and we're going to win this decisively," and with epithets to rally public opinion to the cause. But instead, Lincoln spoke these words: "With malice toward none, with charity for all . . ."

That spirit helped him to keep the remainder of the nation together. It also helped him in his relations with the Senate on the Supreme Court nominations. Within a month of assuming the presidency, Lincoln faced three Supreme Court vacancies, one of which was a holdover from the Buchanan administration.

More than casual attention focused on Lincoln and his Supreme Court appointments in the wake of the *Dred Scott* decision. Even before his election, that case had already become an issue for him. In his widely reported 1858 debates with Stephen A. Douglas during their race for the Illinois Senate seat, Douglas lashed out at Lincoln for launching "warfare on the Supreme Court of the United States" over *Dred Scott.* Newspaper accounts of one Douglas debate speech (together with audience reaction) illustrate both the mood of the times and the reason for Lincoln's care on his Supreme Court nominees. As part of their August 21, 1858, debate, Douglas said:

> We are told by Lincoln that he is utterly opposed to the Dred Scott decision, and will not submit to it, for the reason that he says it deprives the negro of the rights and privileges of citizenship. (Laughter and applause.) That is the first and main reason which he assigns for his warfare on the Supreme Court of the United States and its decision. I ask you, are you in favor of conferring upon the negro the rights and privileges of citizenship? ("No, no.") Do you desire to strike out of our State Constitution that clause which keeps slaves and free negroes out of the State, and allow the free negroes to flow in, ("never,") and cover your prairies with black settlements? Do you desire to turn this beautiful State into a free negro colony, ("no, no,") in order that when Missouri abolishes slavery she can send one hundred thousand emancipated slaves into Illinois, to become citizens and voters, on an equality with yourselves? ("Never," "no.") If you desire negro citizenship, if you desire to allow them to come into the State and settle with the white man, if you desire them to vote on an equality with yourselves, and to make them eligible to office, to serve on juries, and to adjudge your rights, then support Mr. Lincoln and the Black Republican party,

who are in favor of the citizenship of the negro. ("Never, never.") For one, I am opposed to negro citizenship in any and every form. (Cheers.) I believe this government was made on the white basis. ("Good.") I believe it was made by white men, for the benefit of white men and their posterity for ever, and I am in favor of confining citizenship to white men, men of European birth and descent, instead of conferring it upon negroes, Indians and other inferior races. ("Good for you." "Douglas forever.")[1]

Still smarting from the *Dred Scott* decision, Lincoln said in his First Inaugural address: "If the policy of the government, upon vital questions . . . is to be irrevocably fixed by decisions of the Supreme Court . . . the people will have ceased to be their own rulers, having . . . practically resigned their government, into the hands of that eminent tribunal."[2]

Lincoln did not rush into making his Court nominations; he took almost a year to make the first ones. The most widely read historian of the Supreme Court, Henry Abraham, labels it "probably [an] inexcusable delay."[3]

The illness of Chief Justice Taney and one other Justice — in addition to the three vacancies — meant that the Court, for all practical purposes, did not function for much of 1861, except for its work "circuit-riding."

Because of the Civil War, the slavery question and the need to reconcile the nation after the war, Lincoln chose his nominees cautiously, keeping in mind the need to get Senate approval, consulting carefully in the open style that Lincoln followed. His first appointee, Noah Swayne, met all of the criteria. He had freed his slaves while in Virginia and moved north to Ohio. He understood the North and the South. He held strict Quaker beliefs and could be helpful in the reconciliation process. The Senate approved Swayne 38-1.

Lincoln's next nomination was Samuel Miller of Iowa, the first Justice to serve from west of the Mississippi, or as the *Yale Law Journal* reported, "from beyond the Mississippi."[4] Miller practiced medicine as a country doctor in Kentucky but gradually became interested in the law. He joined anti-slavery efforts in

Kentucky and, when they suffered a loss, he moved with his family to Keokuk, Iowa, where he freed his slaves. Miller tried unsuccessfully for the governorship of Iowa and had been endorsed for the Supreme Court by several state bar associations. The parallels between the Miller nomination and the Swayne nomination are intriguing: both were originally from southern or border states, both held strong anti-slavery views, both moved north and freed their slaves and both held somewhat unconventional religious views, Swayne as a Quaker, Miller as a Unitarian.

Miller's personal style also had a touch of the Lincolnesque that may have appealed to the President. Presiding at a trial in St. Louis, Miller told a lawyer who seemed to be proceeding endlessly, "Damn it, man, come to the point!" "What point, your Honor?" the lawyer responded, to which Miller replied, "I don't care; any point, some point!"[5]

The Iowa lawyer had high officials from several states write to Lincoln on his behalf, and he had one other major plus: a petition urging his nomination signed by 129 out of 140 House members and all but four of the Senators. The Senate confirmed him unanimously thirty minutes after Lincoln forwarded his name.

Other Lincoln appointees to the Court — all approved — were his former campaign manager and friend, Judge David Davis; an active Democrat, Stephen Field, who served on the Court for almost thirty-five years; and, following the death of Chief Justice Taney, Salmon Chase, his Secretary of the Treasury, as Chief Justice. Chase wrote Lincoln: "On reaching home tonight I was saluted with the intelligence that you this day nominated me to the Senate for the office of Chief Justice. I cannot sleep before I thank [you] for this mark of your confidence, & especially for the manner in which the nomination was made. I shall never forget either and trust that you will never regret either. Be assured that I prize your confidence & goodwill more than nomination or office."[6]

Lincoln's Supreme Court nominees showed independence, and those with whom he had worked before — Davis and

Chase — kept in contact with him on other matters. Three days before Booth shot Lincoln, Chase sent Lincoln a letter advising him how to handle the Confederate states. Davis advised Lincoln to modify his Emancipation Proclamation, which had caused a political storm. (Gen. John A. McClernand advised him to retract it. Lincoln responded: "To use a coarse, but an expressive figure, broken eggs cannot be mended. I have issued the emancipation proclamation, and I can not retract it."[7])

Lincoln's appointments to the Court were above average and by taking his time, listening to Senators and others, he had minimal difficulty with the Senate. That was not true of his two successors.

President Andrew Johnson

While Lincoln's choices for the Supreme Court are viewed on balance as superior, his choice of Andrew Johnson as Vice President for his second term is not. A Democrat chosen in part because of his party affiliation, in part because of his Tennessee roots, he had courage but lacked some of the other qualities a President needed during this difficult period. Three years after taking office, he faced an impeachment trial in the Senate, which he survived by one vote. Ill will toward Lincoln's successor came quickly after he assumed the presidency.

Six weeks after Lincoln's death, Justice John Catron died. Johnson hesitated almost a year before nominating a candidate, Attorney General Henry Stanbery of Ohio, a respected Republican who presumably would have appeal to the Republicans in the Senate. As Supreme Court historian Henry Abraham has noted, "It is doubtful that the Senate would have approved God himself had he been nominated by Andrew Johnson."[8]

Predictably, the Senate did not assent to the Stanbery nomination, but it went beyond that. It joined the House and eliminated that seat on the Court, as well as the next one that would be created due to death or resignation. Amazingly, Johnson signed the bill into law. So two years later, when another Justice died,

Johnson had no ability to fill that seat. Johnson's contribution to the Court was one he never intended: reducing the size of the Court from ten to nine, and then temporarily to eight.

Grant's Rejections

Ulysses S. Grant did a superb job as a general in the Civil War and the public recognized it. The public assumed that he could also do a superb job as President, and on that they miscalculated. Badly. Grant became one of our worst Presidents, and only half of the eight nominees he sent to the Senate served on the Court.

The Senate rejected his first nominee, Attorney General Ebenezer Hoar, for all the wrong reasons. Hoar had demanded that the nominees for the district courts, traditionally presented to the Justice Department by the Senators, be at least of minimum quality; he also had worked for a merit civil service system, reducing the patronage available for Senators and other party leaders; and, worst of all in their eyes, he had opposed the impeachment of Andrew Johnson, which the Senate had overwhelmingly favored. No one seriously questioned Hoar's legal credentials. He received almost universal press acclaim. He even had the "correct" party label. But his views troubled the Senate, and he had geographical problems. *The Press of Philadelphia* reported: "Southern and Western delegations were already opposed to Massachusetts being so largely represented in the Cabinet, and they were especially opposed to elevating a New England man to the Supreme bench while the Southern States were not represented."[9]

After lengthy debate, the Senate rejected Hoar 33-24. Senator Simon Cameron observed: "What could you expect for a man who has snubbed seventy Senators?"[10]

While the Senate still had the Hoar nomination hanging, Justice Robert Grier resigned because of poor health, nudged not so gently by his Court colleagues to retire. A petition signed by most of the members of the Senate and House went to Grant, favoring the somewhat controversial Edwin Stanton, who had been Secretary of War for Lincoln. Stanton received Senate confirmation 46-11 one day after Grant sent up his name. But a heart attack killed the fifty-four-year-old Stanton four days later, leaving that seat vacant.

Grant then sent nominations for the two vacancies to the Senate at the same time. One nominee, William Strong of Pennsylvania, had experience in the state courts and an excellent reputation. In a matter of a few days, the Senate confirmed him.

The other nominee, Joseph Bradley of New Jersey, ran into difficulty. A highly respected attorney, he had strong ties to the business community he had represented. After several weeks of Senate maneuvering and debate, the Senate confirmed him by a larger than expected vote: 46-9. His votes on the Court reflected his business-oriented background.

When Justice Samuel Nelson resigned, Grant nominated Ward Hunt, who had both judicial and legislative experience. Some Senators opposed him but with less than great vigor, and Hunt went on the Court with a 53-11 vote.

Then Grant headed for some serious difficulties. Chief Justice Salmon Chase died. Grant decided immediately to name someone outside of the Court. At the funeral service for Chase, Grant's wife, Julia, noted the presence of the strikingly handsome Senator Roscoe Conkling of New York. She wrote: "I looked around [at the memorial ceremony] and my choice [for Chief Justice], without hesitation, was Roscoe Conkling. He was so talented and so honorable, and I must say that woman-like I thought the flowing robes would be becoming to Mr. Conkling."[11] Grant chose the bright, powerful and hot-tempered Conkling.

Word leaked out that Grant had chosen the forceful New York Senator. The press reacted negatively. Conkling had never gone out of his way to cultivate reporters — or anyone else, other than political leaders. *The Nation* commented:

> Conkling has not contributed a single useful or fruitful idea; he is not the author of a single measure of value or importance; he has made no speech which any sensible man can bear to read—so that his political claims to the

chief place on the bench of the greatest tribunal in the world are as paltry as his professional ones.[12]

Historian Allan Nevins observed that Conkling "was about as well fitted for the bench as for a monastery."[13] Conkling had the good sense to decline the Grant offer.

At that point Grant selected his Attorney General, George Williams, who otherwise might have quietly continued in that Cabinet office. But when the spotlight of the nomination for Chief Justice hit, the nation and Grant learned much more about him.

Williams had served as Chief Justice for the Oregon Territory and Senator from Oregon and appears to have been a competent but unspectacular public servant. Whatever his personal conduct before his first wife died, he then married a woman with distinctly stronger spending and consuming habits. That soon had a bearing on his nomination.

The hometown press reacted favorably to the nomination, with the *Oregonian* describing it as one "that will not fail to reflect credit upon the Administration,"[14] a massive misjudgment. The rest of the nation reacted negatively. The New York Bar Association and other state bar groups passed resolutions in opposition. The *American Law Review* expressed its "regret that the President in making this, the most important appointment in his Administration, has not . . . a choice from the eminent lawyers of the country as the people had a right to expect."[15] One newspaper commented, "The nomination surprised and disgusted every lawyer in the United States."[16]

The mood of the Senate was not favorable. One Senator suggested that a bill should be introduced to do away with the chief justiceship, and a Senate colleague responded that no bill need pass to achieve that; simply confirm Williams, and that would be the result.

These reactions related only to the competence of Williams to be Chief Justice. Other problems of greater interest soon surfaced.

Mrs. Williams had minimal popularity among the wives of officialdom in Washington. One of the people she offended was the wife of Senator Matt Carpenter of Wisconsin, a member of the Senate Judiciary Committee. At a later White House reception, Mrs. Williams "was received by Mrs. Grant with frigidity."[17] In addition to some personality quirks, Mrs. Williams dressed lavishly. Just prior to the Chief Justice nomination, the Attorney General and his wife moved into a new home he had built on Rhode Island Avenue for $25,000, a substantial sum in 1873, and they did not spare resources in decorating it. Williams's salary as Attorney General was $18,000 a year. At least one woman, Mrs. John A. Logan, widow of the Civil War hero, charged that Mrs. Williams accepted "presents" at her home from those who had cases before the Justice Department. A brochure circulated in Washington made the charge that Williams arrived in Washington "somewhat out at the elbows. He had not the means to pay an hundred thousand dollars for a tract of land upon which to lay the foundation of a palatial residence, nor the ability to expend another hundred thousand dollars in building and furnishing the same."[20]

These and other matters — including charges by Judge John Wright of corruption — were discussed in secrecy by the Senate Judiciary Committee, which recognized that it had a sensitive matter to handle. Over a four-day period, the Judiciary Committee received "specific charges in writing and in print, impugning the conduct of Mr. Williams as Attorney General."[21] The Committee met on December 8, 1873, and "feeling the delicacy of the situation of Mr. Williams and how mortifying it might be to him that a formal examination of such charges should be gone into . . . concluded that [the] meeting [should be] an informal one . . . that the Chairman should have an interview with Mr. Williams and ascertain what reply or explanation he might . . . make to the charges."

The next day the chairman, Senator George Edmunds of Vermont, went to see Williams "and state to him what the substance of those charges was . . . and asked him for any suggestions that he might choose to make upon the subject." The

Judiciary Committee reports on the Edmunds visit: "Mr. Williams having thus been asked for suggestions, stated emphatically that he declined to be put on trial before the Committee or the Senate; that he did not propose to submit himself to any such jurisdiction in any form; and that, of course, the Senate had the right to make any inquiries it thought fit . . . but he must decline to be a party thereto in any form."

On December 14th the Senate's agenda listed the confirmation vote for Williams but it delayed action for one day. The next day the Senate recommitted the nomination to the Judiciary Committee, together with the power to subpoena people and papers.

More accusations surfaced, but the Committee decided to focus on the personal finances of Williams as they related to the Justice Department. The two serious charges: that he took the contingent funds of the Justice Department for his personal use and that he bought a carriage and a span of horses, which he used for personal as well as public purposes. Fanning the flames of public outrage was that Williams's carriage was appreciably grander than the President's.

The carriage dispute sounds similar to the limousine disputes that surface occasionally these days. Williams said,

> No other Department of the Government needs horses and carriages as much as this department . . . . All the carriages of the Department have been used, when not needed for official, for family purposes . . . and I think this is more or less true of all the Departments of the Government.[20]

The Williams defense on the carriage issue may have had some merit, but the question of comingling of personal and public funds was not so easily rebutted. The Committee concluded: "In more than one instance and beside that of the carriage, the public money of the U.S. were used for the private benefit of Mr. Williams." He also took cash from a contingency fund and would place a personal check there, as a sort of IOU.

At the time of the investigation, Williams owed the fund more than $2,000. The Committee report continued:

> Mr. Falls, a disbursing officer of the U.S., had been the private cashier of Mr. Williams; that cash deposited with him by Mr. Williams was put in with the public money in the same manner as money might be deposited in [a] bank, and kept all together . . . . There is no denial or explanation whatever . . . . The point is not whether the Treasury of the U.S. had any security . . . but whether such moneys were taken from the fund and used for private purposes. This fact is indisputable.

The Committee quietly decided to reject Williams, not wanting to add burdens to an already scandal-plagued administration, and notified the President and Secretary of State Hamilton Fish. Grant asked Fish to tell Williams to withdraw, using whatever excuses he wanted. On January 7th, Williams wrote to the President, withdrawing and stating that "the floodgates of columny . . . have been opened upon me, and . . . might embarrass your administration and perhaps impair my usefulness on the bench."[21] An observer wrote to a House member: "Kate has withdrawn George."[22]

A few days later, Williams sent a furious letter to the Judiciary Committee: "I have been tried and practically condemned without the privilege of confronting or cross-examining the witnesses, and without any opportunity to controvert or explain anything stated by them to my injury or prejudice."[23] While the Williams letter may have been good public relations, the Committee had offered him the chance to come before it and he had declined. The record makes clear that the Senate Judiciary Committee performed a valuable service.

He served eighteen more months as Attorney General, and then Grant suggested he should resign, which he did. Williams and his wife moved back to Oregon where she founded a religious cult. She went on long fasts, one for forty days and one for one hundred and ten days, predicting the end of the world. At the age of seventy-nine, the people of Portland elected

Williams mayor. Controversy reigned; prostitution and gambling thrived. He was indicted for malfeasance, but prosecutors never pushed the charge. The voters defeated him when he ran for reelection.

After the Senate rejected Williams for Chief Justice, Grant then named Caleb Cushing, who was promoted by House leader Benjamin Butler. At the age of seventy-three, Cushing had an age liability, but, he also had a substantially greater one: Senators did not trust him. He had wandered from party to party, and Grant knew of the mistrust that existed in the Senate. Then a letter became public that Cushing had sent Jefferson Davis just prior to the Civil War, a relatively innocuous letter asking Davis to consider a young employee, Archibald Rowan, who worked under Cushing. The young man said he felt obligated to work for the Confederacy because of his home state roots. The newspaper publication of the letter reached Capitol Hill while the Republican Senators were caucusing. Someone handed Senator Aaron Sargent of California a copy and he read it to a hushed caucus that erupted after hearing it. However innocent the letter, the wounds of the Civil War had not healed and news of the letter caused a storm. Cushing withdrew his name, perhaps at Grant's suggestion.

The *New York World* commented: "Mr. Cushing's great disqualification for the Chief Justiceship is discovered to be an act of humanity to a poor peaceful young man who had faithfully served him as a clerk."[24]

Grant quickly nominated a less-than-stellar candidate for Chief Justice, with no judicial experience, Morrison Waite. This time before selecting the nominee, he took "the wise precaution of consulting Senate leaders."[25] Two days later the Senate confirmed him 63-6.

Another Justice described Waite as a "man that would never have been thought of for the position by any person except President Grant . . . an experiment which no President has a right to make with our Court."[26] But Waite turned out to be better than expected. Among other decisions, he delivered the opinion in the widely discussed *Reynolds v. United States* case, deciding that polygamy in Utah could be considered a crime against the United States: "Suppose one believed . . . it was her duty to burn herself upon the funeral pile [sic] of her dead husband, would it be beyond the power of the civil government to prevent her carrying her belief into practice?"[27] The decision not only dealt with a constitutional question, it dealt with public opinion inflamed over the issue of polygamy.

Waite's nomination as Chief Justice came as a surprise to him and the nation and came because the Senate Judiciary Committee saved both Grant and the nation from the prospect of a George Williams chief justiceship.

Endnotes

1. *Collected Works of Abraham Lincoln,* (New Brunswick, N.J.: Rutgers University Press, 1953), edited by Roy P. Basler, Vol. III, p. 9.

2. *Collected Works of Abraham Lincoln,* March 4, 1861, Vol IV, p. 268.

3. Henry J. Abraham, *Justices and Presidents,* (New York: Oxford University Press, 1992), 3rd edition, p. 117.

4. "Samuel Freeman Miller," by Charles Gregory, *Yale Law Journal,* April 1908.

5. "Samuel Freeman Miller," by Richard W. Peterson, paper presented to the Lee County (Iowa) Historical Society, October 14, 1990.

6. Salmon B. Chase to Abraham Lincoln, December 6, 1864, *Collected Works of Abraham Lincoln,* Vol. VIII, p. 154.

7. Lincoln to Major General John A. McClernand, Jan. 8. 1863, *Collected Works of Abraham Lincoln,* Vol. VI, p. 48.

8. Henry J. Abraham, *Justices and Presidents,* (New York: Oxford University Press, 1992), 3rd edition, p. 124-125.

9. "Attorney General Hoar," no author indicated, *The Press,* (Philadelphia), February 4, 1870.

10. Quoted in Harris, p. 75.

11. Quoted in *Grant* by William McFeely, (New York: Norton, 1981), p. 388.

12. *The Nation,* October 1, 1873, quoted in Jordan, *Roscoe Conkling of New York,* (Ithaca, New York: Cornell University Press, 1971), p. 199.

13. Allan Nevins, *Hamilton Fish* (New York: Dodd Mead, 1936), p. 660.

14. *The Oregonian,* December 4, 1873, quoted in "Almost Chief Justice: George H. Williams," Sidney Teiser, *Oregon Historical Quarterly,* September/December, 1946.

15. Quoted in Teiser article.

16. *Springfield Republican,* quoted in Teiser.

17. Allan Nevins, Hamilton Fish, *The Inner History of the Grant Administration,* (New York: Ungar, 1936), Vol. II, p. 770.
18. Undated document, printed, "Jno. W. Wright vs. Columbus Delano and George H. Williams," p. 8, National Archives.
19. Judiciary Committee report to the Senate, undated but prior to January 1874, unpublished and written by hand, National Archives. The succeeding quotations are from the Judiciary Committee report unless otherwise noted.
20. George Williams to Senator George Edmunds, January 19, 1874, National Archives.
21. George Williams to Ulysses Grant, January 7, 1874, Grant Papers, Library of Congress.
22. Judge M. P. Deady to J. W. Nesmith, letter in Oregon Historical Society Library, quoted in "Almost Chjief Justice: George H. Williams," Sidney Teiser, *Oregon Historical Quarterly,* Sept./Dec., 1946.
23. George H. Williams to Senator George Edmunds, January 19, 1874, National Archives.
24. Quoted in *Life of Caleb Cushing,* by Claude M. Fuess, (New York: harcourt, Brace, 1923), Vol. II, p. 372.
25. Nevins, p. 665.
26. Justice Stephen H. Field, quoted in *Justices and Presidents,* by Henry J. Abraham (New York: Oxford University Press, 1992), 3rd editions, p. 131, quoted from Howard Jay Graham, "The Waite Court and the Fourteenth Amendment," *Vanderbilt Law Review,* March 1964.
27. 98 U.S. 145, 166 (October 1878).

11

Rough Riding Through the "Teddy" Roosevelt Days

After the corruption-ridden Grant administration, the nation had the benefit of the presidency of Republican Rutherford B. Hayes, elected in the tight 1876 election contest with Democrat Samuel J. Tilden, one of only two contests in the nation's history in which the winner of the electoral college received fewer popular votes than the losing candidate.

The First Justice Harlan

Whatever cloud that cast on Hayes, he at once showed a striking contrast to Grant by simply being a President who wanted everyone in his administration to "play it straight." Hayes served only one term but named three to serve as Justices, the most significant being John Marshall Harlan of Kentucky, grandfather of a future Justice also named John Marshall Harlan. The senior Harlan cast the lone negative vote in the famous 1896 *Plessy v. Ferguson* decision, which permitted "separate but equal," in effect tolerating racial segregation in the nation. History is much kinder to Harlan than to the rest of that Court.

Harlan's nomination did not slide through the Senate as easily as the voice vote in his favor suggests. When Hayes nominated Harlan, a group of rigidly Republican Senators known as the Republican Stalwarts expressed "anger at the President's temerity in daring to nominate anyone not approved by them. The result . . . was that Harlan's confirmation was held up for six weeks."[1] Some opposed him on geographical grounds, the retiring Justice David Davis being from Illinois. The powerful Senator Roscoe Conkling — one of the Republican Stalwarts — opposed Harlan purely on patronage grounds. In a letter to a member of the Court, Conkling wrote that he "would prefer to take the chances of what would come from a Democratic administration after the next election, to yielding any of their ancient rights of controlling public patronage."[2] But Hayes stood firm, and the Senators in opposition saw they would lose. The Senate approved Harlan without a roll call.

Shortly before Hayes's one term as President ended, a final vacancy occurred and the President nominated his Kenyon (Ohio) College classmate, Senator Stanley Matthews. Though he was an able attorney and former judge, many regarded Matthews as politically unpredictable. Matthews also had close ties to the biggest financial interests in the nation. He had served as chief counsel for the Midwest interests of Jay Gould, a financially powerful person but not popular. The *Detroit Free Press* said, "Jay Gould has been appointed to the United States Supreme Court in place of Judge Swayne, resigned."[3] The *New York Herald* called it "a nomination not fit to be made."[4] The Senate did not react favorably; the Senate Judiciary Committee bottled up the nomination.

A few weeks later, when James Garfield became President, he renominated Matthews in an apparent attempt to heal the rifts in the badly divided Republican Party. He had promised Hayes that he would do so, and pressure from financial interests may also have played a role. Factors weighing for Matthews included not only his public service but his service for the Union in the Civil War, as well as a sentimental factor: Matthews had lost three sons suddenly of scarlet fever. But weighing against Matthews were not only his railroad and business ties, but also a "cronyism" charge, since the President's brother-in-law had married Matthews's sister. Nonetheless, the Senate finally confirmed him, 24-23. He turned out to be a respectable, if not superior, member of the Court, so much so that even one of his chief opponents, Senator George Edmunds of Vermont, later praised Matthews's work.

Patronage Appointments

During Garfield's term, cut short by an assassin's bullet, he brought to a head the entire question of senatorial patronage. His Supreme Court nomination was only a minor part of the battle, but the patronage fight over presidential appointees in general would affect the power of future Presidents as it related to Supreme Court nominations.

Garfield's predecessor, Rutherford B. Hayes, had caused a mini-storm when he made clear that he would not automatically approve senatorial suggestions for positions, such as those administering the New York Custom House. A commission of three appointed by Hayes to look specifically at the New York Custom House and its practices issued a devastating report. The report charged that positions requiring technical skills were filled by people who had no qualifications other than their political activities and "that 200 small politicians were supported by the New York custom house without performing any public service whatever; they were Conkling's ward heelers, paid for party work with sinecures."[5] Hayes immediately ordered federal employees to cease partisan activities and directed people who were performing no useful function be discharged. Senator Conkling felt betrayed by the President of his own party, whom he had helped elect and he was furious.

Chester Arthur, a future President then in charge of the Custom House, refused to give up his Republican Party activities and Hayes asked for his resignation. Arthur refused. While his status remained in limbo, the President sent the name of Theodore Roosevelt (father of the future President) to replace Arthur. At Conkling's urging, claiming that the President was trying to take power away from Senators that rightfully belonged to them, the Senate turned down Roosevelt, 31-25, with all but five Republicans voting against the Republican President. Both Hayes and Conkling might have been able to agree on the Hayes diary entry: "I am now in a contest on the question of the right of Senators to dictate or control nominations."[6] When Congress adjourned, the President suspended Arthur and appointed E. A. Merritt, a qualified and experienced person. When Congress reconvened, Conkling tried to stop the Merritt nomination, but after a bitter struggle Hayes prevailed.

Patronage abuses were serious enough that both political party platforms contained pledges to move toward civil service, though many political leaders loathed both the idea and the phrase. Conkling, for example, referred to it as "snivel service" and to Hayes as "His Fraudulency" and "Rutherfraud B. Hayes."[7] Former President Grant spoke for many Republican politicians when he commented:

> As to competitive examinations, they are of questionable utility .... The way to achieve the best civil service, is, first to influence Congressmen, and induce them to refrain from pressure upon the Executive ... then keep the Republican Party in power until the process of education is complete. As it is now, the only danger I see to civil service reform is in the triumph of the Democratic party.[8]

When Garfield succeeded Hayes, the same Senate fights erupted with one major change: In order to bring calm to the Republican Party in the key state of New York, Chester Arthur became Garfield's vice president. President Garfield consulted with Conkling about his Cabinet appointments and, while they did not please Conkling, the personal relationship between Garfield and Conkling remained cordial. At one point the President considered naming Conkling to the Cabinet. But then the President raised Conkling's ire by making appointments in New York, and the Garfield vs. Conkling battle recommenced.

The Republican caucus in the Senate unanimously backed Conkling — at first — in his fights with the President. Garfield tried to placate Conkling with some appointments, then, when newspapers attacked him for that, named one of Conkling's chief opponents, William Robertson, to the key post of Collector at the New York Custom House. When the Republican caucus saw that Garfield would be firm on the matter, support for Conkling started to wither. And when it became clear that Conkling and his fellow New York Senator Thomas Platt would lose, Conkling and Platt took the highly unusual step of resigning from the Senate, stunning the Senate and the nation. Some believe they hoped to be reelected to the Senate by the state legislature of New York, but that does not appear to have been an immediate goal. Vice President Chester Arthur, who owed his office to Conkling, urged the pair to reconsider and let the legislature reinstate them. Arthur went to Albany to lobby the legislature in their behalf. But the effort failed.

Not only did it fail, this marked the end of the high point of Senate influence on presidential appointments, whether for the Supreme Court or the New York Custom House. The abuse of the senatorial privileges had been stopped, thanks to the courage of Hayes and Garfield.

Enter Chester Arthur

Ironically, shortly after Conkling resigned, a mentally deranged patronage seeker shot Garfield, and after two and one-half months the President died and Chester Arthur became President.

During his presidency Arthur had two nominations to the Court. The first, Horace Gray, received high marks from everyone and the Senate approved Gray with no difficulty. When the second vacancy occurred, Arthur offered the court seat to his mentor, Roscoe Conkling. Newspapers denounced both Arthur and Conkling, but the Senate approved him 39-12. Five days later Conkling decided not to take the seat. In the end two thorny problems were now put to rest: Arthur had paid his political debt to the person most responsible for putting him in high office, and the nation had lost the questionable services of Conkling who, as Senator, had been much more interested in patronage than issues. Arthur then nominated the highly regarded Samuel Blatchford, whom the Senate approved by voice vote.

Grover Cleveland

Grover Cleveland's election in 1892 brought the Democrats to the White House for the first time since James Buchanan's presidency, and he nominated the first Democrat to the Supreme Court since 1863. Cleveland selected Lucius Lamar of Mississippi. Lamar resigned his House seat in Congress prior to the Civil War and served as a colonel for the Confederacy. After the Civil War, he eloquently voiced the need for reconciliation between the two sections of the nation.

Republicans controlled the Senate when Cleveland nominated Lamar (thirty-eight Republicans, thirty-seven Democrats and one independent), and it quickly became apparent that there would be a battle for Senate confirmation. Objections to his having fought for the Confederacy arose more than two decades after the Civil War. Publicly stated objections were that he did not have enough legal background, not a valid claim, and that he was too old at the age of sixty-two, though an older nominee had previously been approved. The big hurdle remained his Confederate war record. A few Republicans crossed over, believing that Lamar's earlier plea for reconciliation might be fulfilled in part by his approval. The Senate confirmed him 32-28, with sixteen members abstaining.

Cleveland's struggles with the Senate over Supreme Court nominations were not over. When Chief Justice Waite died suddenly, the President named Melville Fuller of Illinois, and after initial Senate resistance by the chair of the Judiciary Committee, the Senate approved Fuller 41-20. But the battle was not pleasant for Fuller. Opponents distributed a brochure, "The War Record of Melville Fuller," pointing out his political activities during the Civil War and that while only in his twenties he did not serve in the military. But Robert Todd Lincoln, son of the former President, came to the defense of his fellow Chicago attorney, and having a Lincoln backing a Democratic nominee helped. Nine Republicans joined the Democrats in supporting Fuller.

President Cleveland had nomination battles that ended in rejections as well. When Justice Blatchford of New York died, New York's Democratic Senator David Hill made several nominee suggestions to the President, but Hill belonged to the anti-Cleveland faction of the New York Democratic Party, still split from the Conkling days. Cleveland nominated William Hornblower, part of Cleveland's faction of the New York Democratic Party. Hill objected. Hornblower represented corporate interests in his personal practice and had the reputation of being a competent attorney, but on the basis of senatorial courtesy, Hill prevailed, and Hornblower lost 30-24. A Democratic President had lost his nominee in a Democratically-controlled Senate.

Cleveland then nominated Wheeler H. Peckham, who was similar to Hornblower in his political and legal associations. Not only did Peckham have the same political liabilities, he compounded those in the eyes of Senator Hill by having participated in an investigation that did lethal damage to a close political friend of the New York Senator. Again Hill objected, and again the Cleveland nominee lost, 41-32, this time in a Republican majority Senate.

Cleveland decided against naming someone else from New York and tried the near-certain route of nominating a Senator, the Majority Leader of the Senate, Edward White. The third Roman Catholic named to the Court, he later served as Chief Justice. The Senate approved White quickly.

Between Two Cleveland Terms

Benjamin Harrison, grandson of William Henry Harrison, served as President between the two Cleveland terms and named four Supreme Court Justices. Modest opposition developed to only one, David Brewer of Kansas, whom the Senate confirmed 53-11. He served on the Court with his uncle, Justice Stephen Field.

Legal Landscape

Abraham Lincoln and Grover Cleveland bypassed the geography factor in nominating Justices, but Theodore Roosevelt became the first President to say openly that geography would not be a major consideration. More important, Roosevelt consulted with members of the Senate before making nominations and had no difficulty with any of his three nominees to the Court, even though his relationship with the Senate was sometimes troubled.

Roosevelt's most significant contribution to the advice-and-consent process, however, was that he sought quality in his appointments. In his first nomination to the Court, after searching the legal landscape carefully, he nominated Oliver Wendell Holmes Jr., Chief Justice of the Massachusetts Supreme Court, Harvard faculty member and the author of highly respected legal works. Senator Henry Cabot Lodge of Massachusetts strongly urged the appointment of Holmes. He assured Roosevelt that Holmes "is our kind right through," and despite the non-public opposition of the senior Senator from Massachusetts, George Hoar, Roosevelt named Holmes.[9] The sixty-one-year-old Holmes served twenty-nine years on the Court and became one of the giants in its history. His dissents are legal landmarks. (Holmes stood at his desk to write opinions. When asked if that didn't tire him, he responded, "Yes, but it's salutary. Nothing conduces to brevity like a caving in of the knees."[10])

Teddy Roosevelt gets high marks for many aspects of his presidency, but none deserves greater praise than his careful selection of Supreme Court nominees. Historian Joseph Harris notes: "He exercised particular care in making judicial appointments, inquiring from all sources of information until he was certain that the best available man had been chosen."[11] Twice Roosevelt tried to get William Howard Taft to accept the nomination. Although destined to serve on the Court, Taft would reach it through a different path.

Endnotes

1. Loren P. Beth, "President Hayes Appoints a Justice," *Supreme Court Yearbook 1989* (Washington D.C.: Supreme Court Historical Society), p. 73.

2. Senator Roscoe Conkling to Justice Samuel Miller, quoted in *Ibid.*, p. 73.

3. January 27, 1881, quoted in "The Contested Confirmation of Stanley Matthews to the United States Supreme Court," by Harold Helfman, *Bulletin of the Historical and Philosophical Society of Ohio,* July, 1950.

4. January 28, 1881, quoted in above.

5. Quoted in Harris, p. 82.

6. Quoted in Harris, p. 83. A more detailed account of this whole episode is provided in the Harris book.

7. David M. Jordan, *Roscoe Conkling of New York* (Ithaca, N.Y.: Cornell University Press), p. 285.

8. *Ibid.,* p. 269.

9. Quoted in *The Justice from Beacon Hill,* by Liva Baker, (New York: Harper Collins, 1991), p. 348.

10. Catherine Drinker Bowen, *Yankee from Olympus,* (Boston: Little, Brown and Company, 1944), p. 319.

11. Harris, p. 95.

12

President and Chief Justice and Manipulator

Only one person in our history has served as both President and Chief Justice: William Howard Taft. And as a member of the Court, no one in our history has had as much influence with Presidents in filling its vacancies.

Shortly before Taft assumed the presidency, the former Appellate Court Judge wrote:

> The condition of the Supreme Court is pitiable and yet those old fools hold on . . . . The Chief Justice is almost senile; Harlan does no work; Brewer is so deaf that he cannot [hear] and has got beyond the point of the commonest accuracy in writing his opinions; Brewer and Harlan sleep almost through all arguments. I don't know what can be done.[1]

Taft soon would be able to do something about it. As President, he appointed six Justices to the Court in his one term, more than any President since George Washington. Three were Democrats, three were Republicans, but all were conservative or close to it.

When Chief Justice Fuller died, President Taft foreshadowed his own approach to nominations from the bench: He asked the members of the Court whom they would like to see as Chief Justice. In this case, newspapers and political leaders were predicting that Justice Charles Evans Hughes would be named Chief Justice, but the members of the Court indicated a preference for Justice E. D. White, and White received the nomination and Senate confirmation. Some say that Taft chose the elder White rather than Hughes because the President nurtured the hope that he might become Chief Justice someday, but whether that entered into his decision is far from clear.

When he was Theodore Roosevelt's Secretary of War, after a dinner at the White House, the President asked Taft and his wife to join him in his private library. Roosevelt leaned back in an easy chair and closed his eyes. "I am the seventh son of a seventh daughter and I have clairvoyant powers," he said in jest. "I see a man weighing three hundred and fifty pounds. There is something hanging over his head. I cannot make out what it is . . . . At one time it looks like the presidency, then again it looks like the chief justiceship."

"Make it the presidency," said Mrs. Taft.

"Make it the chief justiceship," said Taft.[2]

During the Roosevelt presidency, Taft wrote in his diary: "I am very anxious to go on to the Supreme Bench. The President has promised me a number of times that he would appoint me chief justice if a vacancy occurred in that position and he knows that I much prefer a judicial future to a political future."[3]

After his defeat for reelection to the presidency, Taft's name surfaced briefly as a possible Court nominee during the Brandeis controversy under the Wilson presidency but it did not linger.

Warren G. Harding

When Warren G. Harding became President, Taft already had built a good relationship with the new executive. When Taft had run for reelection in 1912—faced with the opposition of both Teddy Roosevelt and Woodrow Wilson—he had chosen Harding to make the nominating speech at the Republican convention, a significant boost in prestige for the little-known Ohio official who had recently lost a race for governor.

A few days after Harding's inauguration, Taft visited the new President. Taft and Harding had a congenial visit in which the former President made it clear that he would like to be Chief Justice, but otherwise he did not want an appointment to the Court. Harding promised it to him.

Taft then went to the Supreme Court to pay a courtesy call on Chief Justice White, whom he had appointed. To Taft's chagrin, he reported to a friend, "He said nothing about retiring. He spoke of his illness. He said he could still read, though he had a cataract, and he complained of the burden of work that he had."[4] Two weeks later, Taft wrote to a friend:

> It has been reported that the Chief Justice was going to retire . . . . But as a man comes to the actual retirement, after he is seventy years of age, he seems to regard it as an admission of weakness, a singing of the Nunc Dimittis, and he satisfies himself with many reasons why the time has not come. I am getting on myself—shall be sixty-four my next birthday, and it is not wise to appoint a man to that bench at such an age that he has to serve long after seventy . . . . If the position, which I would rather have than any other in the world, is not to come to me, I have no right to complain, for the Lord has been very good to me.[5]

Five weeks after Taft wrote that letter, White died. True to his word, Harding announced six weeks later that he would name Taft, and that same day — without reference to committee — the Senate confirmed the new Chief Justice. Four Senators cast votes against his confirmation. One historian has noted, with probable accuracy: "No person who ever became Chief Justice yearned for that office more than William Howard Taft."[6]

Taft turned out to be a good Supreme Court manager. An early private critic of his appointment, Justice Holmes, later called it "the best appointment that could have been made."[7] During the eight-year period between being President and Chief Justice, Taft had taught at Yale Law School, reflecting on the Court and the law, an experience that added substance to his service. While philosophically conservative in his decisions, history gives him high marks for his leadership, not only of the Supreme Court but also of the federal court system.

Taft's personal influence on the composition of the Court probably exceeded anyone's, with the possible exceptions of George Washington and Franklin Roosevelt. Beyond dispute, he had more influence on who would sit on the Court over a longer period of time than anyone has had, and perhaps ever will have. An activist as Chief Justice, "his view of the appropriate responsibilities of the Chief Justice outside of the Supreme Court . . . departed audaciously from his predecessors."[8] He influenced the composition of lower courts as well as the Supreme Court. He lobbied presidents and attorneys general, members of Congress, newspaper editors — and a long list of others.

When vacancies occurred on the bench, Taft sought the advice of large numbers of people, almost as if he were still President — and much more than some Presidents. He would consult with the President and key players and bring suggestions to the table. Taft became a one-person advisory board to the President. He had a particularly close relationship with Harding and his Attorney General, but he also worked with their successors. A naturally outgoing personality, Taft got along well with his colleagues on the Court as well as key players in decision-making on nominations. It came easily to him.

In the meantime, no one questioned how strong his conservative leanings were. In 1929 he wrote to his brother:

> The only hope we have of keeping a consistent declara-
> tion of constitutional law is for us to live as long as we can
> .... The truth is that Hoover is a Progressive just as Stone
> is, and just as Brandeis is and just as Holmes is.[9]

That belief and the philosophy that nurtured dominated most of Taft's direct and indirect nominations and would influence the course of the nation some years after Taft's death.

Harding nominated three Supreme Court Justices in addition to Taft. One was Senator George Sutherland of Utah, who had been promised a seat before Harding discussed the Supreme Court with Taft. Taft concurred in the idea and may have modestly reinforced the Harding inclination, but that appointment was basically Harding's idea.

When Justice Day retired, Taft already knew who the potential candidates were, met with the President about them and got his choice, Pierce Butler, nominated. He then strategized with Butler and the White House staff on how to get Butler confirmed by the Senate. Butler had offended many when, as a regent for the University of Minnesota, he disapproved of views expressed by some faculty members and had them fired or forced a non-renewal of their contracts. Taft's efforts paid off. While the Senate was unenthusiastic, it confirmed Butler 61-8, with twenty-seven senators not voting.

Harding accepted Taft's next suggestion for a vacancy, Edward T. Sanford of Tennessee, and so did the Senate. At one point Harding considered one of the most distinguished jurists of this country, Judge Learned Hand, but Taft dissuaded him. Taft regarded him as too progressive. Counting his own nomination, nine Justices were either appointed by Taft as President or through his influence with Harding. Under Coolidge as President, a tenth might be listed.

Taft had less leverage with Coolidge than he had with Harding. But he showed no reluctance to contact Coolidge on matters relating to the judiciary: When he learned a Senator planned to make a federal judgeship recommendation that Taft thought unwise, Taft pursued Coolidge onto the Harding funeral train to discuss the matter with the new President.

Justice Stone

For his first Court vacancy, Coolidge appointed his Attorney General, Harlan Stone, later named Chief Justice by FDR.

Stone faced opposition in the Senate because as Attorney General he continued to pursue an oil fraud matter his predecessor had started involving Senator Burton K. Wheeler of Montana. Stone was asked to appear before the Judiciary Committee, becoming the first Court nominee to do so, and under tough questioning made a strong impression on the Senators. The Senate approved him 71-6. Taft wrote to his son,

> I rather forced the President into [Stone's] appointment. The President was loath to let him go, because he knew his worth as attorney general, but I told him . . . that he was the strongest man that he could secure in New York that was entitled to the place.[10]

Stone turned out to be one of the better Justices in the Court's history.

How much of a role Taft actually played in encouraging Coolidge to name Stone is not clear. Taft may have exaggerated his influence, but having the Chief Justice, a former President, backing Stone at least reinforced Coolidge and maybe did more.

Taft resigned during Herbert Hoover's second year in office. Other Chief Justices, such as Marshall and Taney, had greater influence on decisions of the Court but no Chief Justice had greater influence in selecting members of the Court. It is doubtful that the United States will again have a Chief Justice who has served as President. Taft's dual roles put him in a unique position to influence the choice of nominations.

But there is no reason Presidents should not ordinarily consult with members of the Court about possible successors. Besides Taft, others have occasionally done so from our earliest years.

When Franklin Pierce faced a vacancy, the entire Court visited Pierce urging the nomination of John Campbell, and Pierce followed their wishes. Chief Justice Marshall consulted with several Presidents about vacancies, though he was careful about it. When Henry Clay asked Chief Justice Marshall to approach John Quincy Adams on behalf of John Crittenden, Marshall responded that he had a high opinion of Crittenden and had no candidate he preferred more, but that "I cannot venture, unasked, to recommend an Associate Justice to the President."[11] Others, including Taft, were less circumspect. Justice Samuel Miller wrote several Presidents suggesting nominees. Justice Felix Frankfurter played a role in Franklin Roosevelt's nominations. Chief Justice Stone recommended Frankfurter to FDR. Ronald Reagan probably picked Justice Sandra Day O'Connor because of the recommendations of Chief Justice Warren Burger and Justice William Rehnquist. President Kennedy considered naming the first black to the Court, Judge William Hastie, but when Robert Kennedy checked it out with Chief Justice Warren, to Kennedy's surprise Warren "was violently opposed," believing that Hastie would be an impediment to progressive causes. Kennedy then named Byron White, who turned out to be more conservative than Hastie probably would have been.[12]

Several Associate Justices have recommended themselves for Chief Justice when that opening occurred, or had their friends do it for them. Having a self-perpetuating Court that would pick their own successors is not generally regarded as desirable. Presidential selection, with Senate consultation and approval, permits greater diversity both in background and viewpoint. There is a lengthy list of Justices who have tried to play a role — and sometimes did — in influencing a President on Supreme Court nominations, but no one compares with Taft in the influence actually exerted.

Endnotes

1. Quoted in *Justices of the Supreme Court,* Vol. III, p. 1980.
2. Henry F. Pringle, *Life and Times of William Howard Taft,* (Norwalk, Connecticut: Easton Press, 1967), Vol. I, p. 313, quoting from H. H. Kohlsaat, *From McKinley to Harding,* (Scribner, 1923) pp. 161-162.
3. *War Secretary Diaries,* quoted in Pringle, pp. 313-314.
4. Taft to Gus Karger, March 26, 1921, quoted in Pringle, Vol. II, p. 956.
5. Taft to C. S. Shepard, April 11, 1921, Pringle, *Life and Times of William Howard Taft* (Norwalk, Connecticut: Easton Press, 1967), Vol. II, pp. 956-957.
6. "What Heaven Must Be Like: William Howard Taft as Chief Justice," by Jeffrey B. Morris, *Supreme Court Yearbook 1983* (Washington, D.C.: Supreme Court Historical Society), p. 80.
7. Oliver Wendell Holmes to Harold Laski, quoted in *Ibid.,* p. 93.
8. "What Heaven Must Be Like: William Howard Taft as Chief Justice," by Jeffrey B. Morris, *Supreme Court Yearbook 1983* (Washington, D.C.: Supreme Court Historical Society), pp. 84-85.
9. Taft to Horace Taft, December 1, 1929, Pringle, vol. II, p. 967.
10. Pringle, Vol. II, p. 1043.
11. John Marshall to Henry Clay, November 28, 1828, Warren, Vol. I, p. 701.
12. Harris Wofford, *Of Kennedys and Kings* (New York: Farrar, Strauss, Giroux, 1980), p. 169.

13

Wilson's Nominations: A Bigot and Brandeis

Woodrow Wilson distinguished himself with what historians agree is one of the worst appointments in the history of the Court, James McReynolds. Wilson also made one of the best appointments in the history of the Court, Louis Brandeis. But the Brandeis legacy began as the biggest Supreme Court nomination fight in the history of the Court.

McReynolds

McReynolds first came to national attention as an assistant attorney general under Theodore Roosevelt, fighting the business monopolies. In the same post under the Taft administration, McReynolds felt he had been undercut, and he publicly resigned, renouncing the Republican Party in the process. When Wilson became a candidate for President, McReynolds campaigned for him, and when Wilson won, the President named McReynolds Attorney General. But it soon became apparent that Wilson had a problem on his hands in McReynolds, and some theorize that when the Supreme Court vacancy occurred, Wilson thought this an excellent chance to "kick him upstairs." Wilson thought McReynolds's basic progressive tilt, which Wilson sensed, would make him an acceptable member of the Court. Some of the progressive Republicans opposed McReynolds, as did one Democrat, but the Senate confirmed him 44-6, with forty-six senators not voting. Court historian Henry Abraham observed that McReynolds came to be regarded "universally, and justifiably, as a total on-bench failure."[1]

A bachelor, McReynolds turned out to be prejudiced against Jews, blacks, women and a host of others, including people who drink. Brandeis, the first Jew on the court, found his new colleague refused to speak to him for three years. Taft cancelled the annual photograph of the Court in 1924 when McReynolds refused to sit next to Brandeis for the picture.

McReynolds even refused to sign the traditional tribute given by the Court to a fellow Justice when Brandeis retired. When the Court traveled the short distance to Philadelphia for a ceremonial occasion, McReynolds sent a note to Taft: "As you know, I am not always to be found when there is a Hebrew aboard. Therefore, my 'inability' to attend must not surprise you."[2] When rumor spread that President Hoover had under consideration the name of Benjamin Cardozo for the Supreme Court, McReynolds went to Hoover and told the President that it would be a mistake to have two Jews on the Court.

Taft had little respect for McReynolds, regarding him as "one who seems to delight in making others uncomfortable . . . . He has a continual grouch, and is always offended because the court is doing something that he regards as undignified."[3] He fairly consistently voted against everything Wilson wanted and turned out to be one of the most reactionary Justices ever to serve on the Court. Brandeis considered McReynolds to be "lazy" and moved by the "irrational impulses of a savage."[4] As Attorney

General, he had startled Colonel House, chief adviser to Wilson, by opposing a man suggested for a federal judgeship because the potential nominee "had no chin."[5]

Ella Pearson, the woman once engaged to marry Mc-Reynolds, had died suddenly. He frequently visited her grave. But otherwise his relationship with women — and all people — caused comment. He had a huge poster of a naked woman over his bed. When women attorneys approached the bench to speak to the Justices, he walked out. He viewed the use of red fingernail polish by women as "vulgar" and believed men wearing wrist watches showed signs of being effeminate.[6] He had a terrible reputation for the treatment of his clerks. McReynolds asked one clerk about something he had written, "What would you say about a man who had penmanship like that?" The embarrassed clerk said it could be improved. McReynolds responded, "No, I would say that that man's mother was a low woman."[7]

When a new Justice started to smoke a cigar at the regular Saturday conference of the Court, instead of saying something he sent the new man a note: "Smoking makes me sick. Mc-Reynolds."[8] Another Saturday conference discussed the famous *Scottsboro* case, where an all-white jury found nine blacks guilty of raping two white women. "The damn niggers are guilty," McReynolds told his colleagues. "Why don't they just hang them?" Justice Cardozo responded, saying that innocence or guilt was not the question but whether the trial had been fair. After that comment, McReynolds rarely talked to Cardozo.[9]

Justice William O. Douglas recalls that McReynolds asked a black barber who worked at the Supreme Court, "Tell me, where is this nigger university in Washington?"[10] When Justice Stone commented to McReynolds that a brief from an attorney had been the dullest thing he had ever heard, McReynolds responded, "The only thing duller I can think of is to hear you read one of your opinions."[11] One observer noted, "McReynolds and the theory of a beneficent deity are quite incompatible."[12]

McReynolds served on the Court twenty-six undistinguished years. Supreme Court scholar Laurence Tribe calls him "the most obnoxious man who ever served on the Court."[13]

The First Jewish Justice

When Wilson's second Court vacancy occurred, he redeemed himself. On most significant appointments Wilson consulted with Senators of both parties, frequently going to the Capitol to do so. But this time he handled himself carefully and quietly. He talked with his son-in-law, Secretary of the Treasury William McAdoo, and Attorney General Thomas Gregory, asking them whom he should nominate. Both immediately responded, "Brandeis." Gregory called Brandeis "the greatest lawyer in the United States." However, he added that the nomination would cause a storm. The *New York Times* and other newspapers editorially suggested that Wilson nominate Taft, though there is no indication that Wilson ever seriously considered that. Wilson talked to Senator Robert LaFollette, leader of the progressive Republicans in the Senate, to determine whether they would cross party lines to vote for Brandeis, who also called himself a Republican. He then asked Samuel Gompers, leader of the labor movement in the nation. Both LaFollette and Gompers responded enthusiastically. The administration contacted Brandeis in Bridgeport, Connecticut, where he had gone to organize for the American Jewish Congress. Brandeis immediately said he would accept.

Born in Louisville in 1856, Brandeis grew up in an immigrant family that took an active part in anti-slavery politics. Brandeis's uncle went to the Republican convention of 1860 that nominated Lincoln. Brandeis attended Harvard Law School, graduating at the top of his class, and achieved his fame on the national scene primarily through championing consumer causes against utilities and major American corporations. His careful legal work brought him great respect from his profession even though he did not please the "establishment." By the age of thirty-four his income exceeded $50,000 a year, at a time when the average attorney made less than $5,000 annually. The fact that he was the first Jew to be nominated to the Supreme Court stirred some opposition, but he faced significantly greater opposition as a result of "radical" stands. (The first Jew ever offered a Supreme

Court nomination was sixty-four years earlier, when Judah P. Benjamin, who had just been elected to the Senate from Louisiana, received the opportunity from Millard Fillmore. Benjamin said he would prefer the Senate.)

Because Wilson had been so cautious in discussing the possible Brandeis nomination, the news caused the sensation that Attorney General Gregory had predicted. A friend wrote to Taft:

> When Brandeis's name came in yesterday, the Senate simply gasped .... There wasn't any more excitement at the Capitol when Congress passed the Spanish War Resolution.[14]

The United Press wire story started, "President Wilson sent a bomb to the United States Senate ..." The *Wall Street Journal* observed: "In all the anti-corporation agitation of the past years one name stands out conspicuous above all others .... Where others were radical, he was rabid; where others were extreme, he was super-extreme; where others would trim, he would lay the ax to the root of the tree."[15] Brandeis, the leading consumer advocate in the nation, was a Jew in a period when anti-Semitism had deep roots in the nation. Only five months before Brandeis got word that Wilson had picked him, a mob had lynched Leo Frank, the Jewish manager of a pencil factory in Georgia, who had been convicted on thin evidence of murdering a fourteen-year-old Christian. The prosecutor of Frank became a hero and Georgia elected him Governor. A Georgia publication, the *Jeffersonian* (with 87,000 circulation at one point) commented on the Frank case: "Was it not notoriously true that rich Jewish businessmen corrupted the daughters of Gentiles who worked for them?"[16] After the lynching the *Jeffersonian* commented: "Let Jewish libertines take notice. Georgia is not for sale to rich criminals."[17]

Brandeis received the word that he would be nominated on January 24, 1916, ten months before his sixtieth birthday. Four days later Wilson announced it.

Five of the Democratic members of the Judiciary Committee said they would probably vote against Brandeis. Senator Lee Overman of North Carolina, chairman of the Committee, later indicated that if the vote had been taken on the day the President sent the nomination to the Senate, Brandeis would have lost.

The nomination evoked strong responses on both sides. Seven former presidents of the American Bar Association — including William Howard Taft — signed a public statement that Brandeis "is not a fit person to be a member of the Supreme Court of the United States." Taft at no time publicly joined some who alluded to Brandeis's Jewish background; Taft had experienced religious prejudice as a Unitarian. But Taft wrote in a private letter:

> Brandeis has adopted Zionism, favors a New Jerusalem, and has metaphorically been recircumcised . . . . He has gone all over the country making speeches, arousing the Jewish spirit, even wearing a hat in the synagogue . . . . If it were ever necessary, I am sure he would have grown a beard to convince them that he was a Jew of Jews.[18]

Brandeis said that if he had been an attorney for J. P. Morgan, the opposition would have been appreciably less, that most — not all — of the opposition centered on his political beliefs. Brandeis biographer Philippa Strum wrote: "The nomination became a confrontation of interests and ideologies rather than a display of prejudice."[19] Writing in 1953, historian Joseph Harris concluded: "No nominee to the Supreme Court ever faced a stronger and more determined opposition."[20]

The primary opposition centered on and emanated from the Boston community where Brandeis lived. There he fought utilities, insurance companies, financial institutions and the railroads; he tangled with the most prominent law firms and offended "the old Brahmins" of Boston society. They were not about to let him sit on the Supreme Court after he had fought them so vigorously and so often won.

He had a highly successful corporate law practice, but his volunteer law practice offended major businesses with his fighting against railroad mergers, his defenses of lower gas rates, and what they viewed as his radical stands in favor of public ownership of utilities and minimum wage laws. A petition circulated by Harvard President A. Lawrence Lowell in opposition to the confirmation of Brandeis had the big Boston names: Adams, Sargent, Dodge, Gardner, Grew, Pillsbury, Peabody, Endicott, Thorndike, Putnam, Stone and Coolidge. Lowell said the Supreme Court seat should not go to "a man who is believed by all the better part of the bar to be unscrupulous."[21]

But of the eleven members of the Harvard Law faculty, Dean Roscoe Pound and eight others supported Brandeis, one opposed him, and one remained neutral. Seven hundred and thirteen Harvard students sent a petition supporting Brandeis. Even more significant, the revered former president of Harvard, Charles Eliot, responded to the Lowell statement with a ringing endorsement of Brandeis: "Rejection by the Senate of his nomination ... would be a grave misfortune for the whole legal profession, the court, all American business, and the country."[22] About the Eliot letter, a Brandeis law partner told Senator LaFollette, "Next to a letter from God, we have got the best."[23]

In addition to leaders within the administration and in the Senate helping Brandeis, two enthusiastic supporters were Felix Frankfurter, a future Justice, and Walter Lippmann, then editor of the *New Republic.* Lippmann visited with him for an off-the-record session and was amazed at Brandeis's apparent detachment. He "treated the whole fight as if it were happening on the planet Mars."[24]

Hearings in the Senate lasted four months. The Judiciary Committee or the Subcommittee held twenty-eight hearings.

Brandeis kept himself "under wraps" until confirmed. He accepted no new clients, did not answer questions from reporters and avoided almost all public appearances. When a reporter for the *New York Sun* approached him, Brandeis said, "I have nothing to say about anything, and that goes . . . to all newspapers, including both the *Sun* and the moon."[25] At this point nominees did not appear before the Committee. But key Brandeis allies monitored the hearings closely, working with the Attorney General.

In their testimony, opponents of Brandeis tried to stop him because of his political philosophy. Taft spoke for many when he described Brandeis as "a muckracker, an emotionalist for his own purposes, a socialist."[26] But the opponents knew that if they attacked Brandeis because he favored low utility rates and opposed railroad mergers, their cause would be doomed. Instead, they attacked him as a person lacking in ethics. And the more they focused on Brandeis's "unethical activities," the better Brandeis looked.

The first witness against Brandeis before the Committee, Clifford Thorne, chairman of the Iowa Railroad Commission, tried to suggest that Brandeis had been unethical in representing the Interstate Commerce Commission on a railroad hearing. But by the time Thorne finished testifying and after other witnesses on the matter had also testified, the impression — from reading the record of the hearings — is of Brandeis conducting himself both competently and ethically. Brandeis's law partner, Edward McClennan, monitoring the hearings, reported: "Thorne peaked out to less than nothing." Taft's friend Gus Karger reported that Thorne's testimony failed "to make much of an impression on the committee."[27]

Senator Thomas Walsh of Montana reported to the Senate, "The real crime of which this man is guilty is that he has exposed the iniquities of men in high places in our financial system."[28]

Pressure mounted, including from Jewish opponents of Brandeis who urged Wilson to withdraw his name because it was increasing anti-Semitism in the nation.

One of the witnesses against Brandeis, Clarence Barron of Cohasset, Massachusetts, called himself a farmer, but he also published the *Wall Street Journal* and two other newspapers. He said, "I employed in this case a firm of lawyers to look up the record of Mr. Brandeis."[29] Barron apparently volunteered to testify — no subpoenas were issued at this point — to comment on charges made in an editorial he had written for his Boston publication under the title, "An Unfit Appointment," in which he called the Brandeis nomination "an insult to New England and the business interests of the country. There is only one redeeming feature in the nomination, and that is that it will assist to bury Mr. Wilson at the next presidential election."[30] The editorial charged that Brandeis lacked "moral fiber" and had taken clients on both sides on two cases, a matter that other witnesses explained to the apparent satisfaction of the Subcommittee.

Barron testified that Charles S. Mellen, a railroad executive, had material that would be damaging to Brandeis. The Subcommittee sent a telegram to Mellen asking him to testify, and he replied: "I am absolutely without information as to anything that I would be justified to testify under oath. I think it would be a waste of Committee's time and mine for me to go to Washington to testify. I am not at all unfriendly to Brandeis, and I know nothing about his career except hearsay."[31] Mellen was the former president of the New Haven Railroad, which Brandeis had fought and which two historians say subsidized Barron's publications.[32]

The most negative characterization of Brandeis came from several attorneys who used the same phrase, "not trustworthy." When pressed, they said one of the things that bothered them was his refusal to indicate the client for whom he worked on certain matters. Perhaps a more substantial reason remained unexpressed. Brandeis had violated an unwritten code of ethics among attorneys by suing to get back what a client — and Brandeis — felt was an excessive fee charged by a lawyer. Even three-quarters of a century later, lawyers rarely undertake such suits.

One of the witnesses against Brandeis, Dr. James Cannon of Virginia, chaired the Committee on Legislation of the Anti-Saloon League. He had "nothing against the personal character of Mr. Brandeis," except that Brandeis had been employed as legal counsel by the Liquor Dealers Association of Massachusetts and the New England Brewers Association. Cannon and his associates particularly found objectionable the Brandeis statement made to the Massachusetts legislative committee in 1891 — twenty-five years earlier — that "liquor drinking is not wrong; but excessive drinking is."[33] They objected to "the position he took and which we understand he has never changed."

On April 1, the Subcommittee recommended favorable action 3-2. In submitting his views for the Subcommittee report, Senator Walsh said that the nominee

> has awakened unrelenting enmities and fast friendships
> . . . . He has not stood in awe of the majesty of wealth . . .
> . He has written about and expressed views on 'social
> justice' . . . to obtain greater security, greater comfort, and
> better health for industrial workers.[34]

In the minority report in opposition, Senator Albert Cummins, Republican of Iowa, applauded Brandeis's ability but said he cannot "approve his course in many of the matters which have been brought to the attention of the subcommittee, through which he has lost the confidence of so large an element of the profession of which he is a member."[35]

On May 24, the Judiciary Committee approved his nomination 10-8 on a straight party vote. The Brandeis forces were hoping to get the vote of Senator William Borah of Idaho, an independent Republican, but he voted with the other Republicans. They did get the wavering Democrats. A key final factor in the committee vote was an informal gathering at the apartment of Norman Hapgood, editor of *Collier's Weekly*, to which two uncertain Democratic Senators came, James Reed of Missouri and Hoke Smith of Georgia, both intending to stop only briefly. Brandeis visited with them, the only time he is known to have had contact with Senators directly on his nomination other than communication with Senator LaFollette, who championed his cause. Reed left his wife in the car parked outside. He and Brandeis sat down alone in front of the fireplace and had an hour-long conversation — until Reed suddenly remembered his wife waiting in the car. Both Reed and Smith voted for Brandeis.

The Senate vote had been more predictable than the Committee vote, and if the Committee had not acted favorably, it is doubtful the Senate would have taken up the nomination. The Senate voted 47-22 for confirmation, with three Republicans (LaFollette, George Norris of Nebraska and Miles Poindexter of Washington) joining the Democrats. One Democrat, Senator Francis Newslands of Nevada, voted against him. However, twenty-seven members did not vote. "Paired" for him were ten Democrats and two Republicans and against him were twelve Republicans.*

Brandeis was on his way home when word of the Senate vote reached his wife. She greeted him with the words, "Mr. Justice Brandeis." Brandeis's daughter Susan, at a meeting in New York City for the right of women to vote, heard the woman sitting next to her say, "I hear they confirmed that Jew Brandeis to the Supreme Court." Susan replied coolly, "You are speaking to the right person. Mr. Brandeis happens to be my father."[36]

When the next opening on the Court occurred, Wilson told a visitor: "I can never live up to my Brandeis appointment. There is nobody else who represents the greatest technical ability and professional success with complete devotion to the people's interest."[37]

---

*"Pairing" is a procedure which assists absent Senators to cast a vote. For example, if Senator Smith's mother died and he has to be away from the Senate and is opposed to a bill, Senator Jones who is for the bill will "pair" with Smith, one recorded as for the measure, one opposed. Both are recording their views but are not counted in the vote tally that is announced.

Endnotes

1. *Abraham, p. 176.*

2. *Ibid., p. 176.*

3. Taft to Helen Manning, June 11, 1923, quoted in Pringle, Vol. II, p. 971.

4. Quoted in *Louis D. Brandeis: Justice for the People,* by Philippa Strum (Cambridge: Harvard University Press, 1984) p. 371.

5. Lewis J. Paper, *Brandeis* (Englewood Cliffs, N.J.: Prentice-Hall, 1983), p. 250.

6. "James C. McReynolds," by David Burner, *Justices of the United States Supreme Court.* Vol. III, p. 2024.

7. Paper, p. 251.

8. *Ibid.*

9. *Ibid.*

10. *The Court Years: The Autobiography of William O. Douglas* (New York: Random House, 1980) p. 15.

11. Quoted in Abraham, p. 177.

12. Harold Laski, quoted in "Chief Justice Edward Douglass White and President Taft's Court," by Jeffrey E. Morris, *Supreme Court Yearbook 1982* (Washington, D.C.: Supreme Court Historical Society), p. 37.

13. Tribe, p. 53.

14. Strum, Gus Garger to Taft, January 29, 1916, p. 293.

15. Quoted in Paper, p. 213.

16. Quoted in *The Jewish Seat,* by Thomas Karfunkel and Thomas W. Ryley, (Hicksville, N.Y.: Exposition Press, 1978), p. 34.

17. *Ibid.,* p. 35.

18. William Howard Taft to Gus J. Karger, January 31, 1916, Taft papers, Library of Congress.

19. Strum, p. 294.

20. Harris, p. 99.

21. Quoted in "The 'Outragous' Brandeis Nomination," by Melvin Urofsky, *Supreme Court Yearbook* 1979 (Washington, D.C.: Supreme Court Historical Society), p. 12.

22. Quoted in Paper, pp. 237-238.

23. *Ibid.,* p. 238.

24. Quoted in *Walter Lippmann and the American Century,* by Ronald Steel (Boston: Little, Brown, 1980), p. 102.

25. New York *Sun,* January 29, 1916.

26. Quoted in Harris pp. 102-103.

27. Paper, p. 216.

28. *Nomination of Louis D. Brandeis,* Senate Hearings (Washington: Government Printing Office, 1916), Vol. II, p. 234.

29. Senate Hearings, Vol. I, p. 118.

30. Quoted in Senate Hearings, vol. I, p. 123.

31. Senate Hearings, Vol. I, p. 136.

32. Harris, p. 105. Paper, p. 217.

33. Senate Hearings, Vol. I, p. 1057.

34. Senate Hearings, Vol. II, p. 234.

35. Senate Hearings, Vol. II, p 323.

36. David C. Gross, *A Justice for All the People: Louis D. Brandeis* (New York: E. P. Dutton, 1987), p. 64.

37. Wilson to Norman Hapgood, quoted in Strum, p. 299.

14

Hoover's Battles

Most people associate Herbert Hoover with the Great Depression or, possibly, with his pre-presidential relief efforts. Few would mention his significant — though not battle-free — impact on the United States Supreme Court.

Taft resigned as Chief Justice one month before he died. Hoover and Stone played "medicine ball" early each morning, and Sunday evenings they and their wives had dinner together. The Chief Justice's health had worsened to the point that Hoover had asked his Attorney General to determine through Justices VanDevanter and Butler whether former Justice Charles Evans Hughes would accept the position. Some believed that at the age of sixty-eight Hughes might decline the responsibility. He accepted. Only hours after Taft's resignation, Hoover announced the nomination of Hughes as Chief Justice.

Justice Hughes's original appointment to the Court by President Taft had gone through the Senate without difficulty. But his resignation from the Court to pursue the presidency in what turned out to be a bitter contest with Wilson had changed the political climate surrounding him. Hughes, by any standard one of the top attorneys in the nation, had left the Court for a partisan battle, and it would take another partisan battle—though not a lengthy one—to get him back in.

Not only were Democrats skeptical of this one-time resignee, but the small band of progressive Republicans also had serious questions about Hughes and his law practice for the financially powerful. Senator Norris pointed out that as a Wall Street lawyer, Hughes appeared before the Supreme Court fifty-four times from 1916 to 1928 "for corporations of untold wealth.... He looks through glasses contaminated by the influence of monopoly as it seeks to get favors by means which are denied to the common, ordinary citizen."[1] After lengthy floor debate Norris moved to recommit the nomination to the Judiciary Committee, which would have killed it, but that lost 49-31. New York's two Democratic senators came to the rescue of their constituent, and Hughes received Senate approval 52-26. It was more of a brawl than the ten-day period between nomination and approval might suggest, but still not a major fight in the history of Supreme Court nominations. Hughes ranks high in the history of the Court.

A Key Battle—And Loss

The next struggle Hoover lost. Justice Edward T. Sanford, a Harding appointee, died suddenly. Hoover chose Judge John J. Parker of North Carolina, a member of the U.S. Court of Appeals. Hoover had considered him for Attorney General and asked the advice of his friend Justice Stone, who replied:

> I should say that he does not possess the intellectual acuteness or range of legal knowledge of the present Solicitor General, for example.... My doubt would be... whether he would have the success of judgment and keenness of perception which would save him from having things put over him.[2]

The President passed over him for Attorney General but later picked him for the Court.

Initially there appeared to be no opposition to Parker. Even though one scheduled and one unscheduled witness appeared against him, the Judiciary subcommittee had only one meeting, which lasted four hours. They reported Parker favorably by a 2-1 vote, with Senator Borah casting the negative vote. Opposition gradually grew as the appointment headed to the full Senate.

Parker had two problems, labor relations and race relations. His decisions on labor-management cases caused controversy, particularly a judicial injunction upholding what were then known as "yellow-dog contracts." These anti-union contracts, which some employees were required to sign before they could be employed, had been questioned all the way to the Supreme Court, and in a divided opinion the Court had ruled them valid. Here is one "yellow-dog contract" that reached the high court:

> I am employed and work for the Hitchman Coal and Coke Co. with the express understanding that I am not a member of the United Mine Workers of America and will not become so while an employee of the Hitchman Coal and Coke Co.; that the Hitchman Coal and Coke Co. is run nonunion and agrees with me that it will run nonunion while I am in its employ. If at any time I am employed by the Hitchman Coal and Coke Co. [and] I want to become connected with the United Mine Workers of America or any affiliated organization, I agree to withdraw from the employment of said company, and agree that while I am in the employ of that company I will not make any efforts amongst its employees to bring about the unionizing of that mine against the company's wishes. I have either read the above or heard the same read.[3]

Judge Parker had ruled in favor of an injunction supporting the "yellow-dog contract," upholding a Supreme Court decision which as a lower court judge he had an obligation to do. Opponents charged he went further than the Supreme Court, and even if he were upholding the highest court, he could have indicated some disagreement while following it.

Parker sent a letter to Senator Lee Overman of his home state of North Carolina, chair of the Judiciary subcommittee handling the nomination, defending himself on the issues. In that letter he easily could have expressed a view of whether the "yellow-dog contracts" are sound policy or not, but he refrained from even a hint at a question.[4] Neither in his opinions nor in other letters to members did he suggest any possible disagreement with Court decisions.

The country divided sharply on his nomination. Labor, under the leadership of William Green, opposed Parker, as did the more liberal press. John L. Lewis, the powerful and colorful leader of the United Mine Workers, wrote to Overman:

> Why, from all that long list of eminent legal minds ... was it necessary for the President to appoint the judge ... who delivered 50,000 free Americans into indentured servitude [through an injunction]? Why lay another lash across the tortured shoulders of the struggling mine workers by placing in a position of vastly increased power a man who regards them as industrial bondmen? Why should any consideration of politics or statecraft impel any Senator to vote for the confirmation?[5]

The *Washington Daily News* joined the opponents:

> No judge who enslaves workers with a yellow-dog injunction should be appointed to the Supreme Court .... There is very good legal opinion that Parker went far beyond the Supreme Court decision .... If the Senate Committee has any doubt, let it call Parker to explain in his own words .... The curse of this country is that there are too many Parkers on the Supreme Court already.[6]

But the *New York Sun* editorialized: "When Mr. Hoover named Judge Parker he knew that he was naming another conservative and he named him because the Supreme Court ought to be highly conservative. With a Senate and a House well stocked with radicals, why should the conservative President of a conservative people do anything to turn the judicial department of the Government in the direction of radicalism?"[7] The *New York World* commented: "The presence of Judge Parker on the bench would increase, rather than lessen, the top heavily conservative bias of the Supreme Court as now constituted."[8]

The other issue Parker faced grew out of comments he made as the Republican candidate for governor of North Carolina ten years earlier. In one speech he said:

> The Negro, as a class, does not desire to enter into politics. The Republican party of North Carolina does not desire him to do so. We recognize the fact that he has not yet reached the stage in his development where he can share in the burdens and responsibilities of government. This being true, and every intelligent man in North Carolina knows that it is true . . . the participation of the Negro in politics is a source of danger to both races.[9]

He made similar comments in other political speeches around the state.

The National Association for the Advancement of Colored People, headed by Walter White, took on its first major national fight and opposed Parker. The *Christian Science Monitor* observed: "This is the first time that the negro in an organized campaign is making himself felt in a powerful political manner. That this influence will be exercised in many other matters henceforth is regarded as inevitable."[10] White sent a telegram to Parker and asked if he still held the views expressed ten years earlier; the nominee failed to respond. But the nation responded, on both sides. The conflict illustrated how far the United States had yet to go in its treatment of minorities.

The Society of Friends joined the NAACP in its concerns, but most journals were critical of the NAACP. The *New York Times* commented:

> Let it be said at once that negro associations, anxious to show their political strength, are entitled to make use of Judge Parker to further their aims . . . . Negro leaders . . . have found a lot of timid Senators at Washington whom they can frighten . . . . No principle is at stake. Only a political self-interest is driving on these Republican Senators. Full in the eye of the public, they write themselves down as what they are—men afraid of doing anything to injure their own chances at the polls, even if they know it to be the right thing to do. Compared with them, the negro agitators, hot on their trail, are straightforward and honorable.[11]

"These Republican Senators" the *Times* referred to disdainfully in its editorial were headed by the highly principled Senator George Norris of Nebraska and Senator William Borah of Idaho.

In those pre-FDR days, African-American votes were still strongly Republican, as they had been since Abraham Lincoln's leadership. Republican leaders in key states were expressing concern as to how the Parker nomination might change that. The Republican Party chairman of Missouri sent a telegram to his two Senators warning "that the Republican party might just as well say good-bye to Missouri for the next two or three elections at least. It will be the first great affront given by a Republican Senate to the Negro race since the days of Abraham Lincoln."[12]

Six weeks after Hoover sent the nomination to the Senate, as political leaders sensed mounting opposition, the Judiciary Committee met. Overman, ranking member of the Judiciary Committee among the minority Democrats, moved to allow Parker to appear before the full Committee — as Harlan Stone had in 1925 — to answer the charges against him. The Committee voted that down 10-4. The Senate Judiciary Committee then voted 10-6 against confirming Parker. Six Republicans and four Democrats voted against Parker; four Republicans and two Democrats voted for him. The bitter fight then went to the full chamber. Watching the debate on the floor was the nation's only African-American congressman, Oscar DePriest of Illinois.

Overman headed the Senate forces supporting Parker. He inserted into the *Congressional Record* letters of support for Parker from African-Americans and statements from white leaders about how well they were treating blacks in North Carolina. M. K. Tyson, executive secretary of the National Association of Negro Tailors, Designers and Dressmakers, for example, sent Overman a letter in which he said, "The reason that the negro is out of politics in North Carolina is because he brought it upon himself. If the negro had acted right, he would have been in politics in North Carolina this very day."[13] An industrial leader, A. M. Carter, wrote Overman:

> If there is anybody in North Carolina who understands labor conditions I believe that it is the writer. You know the Bible refers just as much to the servant being loyal and worthy of his master as it does to the master being worthy of the servant.... We are spending more money in North Carolina for the welfare and education of the colored people than our entire educational system cost in 1900. In connection with this, which is personal, there is a negro boy in Chatham County who slept at the foot of my bed for many years, whom I love and respect, and whom since I have been able to assist every year during lean crops.[14]

Another North Carolina business leader wrote that he had listened to the most controversial Parker speech and said that it

> was of a very high-tone character, there being not an iota of race or class prejudice exhibited. It is a fact that the negro race is being taken care of and educated for better conditions ... by the taxpayers of the State.... We have negro men in our employ who have lived in Ohio and other Northern states, and who state to us that the southern 'white folks' know them and are their friends.[15]

The *Richmond Times-Dispatch* dismissed as insignificant the comments of Parker but added: "This might not be important, but a number of Senators who come from States which have large negro votes are showing signs of panic. When the pinch comes it is almost certain that these Senators . . . will yield to the demand of the dark brother."[16] The *Atlanta Constitution* thought Parker's observations on race were sound and that it "is the political right of a citizen to believe it unwise for the interests of both races for negroes to seek political power in a Southern State committed to white supremacy . . . . It is the hell-raising negro political vampires of New York and Boston who are fighting the Parker nomination."[17] *The Washington Post* commented: "How any southern Senator can oppose him and thus help racial and radical prejudice to defeat him is beyond understanding."[18]

Southerners were able to trot out pressured black college presidents to endorse Parker. At least two African-American newspapers did the same. But the *Chicago Defender* and the *Afro-American* newspapers headed by Carl Murphy of Baltimore, as well as others, protested. The *Black Dispatch* of Oklahoma City commented:

> Judge John Parker . . . does not think the negro has reached the stage in his development where he should participate in politics. Two great minds seem to be running in the same channel. The negro does not think that Judge Parker has reached the place in his development where he should be allowed to sit on the Supreme Bench.[19]

As the racial issue intensified, Parker sent a letter to Overman, "The protest of the colored people seems to be based upon the fear that I might not enforce the provisions of the Constitution in so far as same guarantees their rights. Needless to say such fear is entirely groundless."[20] He also defended his judicial decision in the "yellow-dog contract" injunction. But as a Parker biographer states: "What Parker apparently did not fully appreciate was that his value system and attitude was [sic] under attack, not just his decision in one case."[21]

Two other issues surfaced briefly in Senate debate: a charge that the Hoover administration offered a Senator a federal judgeship to get a vote, apparently not true; and a Scripps-

Howard story that Parker as a prosecutor had withheld information that would have proven the innocence of an indicted man. The attention of the Senate, however, focused almost totally on the labor and race issues.

Parker lost 41-39. Senator Robert Wagner of New York summed up the feeling of many: "I see a deep and fundamental consistency between Judge Parker's views on labor relations and his reported attitude toward the colored people of the United States. He is obviously incapable of viewing with sympathy the aspirations of those who are aiming for a higher and better place in the world."[22] A bipartisan coalition — twenty-three Democrats, seventeen Republicans and one Farmer-Laborite, Senator Henrick Shipstead of Minnesota — voted against him. Twenty-nine Republicans and ten Democrats voted to confirm him. Sixteen Senators were paired. The younger Senators tended to vote against Parker, the older Senators for him.

Afterward, the *New York Times,* which had supported Parker, said that he "showed himself too anxious, too small minded. He fairly rained letters and telegrams upon the Senate . . . . His activities [were] too much like those of a candidate for the office of sheriff."[23] The *Savannah* (Ga.) *Hawkeye* observed:

> The southern Democratic Senators who voted against confirmation . . . have delivered an unpardonable blow to the south and jeopardized white supremacy. Our own Senator, W. J. Harris, rushes into print and undertakes to explain his colossal blunder . . . . Congressman Oscar DePriest, the Chicago mulatto nigger, who hates every drop of Caucasian blood in the South, applauded the vote of a Democratic Senator representing a Southern white Democratic State . . . who [once] had stood for the preservation of purity of a race that swears by the eternal gods, that neither DePriest nor any of his litter shall ever debauch any of their blood.[24]

Hoover, in his *Memoirs,* states that Parker was "denounced by a Negro association upon the wholly fictitious statement that, when twenty-one years old, he had made some remark bearing on white supremacy in the South."[25] Hoover was inaccurate. No one questioned the validity of the remarks, including Parker; and Parker was thirty-five — not twenty-one — and the Republican candidate for Governor of North Carolina when he spoke. In adddition, the controversy involved a series of statements, not one.

However, Parker stayed on the Court of Appeals and wrote several opinions upholding the Supreme Court decisions on desegregation.

Chief Justice William Rehnquist, while a young attorney, wrote an article contrasting the Senate's "dearth of inquiry or even concern over the views of the new Justice [Charles Whittaker] on constitutional interpretation" with the Senate's careful examination of the views of Parker.[26] The clear suggestion of the future Chief Justice is that the earlier, more careful examination of Parker is to be preferred.

Justice Cardozo

Early in 1932, Justice Holmes resigned at the age of 90. The demand for a stellar nomination to replace a Supreme Court great became evident all over the nation. The name most frequently mentioned: Benjamin Cardozo, Chief Judge of the New York Court of Appeals. Academicians in the field of law throughout the country urged his nomination. The evening that Holmes resigned, five Senators and a larger number of House members met to discuss pensions for older Americans, but the talk quickly turned to the Supreme Court and centered on the desirability of getting Cardozo nominated. Word spread that Hoover had in mind Newton D. Baker, Wilson's Secretary of War. Rabbi Stephen Wise of New York, a leader on social causes, called Baker and asked if he was interested in Holmes's seat. "Yes," he responded, "but not for myself." Wise suggested Cardozo, and Baker responded enthusiastically. Baker said he would contact the President within the hour.

But the sixty-two-year-old Cardozo had three strikes against him: He came from a state already represented by two seats,

Hughes and Stone; his nomination would add a second Jew to the Court; and he was philosophically not as conservative as Hoover.

Cardozo had been recommended to the two previous Presidents, once by Harlan Stone to Harding, when Stone served as Dean of Columbia Law School, and once by Stone to Coolidge, when Stone was Coolidge's Attorney General. Stone recalled that Coolidge asked him whom he would recommend, and Stone replied, "I can give you my recommendation right now . . . . Benjamin Cardozo, the outstanding jurist of our times."[27] After some discussion, Coolidge indicated to his Attorney General that he had Stone himself in mind and named him.

Senators Norris and Borah, the two who had played key roles in the rejection of Parker, were pushing Cardozo strongly. When Borah visited the President to discuss the nomination, Hoover showed him a list of five names. Borah told Hoover it was a good list but it was upside down; Cardozo's name was on the bottom. Hoover finally, with some reluctance, nominated Cardozo and received wide praise. The Senate quickly approved Cardozo, who lived up to the high expectations. Cardozo died during FDR's presidency, and Judge Learned Hand said of him:

> In this America of ours when the passion for publicity is a disease, and where swarms of foolish, tawdry moths dash with rapture into its consuming fire, it was a rare good fortune that brought to such eminence a man so reserved, so unassuming, so retiring, so gracious to high and low, and so serene.[28]

Hoover has been quoted as saying that the Cardozo appointment was the high point of his presidency. It may be that historians will judge it that way but it is doubtful that Hoover honestly believed that. In his *Memoirs,* Hoover gives Cardozo only perfunctory attention, with two sentences: "On February 15, 1932, when a third vacancy occurred, I nominated Chief Justice Benjamin N. Cardozo of the New York Court of Appeals, a Democrat. The appointment met with Senate approval."[29]

As with the Parker nomination, "advice and consent" had again served the national interest.

Endnotes

1. Quoted by David J. Danelski, "Ideology As a Ground for the Rejection of the Bork Nomination," *Northwestern University Law Review,* 1990, Vol. 84, Nos. 3 and 4.

2. Hoover Library Papers, quoted in *The NAACP Comes of Age,* by Kenneth W. Goings, (Bloomington, Indiana: Indiana University Press, 1990), pp. 20-21.

3. *Congressional Record,* Senate, April 28, 1930, p. 7814.

4. John Parker to Lee Overman, *Congressional Record,* Senate, pp. 7793-7794.

5. John L. Lewis to Lee Overman, April 19, 1930, *Congressional Record,* Senate, April 21, 1930, pp. 7301-7302.

6. "Yellow Dog," editorial, *Washington Daily News,* April 8, 1930.

7. "The Case of Judge Parker," *New York Sun,* April 16, 1930.

8. April 28, 1930. Quoted in "The Making of a Supreme Court Justice," *Congressional Record,* Senate, pp. 7793-8894.

9. *Congressional Record,* Senate, May 5, 1930, p. 8338.

10. Quoted in *Congressional Record,* Senate, May 5, 1930, p. 8338.

11. "Judge Parker and Negroes," editorial, *New York Times,* April 21, 1930.

12. B. G. Voorhees to Senator Roscoe C. Patterson, quoted in "The Defeat of Judge Parker," by Richard Watson, Jr., *Mississippi Valley Historical Review,* September, 1963.

13. M. K. Tyson to Lee Overman, *Congressional Record,* Senate, April 28, 1930, p. 7813.

14. A. M. Carter to Lee Overman, *Congressional Record,* Senate, April 28, 1930, p. 7813.

15. C. C. Burns to Lee Overman, *Congressional Record,* Senate, April 28, 1930, p. 7813.

16. "The Fight on Parker," editorial, *Richmond Times-Dispatch,* April 4, 1930.

17. "The Judge Parker Case," editorial, *Atlanta Constitution,* April 4, 1930.

18. "To Southern Senators," editorial, *Washington Post,* April 23, 1930.

19. Quote in *Congressional Record,* Senate, May 5, 1930, p. 8339.

20. John Parker to Lee Overman, *Congressional Record,* Senate, April 28, 1930, p. 7793.

21. William C. Burris, *Duty and the Law: Judge John J. Parker and the Constitution,* (Bessemer, Alabama: Colonial Press, 1977), p. 84.

22. Quoted in Goings, p. 42.

23. "Parker Only an Incident," editorial, *New York Times,* May 8, 1930.

24. "Defeat of Parker Deadly Blow to Southern White Supremacy," editorial, *Savanah Hawkeye,* Pembroke, Ga., May 15, 1930, quoted in *Congressional Record,* Senate, June 4, 1930, pp. 10010-10011.

25. Herbert Hoover, *Memoirs, The Cabinet and the Presidency, (New York: Macmillan, 1952), p. 269.*

26. "The Making of a Supreme Court Justice," by William Rehnquist, *Harvard Law Record,* October 8, 1959.

27. "Justice Cardozo: One-Ninth of the Supreme Court," by Milton Handler and Michael Ruby, *Supreme Court Yearbook 1988,* (Washington, D.C.: Supreme Court Historical Society). The article originally appeared in the *Cardozo Law Review.*

28. Quoted in Abraham, p. 204.

29. Hoover, p. 269.

15

The Senate Resists FDR's Court Plan

Franklin Roosevelt — like all Presidents — had his difficulties with the Senate. On Supreme Court nominations, he had only one struggle, but on his "Court-Packing Plan" he ran into a buzz saw of opposition.

The Supreme Court in 1936 had a strong conservative tilt. In 1920, it ruled child labor laws unconstitutional. In 1923, it called minimum wage laws unconstitutional. When FDR became President, he headed a nation mired in deep economic problems. As he proposed changes, and Congress passed them, the nation seemed to be moving in a better direction economically — except that some of FDR's solutions were ruled unconstitutional by the conservative Supreme Court.

To make matters worse for the President, no vacancies occurred on the Court during his first four years, so those 6-3 and

5-4 rulings against his administration could not be changed. The Court had Justices Brandeis, Stone and Cardozo usually voting on the "liberal" administration side, and Justices VanDevanter, McReynolds, Sutherland and Butler on the "conservative," anti-administration side. Chief Justice Hughes and Justice Roberts tilted against the administration, though occasionally they broke from that pattern.

Shortly before his second-term inauguration, Roosevelt sent a message to Congress calling for a massive "judicial reorganization" that did not have even a thin veil to disguise its purpose. If the bill passed, the President would be authorized to appoint an additional federal judge for each sitting judge who had at least ten years on the bench and who had failed to retire within six months of that jurist's seventieth birthday. The additional judge would serve on the same Court on which the septuagenarian sat. That would mean the appointment of approximately fifty additional federal judges throughout the system, but the plan too obviously had only the Supreme Court in mind. The four solidly anti-administration justices — VanDevanter, McReynolds, Sutherland and Butler — all met the age and service criteria — as did Hughes and Brandeis. It would have permitted FDR to add six additional Justices to the Supreme Court.

Senator Huey Long, the colorful Louisiana leader, had first mentioned the idea to a White House staff member: "Did it ever occur to you that Congress could increase the membership of the Supreme Court?"[1] What initially seemed like a ridiculous idea took on more and more appeal within the FDR inner circle. Coming after the huge 1936 election victory, and with a large majority of Democrats in Congress, it seemed a natural. The President called congressional leaders to the White House at ten in the morning to give them information about a noon address he would make to the nation. The press had already been given the information. Vice President John Nance Garner and the legislative leaders reacted negatively. It turned out to be FDR's worst political miscalculation.

FDR's Attorney General said the bill would assure Justices "of a type and age" that would reduce the heavy Supreme Court burden.[2] But Chief Justice Hughes, writing for the Court, sent statistics to the Senate Judiciary Committee pointing out that the Supreme Court had no backlog. The excuse used by the President, that the additional Justices would add to the efficiency of the Court, was attacked by Hughes:

> An increase in the number of Justices . . . would impair the efficiency [of the Court]. There would be more judges to hear, more judges to confer, more judges to discuss, more judges to be convinced and to decide.[3]

To Save the Constitution from the Court

The President went on national radio, making the first electronic appeal a President had ever made regarding the Supreme Court: "We have reached the point . . . where we must save the Constitution from the Court."[4] In a pointed message to Congress that stirred the ire of the Justices, FDR said: "In exceptional cases . . . judges, like other men, retain to an advanced age full mental and physical vigor."[5]

Not surprisingly, the Supreme Court, the lawyers and the press of the nation, as well as Congress, reacted overwhelmingly against the plan. Liberals and conservatives denounced the proposal. Oswald Garrison Villard, publisher of the liberal *Nation,* testified before the Senate Committee that the Court-packing bill "opens the way for dictatorship,"[6] and there were many who felt that way. The Judiciary Committee held lengthy hearings; eighty-two witnesses testified. Even religious groups unaccustomed to appearing before Congress came forward. On behalf of Missouri Synod Lutherans, theology Professor Theodore Graebner testified that he saw "no implication of a religious nature in the proposal" but believed that it ultimately could be a threat to the guarantees of religious liberty.[7]

One of the ironies in the entire five-month fight is that one of the Justices affected, McReynolds, had suggested to Wilson something similar when he served as Wilson's Attorney General.

The Senate's Independence

Four months after the FDR proposal surfaced, the heavily Democratic Senate Judiciary Committee (14 Democrats, 4 Republicans) turned it down 10-8. In vigorous language, the Committee reported to the Senate that the proposal "does not accomplish any one of the objectives for which it was originally offered. It . . . would undermine the independence of the courts . . . . It would be a dangerous precedent for the future."[8] The next month, the Senate voted it down 70-20. FDR had badly calculated his political power after the sweeping 1936 win.

Yet many believe he won even as he lost. Seven weeks after Senators introduced the President's Court-packing bill and before the Committee voted on it, the Court ruled on the question of a minimum wage for women enacted by the State of Washington. In what many viewed as a Court "about-face," Brandeis, Holmes and Stone were joined by Roberts and Hughes to approve this minimum wage law 5-4, though Roberts had indicated before FDR made the Court-packing proposal that he might reverse himself on the minimum wage law. Two weeks later, the Wagner Labor Relations Act, which many thought had no chance for Court support, received a 5-4 stamp of approval. "A switch in time saved nine," noted a Court observer.[9] The dam had been broken. Soon the Social Security tax and benefits were approved by the Court, as were other New Deal measures designed to get the moribund economy moving. All of these rulings came before the Senate Judiciary Committee voted on the Court-packing proposal. While Roberts and Hughes denied it — perhaps accurately — others believe their shift only weeks before the Committee had scheduled a vote was more than coincidental.

FDR's First Appointment

What could not have been coincidental with the Court-packing proposal was the resignation of Justice VanDevanter on May 18, four weeks before the Committee vote. The President finally had his first chance to fill a Court seat.

The Senate made FDR's first Court nomination awkward. In an unusual move, the Senate decided to give its advice in a formal manner and unanimously passed a resolution urging that the Majority Leader of the Senate, Joseph T. Robinson of Arkansas, be named. While Robinson had been helpful to the President and headed the efforts on the floor on the Court-packing proposal, Robinson was more conservative than the type of person FDR wanted to name. Just as President Grant's problems had been relieved when the Senate had pushed Stanton onto Grant and Stanton suddenly died, so Roosevelt found his dilemma solved when on July 14 — six days before the Senate floor vote on the Court-packing measure — Robinson had a heart attack and died.

FDR then made his most controversial nomination to the Court and, many believe, his best: Hugo Black, U.S. Senator from Alabama. On paper Black did not look like a strong nomination. He had served at the municipal and county level as a prosecutor and judge, but Senate colleagues knew him also as a person widely read and thoughtful. From FDR's point of view, he had one other major virtue: In the Senate, Black championed the cause of those less fortunate, and the President had reason to believe he would do the same on the Supreme Court.

The press, which generally hated Roosevelt, did not take kindly to Black, either. The *Chicago Tribune,* headed by the extremely conservative Col. Robert McCormick, said the President chose "the worst he could find."[10] The New York *Herald-Tribune* called the nomination "an affront to the Court and to the people .... The nomination is as menacing as it is unfit."[11] While Black championed civil rights in the Senate — no small thing for an Alabama Senator then — the debate brought out the fact that he had once been a member of the Ku Klux Klan. Despite that knowledge, the Senate confirmed its colleague 63-16, after a Judiciary Committee vote of 13-4. After the Senate confirmed him, Hoover commented that the Court had become one-ninth packed.

Between the time of the Senate action and his formal swearing-in ceremony, the *Pittsburgh Post-Gazette* charged that not only had Black been a member of the Klan, he had been elected a life member of the Klan and so still retained his Klan ties. Black issued a terse statement:

> I did join the Klan. I later resigned. I never rejoined. I have never considered and I do not now consider the unsolicited card given to me shortly after my nomination to the Senate as a membership of any kind in the Ku Klux Klan. I never used it. I did not even keep it. Before becoming a Senator I dropped the Klan. I have had nothing whatever to do with it since that time.[12]

But the real opposition to Black did not come from his one-time Klan membership, a tool used by those who tried to stop him; his critics were the business leaders and conservative elements.

A group called the Independent Young Americans distributed a flier after he assumed a seat on the Court calling October 4, the Justice's first day on the high court, "Black Day," which would be "mourned each year as the Blackest Day in the history of American Justice."[13] If "Black Day" were celebrated today, it would be because Black became a giant on the Court on behalf of civil liberties over his thirty-four years of service.

The Roosevelt Legacy

As each Court vacancy occurred, women around the nation commenced letter-writing campaigns to urge the nomination of Judge Florence Allen, the first woman named to the federal bench, placed there by FDR. Within weeks of being named to the Court of Appeals she wrote: "My friends delightfully tell me that they hope to see me upon the Supreme Bench of the U.S. I know ... that will never happen to a woman while I am living."[14]

When Hughes stepped down as Chief Justice, Roosevelt named the Coolidge-appointed Justice Harlan Stone as the Chief Justice and ultimately named more people to the Court than any President other than Washington. His other appointees were Stanley Reed, Felix Frankfurter, William O. Douglas (who served thirty-six years), Frank Murphy, James F. Byrnes (who served fifteen months), Robert Jackson and Wiley B. Rutledge. All were confirmed by the Senate without controversy. In terms of quality, Roosevelt's record stands high.

The only one of these to experience modest difficulty was Frankfurter. At first reluctant to testify before the Judiciary Committee, his friends persuaded him that he should, following the example of Harlan Stone. He became the second nominee in the history of the Supreme Court to come before the Committee. Stone testified for less than one day.

Frankfurter said, "I, of course, do not wish to testify in support of my own nomination." Then he added, "I should think it improper for a nominee, no less than for a member of the Court, to express his personal views on controversial political issues affecting the Court. My attitude and outlook on relevant matters have been fully expressed over a period of years and are easily accessible."[15]

Committee members, however, were not seeking his views on Court matters. Frankfurter, a friend of Roosevelt, had been pictured in some of the press as a radical, even though he served as an Assistant Attorney General under Theodore Roosevelt and Taft. A prominent Republican member of the House Un-American Activities Committee, Rep. J. Parnell Thomas, said that Frankfurter belonged to radical organizations and that he "could not conceive of a worse appointment.... [The President] might as well have appointed Earl Browder [national leader of the Communist party]."[16] The first question asked of Frankfurter: "How long were you a member of the National Committee of the American Civil Liberties Union?"[17]

Then Senator Pat McCarran, Democrat of Nevada, moved to the heart of the matter:

McCarran: I take it that you are acquainted with the names of that [National ACLU] committee, of which you were one?

Frankfurter: I know some of the names. I have some of them in mind.

McCarran: Did you notice that you were on that committee with Mr. [William] Foster [a nationally prominent Communist]?

Frankfurter: I believe Mr. Foster was at one time a member of that committee. I do not know whether he is at this time or not.

McCarran: You knew he was a member of that committee, which, I take it, is in the nature of a sort of advisory committee of the American Civil Liberties Union? ...

Frankfurter: It is a body that gives whatever strength those names give, and they are all responsible for having their names on the letterhead. . . .

McCarran: I take it that you have had drawn to your attention the various reports and statements that have been made with reference to the American Civil Liberties Union . . . .

Frankfurter: That is a rather tall order, Senator McCarran. If you mean have I read the report of the Dies committee, I have not. Like every good lawyer, I pay very little attention to newspaper accounts of a trial or proceeding unless I read the whole record. I would not want to be charged with knowledge of everything that took place before a congressional committee. I have not read the report of the Dies committee; I have not read the report of the Fish committee; and I have not read the many volumes of the report of the Lusk committee of the New York Legislature. There are only 24 hours in a day.

McCarran: Have you read any of the reports of the American Legion?

Frankfurter: I am sorry; I have not.

McCarran: All those reports bear upon the activities of the American Civil Liberties Union as regards Communism, and quite broad and emphatic statements are made in some of those reports. I take it from what you have said that you have not taken it upon yourself to become familiar with any of those reports?

Frankfurter: I have not read them. I will have to leave it to the committee to judge what responsibility is upon me to read all of such reports. I shall only say that the repetition of an error does not make it true.

McCarran: No; the repetition of an error does not make it true; but I should think it would cause one of your high place to investigate his associates . . . . Doctor, are you acquainted with Harold Laski [a British Socialist]?

Frankfurter: Oh, yes.

McCarran: Quite well?

Frankfurter: Very well.

McCarran: Was he one of your students?

Frankfurter: No; he is an Englishman who graduated from Oxford University. He was disqualified for service in the war for physical reasons. He was a teacher in McGill University in Montreal when I first heard of him through my friend, Mr. Norman Hapgood, who is, perhaps, known to members of the committee. Having been a Harvard man, he spoke to me about this young man, and eventually Mr. Laski became a teacher at Harvard University. He later returned to England, and become professor of political science at the University of London, and has been there ever since.

McCarran: Have you ever read any of his publications?

Frankfurter: Oh, certainly.

McCarran: Do you agree with his doctrine?

Frankfurter: I trust you will not deem me boastful, if I say I have many friends who have written many books, and I shouldn't want to be charged with all the views in books by all my friends.

McCarran: You can answer that question simply.

Frankfurter: No; I cannot answer it simply. If you have a recent book of his, you will find the list of books he has written, some 12 or 15 or 20. He is an extraordinarily prolific writer. How can I say I agree with his doctrine? That implies that he has a doctrine.

McCarran: Do you know whether or not he has a doctrine?

Frankfurter: I assume he has more than one. All people have.

McCarran: I refer now to a publication entitled "Communism," and ask you whether you have read that?

Frankfurter: I have read it.

McCarran: Do you subscribe to his doctrine as expressed in that volume?

Frankfurter: Senator McCarran, how can I answer that question without making a speech about my views on government and the relations of the various branches of government to one another?

McCarran: You say you have read it and know the author, and you know the sentiment prevailing in this country now in regard to Socialism and Communism. If you have read this small volume, you can surely answer whether you subscribe to the doctrine?

Frankfurter: Have you read the book?

McCarran: I have just casually glanced at it.

Frankfurter: What would you say is its doctrine?

McCarran: The doctrine is the advocacy of Communism.

Frankfurter: You see, we could debate all day on whether that is in fact the doctrine of that book . . . .

McCarran: Do you believe in the doctrine set forth in this book?

Frankfurter: I cannot answer, because I do not know what you regard as the doctrine. You have never read it. I understand that it is a study of certain beliefs, of a theory called Communism. So far as I know, it would be impossible for me to say whether I agree with the doctrine in that book or not, because I think it is impossible to define what the doctrine is.

McCarran: If it advocates the doctrine of Marxism, would you agree with it?

Frankfurter: Senator, I do not believe you have ever taken an oath to support the Constitution of the United States with fewer reservations than I have or would now, nor do I believe you are more attached to the theories and practices of Americanism than I am. I rest my answer on that statement.

McCarran: Is that all the answer you want to make? Do you prefer to let your answer to the question I propounded rest in that form?

Frankfurter: I do, sir.[18]

Senator Matthew Neely of West Virginia, who chaired the subcommittee, concluded the hearings by asking: "Some of those who have testified before the committee have, in a very hazy, indefinite way, attempted to create the impression that you are a Communist. Therefore, the Chair asks you the direct question: Are you a Communist, or have you ever been one?"

Frankfurter replied, "I have never been and I am not now." Neely pursued it further: "By that do you mean that you have never been enrolled as a member of the Communist Party?"

Frankfurter closed the hearing by responding: "I mean much more than that. I mean that I have never enrolled, and have never been qualified to be enrolled, because that does not represent my view of life, nor my view of government."[19]

Twelve days after the hearing, the Senate confirmed Frankfurter by unanimous voice vote, though it is obvious some Senators were still reluctant to see him on the Court. The fears of the few proved unfounded: Frankfurter turned out to be a superior Justice.

Endnotes

1. Ted Morgan, *FDR* (New York: Simon and Schuster, 1985), p. 468.

2. Homer Cummings to Franklin Roosevelt, February 2, 1937, *Guide to the U.S. Supreme Court* (Washington: Congressional Quarterly, 2nd Edition), p. 958

3. Charles Hughes to Burton Wheeler, March 21, 1937, *Ibid.*, p. 964.

4. March 9, 1937, *Ibid.*, p. 961.

5. February 5, 1937, *Ibid.*, p. 959.

6. Quoted in *Walter Lippmann and the American Century,* by Ronald Steel (Boston: Little, Brown, 1980), p. 320.

7. March 24, 1937, *Reorganization of the Federal Judiciary,* Senate Judiciary Committee Hearings (Washington: Government Printing Office, 1937), p. 679.

8. *Reorganization of the Federal Judiciary,* Senate Judiciary Report, June 7, 1937, p. 3.

9. Bernard Bailyn et al, *The Great Republic* (Boston: Little, Brown, 1977), p. 1095. Person making the statement is not identified.

10. Quoted in Abraham, p. 212.

11. Quoted in Harris, p. 307.

12. *New York Times,* October 2, 1937.

13. Quoted in *Mr. Justice Black and His Critics,* by Tinsley Yarbrough (Durham: Duke University Press, 1988) p. 1.

14. Quoted in "The First Woman Candidate for the Supreme Court," by Beverly Cook, *Supreme Court Yearbook 1981* (Washington: Supreme Court Historical Society), p. 19.

15. *Nomination of Felix Frankfurter,* hearings before a subcommittee of the Committee on the Judiciary, United States Senate (Washington: Government Printing Office, 1939), January 11 and 12, 1939, pp. 107-108.

16. Quoted in Harris, p. 309, from *New York Times*, January 6, 1939.

17. *Nomination of Felix Frankfurter,* Hearings before a sub-committee of the Committee on the Judiciary, United States Senate (Washington: Government Printing Office, 1939), January 11 and 12, 1939, p. 108.

18. *Ibid.,* pp. 123-126.

19. *Ibid.,* pp. 128.

16

The Warren Court

Dwight Eisenhower, whose political star has risen since his presidency, performed the function of selecting Supreme Court Justices well above the presidential average.

His first nomination was Earl Warren to be Chief Justice. Warren, former Governor of California and Republican candidate for Vice President with Thomas E. Dewey in 1948, received widespread support for his nomination to the Court. However, a few Senators were able to delay it for two months, led by Senator William Langer of North Dakota, who complained bitterly that there had never been a Supreme Court Justice from North Dakota.

When the vote came, the vocal minority of critics was overwhelmed, and the Senate confirmed Warren by voice vote, without a roll call. The year after his nomination, Warren led a unanimous Supreme Court in the landmark *Brown v. Board of Education of Topeka* decision outlawing segregated schools. It began what Court observer Anthony Lewis describes as "a revolution made by judges."[1] The Court became more sensitive to the powerless in our society than at any time in its history. The sweeping decisions by what became known as the Warren Court often stunned the public. "Impeach Earl Warren" billboards dotted the national landscape, but history is appreciably kinder to Earl Warren than to those billboards.

Harlan and Brennan

A small group of senators waged a mini-battle against Eisenhower's next nominee, John Marshall Harlan, grandson of the Justice with the same name who had provided the lone dissent in the 1896 *Plessy v. Ferguson* decision, which legalized "separate but equal" and sanctified segregation. In selecting Harlan, the President said that his "qualifications . . . are of the highest. Certainly they were the highest of any I could find."[2] The Senate approved Harlan 71-11.

Eisenhower's next nominee, William Brennan, a member of the New Jersey Supreme Court, also received high marks in the legal field. A liberal Democrat, he ran into the senatorial slasher, Joseph McCarthy, who questioned Brennan — already serving on the Court in a recess appointment — for much of one day. As a New Jersey Supreme Court justice, Brennan had made speeches in defense of freedom that were pointed at the abuses fostered by McCarthy, a fire-and-brimstone senator who often questioned the patriotism of those who differed with him philosophically.

At the start of the hearing, McCarthy said: "I believe that Justice Brennan has demonstrated an underlying hostility to congressional attempts to expose the Communist conspiracy. I can only conclude that his decisions on the Supreme Court are likely to harm our efforts to fight Communism."[3] McCarthy's questions centered on two Brennan speeches that appeared to be directed at McCarthy without naming him. McCarthy told Brennan: "You have adopted the gobbledegook that Communism is merely a political party, is not a conspiracy."[4] Brennan replied that he recognized that international Communism is a conspiracy, but that questions pending before the Court were to determine matters relating to individuals who were Communists, and therefore he must decline to answer more specific questions. That did not please McCarthy, but the other Committee members rallied to Brennan's defense. On the Senate floor McCarthy said: "I shall not ask for a yea-and-nay vote . . . . I assume — because of Mr. Brennan's attacks on anyone who dares fight subversives in this country — that perhaps he qualified in the minds of some Senators for a position on the Supreme Court."[5]

McCarthy's Senate colleagues were tiring of his antics and confirmed Brennan easily.

Thurgood Marshall

Lyndon Johnson's dramatic nomination of the first African-American to sit on the Court, Thurgood Marshall, stirred opposition, not primarily on the basis of race — though that entered into it — but because as a legal giant on the national scene, he had argued many celebrated cases and had led the fight on the watershed *Brown* school desegregation decision. He had argued thirty-two cases before the Supreme Court prior to sitting on it, winning most of them. He planned and directed the entire historic legal battle against segregation, often facing hostile courts. "He has already earned his place in history," the President said in announcing his nomination, and no one could dispute that.[6]

But they could and did dispute Marshall's assumption of a Court seat. His championing of civil rights made him no hero to most southern senators. When they charged him with being a Communist, he pointed out that he led the fight for anti-Communist resolutions within the National Association for the Advancement of Colored People. For Thurgood Marshall, as for almost every nominee who faces the Judiciary Committee, the tug-of-war took place between Senators asking specific questions and the nominee declining to be specific. He said he opposed forced confessions but would not comment on the

Miranda case that requires those arrested to be informed of their right to an attorney before saying anything. He did say that he felt that the *Miranda* decision had not contributed to an increase in crime. The tug-of-war continued, with Senator Sam Ervin, Democrat of North Carolina, questioning:

Ervin: [I]f you are not going to answer a question about anything which might possibly come before the Supreme Court some time in the future, I cannot ask you a single question about anything that is relevant to this inquiry.

Marshall: All I am trying to say, Senator, is I do not think you want me to be in the position of giving you a statement on the fifth amendment, and then, if I am confirmed and sit on the Court, when a fifth amendment case comes up, I will have to disqualify myself.

Ervin: If you have no opinions on what the Constitution means at this time, you ought not to be confirmed. Anybody that has been at the bar as long as you have, and has as distinguished a legal career as you have, certainly ought to have some very firm opinions about the meaning of the Constitution.

Marshall: But as to particular language of a particular section that I know is going to come before the Court, I do have an opinion as of this time. But I think it would be wrong for me to give that opinion at this time. When the case comes before the Court, that will be the time.[7]

Senator John McClellan of Arkansas pushed hard on the *Miranda* decision, and Marshall persisted: "On decisions that are certain to be reexamined in the court, it would be improper for me to comment." McClellan came back: "I am not talking about cases pending. Here is a decision that changed the law of the land." Marshall again refused and said, "I appreciate your difficulty, and I have one too." McClellan responded: "I grant you that. We both have one."[8]

Marshall appeared before the Committee on five different days, but they were not the full-day hearings that have become more common recently.

Three months after the nomination, the Senate Judiciary Committee approved it 11-4. All four opponents were southern Democrats.

Senator Ervin summed up the floor debate opposing Marshall: "This is no time to add another judicial activist to the Supreme Court."[9] The Senate went on to confirm him 69-11, with all eleven negative votes coming from southern Senators, including three members still in the Senate: Robert Byrd, Ernest "Fritz" Hollings and Strom Thurmond. Paired against the nomination were four southern Democrats, and paired for him were three northern Democrats and one border-state Democrat, Fred Harris of Oklahoma. Public opinion in the white South, still reeling from the social changes imposed by the high court, strongly opposed Marshall. An indication of the gradually changing times, however, came from the six southern Senators who voted for Marshall.

Abe Fortas

Less significant in the history of the Court, but also the center of controversy, was Johnson's nomination of his good friend Abe Fortas. They became friends when Johnson served in the U.S. House, and Fortas worked as Under Secretary of Interior with Harold Ickes. After Kennedy's assassination, Fortas "was constantly on the scene, writing speeches, giving advice, keeping Johnson company."[10] Johnson's first speech to the nation, five days after Kennedy's death, was written by Fortas, Ted Sorensen and John Kenneth Galbraith. Johnson offered Fortas the position of Attorney General, but Fortas declined. When United Nations Ambassador Adlai Stevenson died, the President flew to Bloomington, Illinois, for the funeral with an unlikely pair: author John Steinbeck and Justice Arthur Goldberg. An effective persuader, Johnson pleaded with Goldberg to leave the Court and become the new UN Ambassador. Reluctantly

Goldberg agreed, a decision he regretted for the rest of his life.[11] That left an opening for Fortas, an able attorney in addition to trusted friend of the President. The Senate approved his initial nomination quickly, with three Senators expressing opposition.

The consultations with Fortas that the President enjoyed before Fortas went on the Court continued after he took his seat there. It seemed only natural to the President, when Chief Justice Earl Warren announced he would retire, to name his longtime friend Justice Abe Fortas. Before he made his choice public, he consulted with Senator Everett Dirksen, the Republican leader, asking whom Dirksen might suggest. Dirksen played just as coy, asking LBJ whom he had in mind. Johnson mentioned Cyrus Vance, later Secretary of State under Jimmy Carter, but Johnson quickly added that while he "would make a great Chief Justice," he had substantial family responsibilities and probably wouldn't take it.[12] Dirksen suggested Secretary of the Treasury Henry Fowler, popular on both sides of the aisle. Johnson said he couldn't afford to lose him from that position. Johnson then asked Dirksen if he himself would be interested, feeling virtually certain that the Illinois Senator would not be. Finally, Johnson tossed out the name of Fortas to the GOP leader, and Dirksen agreed that would be a good choice. Johnson had similar semi-consultations with others, including Senator Eastland, before he nominated Fortas.

The Thornberry Nomination

At the same time, the President named another old friend, Judge Homer Thornberry, to the vacant seat on the Court. Johnson and Thornberry had been friends since they were teenagers. Supreme Court reporter Fred Graham pointed out: "Between them, the two nominees had known Lyndon Johnson a total of seventy-five years."[13] Immediately the critics cried "cronyism," a charge that is more damaging for Court nominees than for members of a President's administration. People expect a President to name "his people" to the Cabinet and other key positions, but loftier standards are expected for the lifelong positions on the Court.

Clark Clifford, then the Secretary of Defense but also a close advisor to the President on other matters, had counseled naming a Republican rather than Thornberry, along with the elevation of Fortas, believing this would receive a more favorable Senate response. Clifford recommended a nationally respected Republican lawyer of moderate philosophy, Albert Jenner of Chicago. But Johnson rejected the suggestion, not anticipating a struggle ahead with Fortas. Clark Clifford described Abe Fortas "as intellectually fit for the Supreme Court and the Chief Justiceship as any man in this century."[14] The retiring Chief Justice, Earl Warren, told the press: "I feel Justice Fortas will be a great Chief Justice. He has a great record as a lawyer, Government administrator, as a teacher of law, and as a Justice . . . . I can't imagine a better background for a Chief Justice."[15]

Senator James Eastland, chair of the Judiciary Committee, advised Johnson, however, that he "had never seen so much feeling against a man as against Fortas," signaling that the nomination had troubles.[16] And before the hearings started, Senator Richard Russell of Georgia, who had told LBJ that he would back Fortas, sent a furious letter to the President because Attorney General Ramsey Clark would not approve a Russell choice for a district judgeship. Russell said he would now vote against Fortas. (A Justice Department check found Russell's choice had made a speech ten years earlier "that was anti-desegregation and [opposed to] judicial desegregation decisions."[17])

When Warren's resignation was announced, Senator Robert Griffin, a Republican from Michigan, stated on the Senate floor that since Johnson had already said he would not seek another term, the choice of the Chief Justice should be left to the new President. "I would hope and expect that [President Johnson] would not seek to deny the people and the next President of their appropriate voice in such a crucial decision," Griffin told the Senate.[18] Seventeen Senators joined in the Griffin position.

The Fall of Fortas

Fortas became the first nominee for Chief Justice to appear before the Judiciary Committee. The initial witness before the Committee was Senator Griffin, not a member of the Committee. The custom in the Senate is to let any Senator who wishes to testify do so first. Griffin attacked Fortas for regularly giving advice to the President, a practice he asserted violated the separation of powers and the independence of the judiciary. Privately, of course, Griffin's big complaint centered on the fact that the Republicans were likely to win the presidential election in four months, and he wanted a Republican to name the Chief Justice.

Fortas denied ever having made policy suggestions to the President. When pressed by the members, Fortas readily admitted that he had participated in some of the major White House decisions but said they were matters that would not come before the Court, such as the Vietnam War. In the words of Fortas's biographer Laura Kalman, "He simply lied."[19] Fortas did not appear before the Committee until the third day of hearings. A negative atmosphere had been created by the previous witnesses, and Fortas found himself in difficulty from the first questions about his role with the President. At one point, the nominee said, "My role has been solely that of one who sits in the meeting while other people express their views. The President always turns to me last, and he then expects me to summarize what has gone on."[20] Understandably, the Senators found that hard to believe. Then Fortas found himself defending the decisions of the Warren Court, decisions looked upon favorably by historians but not by some Senators, particularly southern Senators who resented the desegregation decisions.

The nominee refused to answer questions that he felt were improper. Over and over, he faced questions such as Senator Thurmond's: "Would the proper thing to do [be] to let the Congress legislate on [that] rather than the Supreme Court?"[21] Fortas spent four days before the Judiciary Committee, and although he showed himself an able advocate, the tension between Fortas and some of the members did not augur well for the future. When he told the Committee that he did not recall making any personnel recommendations to the White House, Lyndon Johnson became concerned, knowing that Fortas had regularly made recommendations. The President told the White House staff to destroy all notes, memoranda and letters from Fortas to LBJ.

Shortly after his appearance before the Committee, newspapers reported that Fortas earned $15,000 that summer lecturing at the American University Law School, and that the money had been solicited by his former law partner from five business leaders, though Fortas apparently was not aware of the source of the funding. Fortas refused to go back to the Judiciary Committee and provide an explanation. In a letter to Senator Eastland, Fortas said he had testified "because of my profound respect for the Senate," but added: "I believe that now my proper course of action is respectfully to decline to appear again."[22]

The Warren Court decisions on race and criminal rights played a significant role in the mounting opposition, and to a lesser degree, so did anti-Semitism. (Fortas was Jewish.) Fortas wrote to his colleague on the Court, William Douglas, that he thought anti-Semitism "is quite small a factor, but it would be pointless to say that it doesn't play some part."[23] Adding to the swelling undercurrent of confrontation, opponents of Fortas concentrated on his decisions on pornography cases, an area of controversy where the defense of freedom is never popular.

But the Judiciary Committee reported the nomination favorably, 11-6. Senator Joseph Tydings of Maryland wrote for the majority on the Committee: "It is our opinion that Justice Fortas is extraordinarily well qualified for the post to which he has been nominated."[24] An ominous note came a few pages later, however, when the Committee chair, Senator Eastland, wrote: "The Senate should refuse to advise and consent to this nomination."[25]

The next day, the *New York Times* carried the headline: "Fortas Approved By Senate Panel," with the sub-head: "Possible Obstacle Arises Over Fund for Seminar."[26] The story quoted from the Canons of Judicial Ethics of the American Bar Association: "A judge should not accept any presents or favors from litigants, or from lawyers practicing before him or from others whose interests are likely to be submitted to him for judgment."

When the nomination came to the floor, several Senators started a filibuster, the time-honored method for a minority of Senators to block any Senate action. The outlook became so grim for the nomination by this time that only one person could have stopped the filibuster: Richard Nixon, the Republican candidate for President, and he remained silent.

Stopping this talkathon required a two-thirds vote (the number has since been reduced to sixty votes from sixty-seven), and when the Senators cast their votes, it was 45-43 to cut off debate, far short of two-thirds. Some Senators who had promised support, including the GOP leader Everett Dirksen, abandoned the cause. But those voting against cutting off debate — in essence against Fortas — included not simply southern Democrats and the more conservative Republicans. Democratic Senator Ernest Gruening of Alaska, one of two Senators to vote against the resolution that authorized the use of force in Vietnam, voted against cutting off debate, as did Democratic Senator Thomas Dodd of Connecticut and Republican moderate Senator Margaret Chase Smith of Maine.

Fortas became the first nominee to the Court to be rejected through the mechanism of a filibuster.

Lyndon Johnson later wrote: "In the end, Abe Fortas's chief assets — his progressive philosophy, his love of country, his frank views always spoken from the heart, and his service to his President — brought his downfall."[27]

An unfortunate postscript to the Fortas career occurred in the early months of the succeeding Nixon administration when *Life* magazine — with the secret help of the Justice Department under Attorney General John Mitchell — disclosed that Fortas had signed a $20,000-per-year contract with the family foundation of Louis Wolfson in prison for stock manipulation at the time of the magazine publication. Fortas had signed the contract before

Wolfson's indictment. While apparently technically legal, it left an unsavory impression and Fortas resigned from the Court.

He is regarded as having been one of the abler members of the Court, making contributions particularly in areas that affect juveniles. But his resignation under less than favorable circumstances will probably cloud history's memory of him.

Endnotes

1. "Earl Warren," by Anthony Lewis, *The Justices of the Supreme Court,* Vol. IV, p. 2721

2. Quoted in "John Marshall Harlan," by Norman Dorsen, *Justices of the Supreme Court,* Vol. IV, p. 2805.

3. *Nomination of William Joseph Brennan, Jr.,* Senate Judiciary Committee Hearings (Washington: Government Printing Office, 1957), p. 5.

4. *Ibid.,* p. 18.

5. *Congressional Record,* Senate, March 19, 1957, p. 3945.

6. Quoted in "Thurgood Marshall," by Fred Graham, *Justices of the Supreme Court,* Vol. IV, p. 3064.

7. *Nomination of Thurgood Marshall,* Senate Judiciary Committee Hearings (Washington: Government Printing Office, 1967), p. 53.

8. *Ibid.,* pp. 9-10.

9. *Congressional Record,* Senate, August 30, 1967, p. 24589.

10. Robert Novak and Rowland Evans, *Lyndon B. Johnson: The Exercise of Power* (New York: New American Library, 1966), p. 346.

11. Johnson paints the picture of a much less reluctant Goldberg in his account, differing appreciably from the recollection of Goldberg and others. *The Vantage Point,* by Lyndon Johnson (New York: Hold, Rinehart and Winston, 1971), pp. 543-544.

12. Quoted in *Fortas,* by Bruce Murphy (New York: William Morrow, 1988), p. 280.

13. "Abe Fortas," by Fred Graham, *Justices of the Supreme Court,* Vol. IV, p. 3024.

14. Clark Clifford, *Counsel to the President* (New York: Random House, 1991), p. 559.

15. "News Conference With Chief Justice," *U.S. News and World Report,* July 15, 1968.

16. Quoted in *Abe Fortas: A Biography,* by Laura Kalman (New Haven: Yale University Press, 1990), p. 32.

17. Neil McFeeley, *Appointment of Judges: The Johnson Presidency* (Austin: University of Texas Press, 1987), p. 123.

18. *Congressional Record,* Senate, June 21, 1968, p. 18171.

19. Kalman, p. 337.

20. *Nominations of Abe Fortas and Homer Thornberry,* Senate Judiciary Committee Hearings (Washington: Government Printing Office, 1968), July 16, 1968, p. 106.

21. *Ibid.,* July 18, 1968, p. 201.

22. *Nomination of Abe Fortas and Homer Thornberry,* Senate Judiciary Committee Hearings (Washington: Government Printing Office, 1968), Part 2, p. 1285.

23. Kalman: p. 348.

24. Report of the Senate Judiciary Committee, September 20, 1968, p. 12.

25. *Ibid.,* p. 19.

26. Story by Fred Graham, *New York Times,* September 18, 1968.

27. Lyndon Johnson, *Vantage Point* (New York: Holt, Rinehart and Winston, 1971), p. 546.

17

Nixon: Haynsworth and Carswell

When the Fortas nomination for Chief Justice imploded, Warren changed his retirement plans, staying on the Court an additional year, but the following June, he submitted his resignation to the new President, Richard Nixon, with whom he had a less than cordial personal relationship. During his political campaigns, Nixon had issued bitter verbal blasts at the Court, though their unhappiness with each other went back to California politics. The President chose Warren Burger, judge of the U.S. Court of Appeals in Washington, not widely known but highly respected, for Chief Justice. Nixon specifically said that he had not "cleared" the nomination with any Senators or political leaders. The Senate Judiciary Committee approved Burger unanimously, and the whole Senate did 74-3.

Clement Haynsworth

When Fortas resigned, Nixon named another judge of the Court of Appeals, Clement Haynsworth of South Carolina. A Nixon "Southern Strategy" had emerged on the political scene, causing a series of moves intended to shore up Nixon's reelection chances in the South, cutting into the areas that had been Democratic. Accurately or inaccurately, political leaders viewed the Haynsworth nomination as part of the widely acknowledged Southern Strategy. Unlike with the Burger nomination, Nixon checked Haynsworth with at least three Senators before submitting the Haynsworth nomination.

The Judiciary Committee questioned Haynsworth closely on his financial affairs. This surprised no one, on the heels of the Fortas financial dealings. From the opening moments of the hearing, the focus of attention became the nominee's financial dealings, not his ability or his political philosophy.

Haynsworth, acknowledged to be an able jurist, had not been as careful as he should have been in the conflict-of-interest area. Senators learned that Haynsworth served on the bench for two marginal cases indirectly affecting two corporations in which he owned stock and did not recuse himself. Worse, he bought stock in a corporation after a favorable decision had been made for it by his court but before the decision had been publicly announced. The American Bar Association committee, which had found Haynsworth highly qualified, met again on his nomination and, once again, endorsed him, but now by a split 9-3 vote. Haynsworth had the opposition of labor and the National Association for the Advancement of Colored People, but the ethical considerations in the wake of the Fortas matter brought about his defeat, 55-45. Seventeen Republicans were among the majority voting against his nomination, including both GOP leaders, Hugh Scott of Pennsylvania and Robert Griffin of Michigan.

Justice Lewis Powell Jr., after his retirement from the Supreme Court, noted that Haynsworth "accepted his defeat with grace and without bitterness." Powell felt the defeat "reflected adversely on the Senate." Powell also resented the tie-in of the Haynsworth name with the next nominee, G. Harrold Carswell of Florida. "Two more dissimilar judges would not be easy to find." He called it a "mindless misjoinder of names."[1]

Nixon's Revenge

The President was furious at the loss, blaming anti-southern prejudices for the defeat. He submitted the name of Carswell, another southern jurist and also a member of a U.S. Court of Appeals.

Originally from Georgia, as a twenty-eight-year-old candidate for the state legislature, he said: "I yield to no man as a fellow candidate or as a fellow citizen in the firm, vigorous belief in the principles of White Supremacy, and I shall always be so governed."[2] In his speech, he also said that "the so-called civil rights program [would] better be called the civil wrongs program."[3]

That might have been forgiven as youthful excess, but later, while serving as a U.S. Attorney in Florida, he assisted in transferring a publicly owned Tallahassee golf course, which had been built in part with federal funds, to a private club. The clear aim: to avoid Supreme Court decisions on discrimination. He had also handed down judicial decisions favoring a slow-down of integration. The Leadership Conference on Civil Rights sent the Judiciary Committee a memorandum stating that Carswell "has been more hostile to civil rights than any other federal judge in Florida."[4]

The first Senator to take the floor and declare he would not support Carswell was William Proxmire, Democrat of Wisconsin. Another early Senator to announce his opposition, Senator Edward Brooke, a Republican of Massachusetts and an African-American, told the Senate, "I do not think this nation can afford G. Harrold Carswell on the Supreme Court."[5] And even though the Senate had just been through a grueling battle on Haynsworth, anti-Carswell sentiment started to grow.

The Republican Leader, Senator Hugh Scott of Pennsylvania, came out for Carswell, after having voted against Haynsworth. He had not been told the background of the nominee, but he was eager to show his GOP credentials after offending some of his Republican colleagues with his Haynsworth vote. Adding to Carswell's difficulties, Senator Charles Mathias, Republican of Maryland, found a pre-nomination memorandum about federal judges that had been prepared by his staff, which referred to Carswell as a "segregationist District Court Judge."[6]

Two months before being nominated, Carswell spoke to the Georgia Bar Association and began his talk with a story: "I was out in the Far East a little while ago, and I ran into a dark-skinned fella. I asked him if he was from Indo-China and he said, 'Naw, suh, I'se from outdo' Gawgee.'"[7] Clarence Mitchell testified for the National Association for the Advancement of Colored People and concluded: "The Negroes of America are waiting to see whether the Senate of the United States will ratify racism by confirming this nominee."[8] Senator Birch Bayh of Indiana, a member of the Judiciary Committee, had led the fight against Haynsworth and found himself unexpectedly being a leader in a second fight.

In the meantime, the American Bar Association Committee on the Federal Judiciary unanimously approved Carswell.

While there were fairly routine character witnesses for the nominee, others painted a picture of a man with strong prejudices. Law school deans and legal scholars suggested that the nominee's credentials for such a high post were slim. One of the most eloquent witnesses, civil rights leader Joseph Rauh, urged the Judiciary Committee to delay voting and extend its hearings.

Senator Joseph Tydings, Democrat of Maryland, who played an increasingly strong role on the nomination, moved in Committee to bring Carswell back to address matters that had been raised since his opening testimony. The Committee turned that down 9-6. But it did delay a final vote. Before that came, a few influential newspapers around the nation editorialized against Carswell, although not as many as endorsed him. Editorial opponents included the significant *Washington Post,* and Herblock political cartoons in that newspaper whittled away at the Carswell support.

After a 13-4 vote for Carswell in the Judiciary Committee, the debate shifted to the floor. In a television interview, Senator Roman Hruska, Republican of Nebraska, told a newsman who used the word "mediocre" to describe Carswell, that "there are a lot of mediocre judges and people and lawyers and they are entitled to a little representation, aren't they?"[9] However he may have meant the remark, it caused a furor. On the floor, Hruska tried to quiet the storm, saying that the "television interview — which I confess I made in a rather mediocre way" had distorted his message.[10] But the damage had been done, reinforcing the image that Carswell had acquired through the media. Senator Bayh summed up the growing mood: "The President has confronted the Senate with a nominee who is incredibly undistinguished as an attorney and as a jurist."[11]

Future U.S. Senator Mitchell McConnell Jr., then legislative aide to Senator Marlow Cook, Republican of Kentucky, wrote an article for the *Kentucky Law Journal* in which he commented on Carswell's lack of skills:

> A study of the nominee's reversal percentage by a group of Columbia law students revealed that while a U.S. District Judge he had been reversed more than twice as often as the average federal district judge .... He had no publications, his opinions were rarely cited . . . and no expertise in any area of the law was revealed .... A telling factor . . . was Judge Carswell's inability to secure the support of his fellow judges on the Fifth Circuit.[12]

The Senate rejected Carswell 51-45, the President losing thirteen Republican votes along with Democratic opponents. Carswell resigned from the appellate court on which he served, ran for the U.S. Senate in the Republican primary in Florida and lost badly. A few years later, newspapers reported his arrest for soliciting sex from an undercover policeman. His attorney reported that he was not well and would be under the care of a physician.

The Carswell defeat heightened Nixon's fury at the Senate. He told the nation in a television address: "I cannot successfully nominate to the Supreme Court any federal appellate judge from the South who believes as I do in the strict construction of the Constitution."[13] Suffering from self-inflicted wounds, the President attempted to portray the two confirmation battles as regional fights, which they were not. While Nixon and much of the media harshly criticized the Senate, it is now clear that the Senate performed a public service, using its powers as those who wrote the Constitution intended.

Justice Blackmun

After some inept handling of trial balloons on other possible nominees by the White House staff, Nixon turned to a soft-spoken jurist, another member of a U.S. Court of Appeals, Harry Blackmun of Minnesota, originally from southern Illinois. A longtime friend of Chief Justice Burger and highly regarded by his fellow judges, Blackmun received quick Senate approval, 94-0. No one had any idea at the time what a large role he would play in the future of the nation. The author of the *Roe v. Wade* decision, he quietly moved to the forefront of those championing civil liberties and the rights of the less fortunate.

The President's next opportunities came with the resignations of Justices Hugo Black and John Harlan II. After trial balloons on six possibilities that were quickly semi-deflated, the President chose a Democrat of moderate tilt, sixty-four-year-old Lewis Powell Jr. of Virginia, a former president of the American Bar Association and highly esteemed in the profession. Powell twice told Attorney General John Mitchell he would not accept, but a call from the President to his Richmond home changed his mind.

Once the President had named Powell, the nominee went with Senator Harry Byrd Jr. and a White House staff person to see Eastland, who still chaired the Committee. They told Eastland of all the groups and committees who would come out for Powell, and Eastland replied, "You're going to be confirmed because you're going to die pretty soon, not because of all these endorsements."[14] But the endorsements helped. His confirmation went smoothly, passing the Senate 89-1. Powell served until June, 1987.

William Rehnquist

More controversial was the next nomination, a forty-seven-year-old with Justice Department experience, William Rehnquist of Arizona, a former aide to Arizona Senator Barry Goldwater in his presidential bid and in many ways a philosophical soulmate of the Arizona Senator. Before selecting Rehnquist, the President had sounded out Senator Howard Baker of Tennessee — popular, able and moderate member of the Senate, but Baker expressed no interest in the seat, and Nixon offered it to Rehnquist, more conservative than any of Nixon's nominees.

His legal credentials were first-rate and the Senate debate centered on his philosophy rather than his ability. The traditional liberal groups opposed him, including the Leadership Conference on Civil Rights, an umbrella group of civil rights organizations; and for the first time ever on a Supreme Court nomination, the American Civil Liberties Union formally entered the fray, opposing the nominee.

The Senate approved Rehnquist 68-26.

A Well-Handled Nomination

Richard Nixon's hasty and unhappy departure from the White House brought Gerald Ford to the presidency. He had been appointed Vice President after Spiro Agnew resigned. Ford brought a sense of decency and confidence to the White House that was no small contribution to a nation beginning to drown in cynicism.

Ford also provided the presidency with an almost picture-perfect method to appoint a Supreme Court justice when Justice William Douglas resigned.

Playing a key role in most Supreme Court nominations is the Attorney General. Ford had chosen Edward Levi as his Attorney General, not a close friend but president of the University of Chicago and former dean of its law school. Everyone knew that Levi administered the Justice Department to provide justice, not to advance a presidential political agenda. The son and grandson of rabbis, Levi had stressed to Ford he intended to be "a nonpolitical head" of the Justice Department and believed it had to be "depoliticized."[15] Observers also knew there would be no questionable activities for political purposes under Levi.

A careful study of the Ford selection process by Professor David M. O'Brien of the University of Virginia concluded that "neither Ford nor Levi entertained making an ideological appointment,"[16] though ideology is at least of some consideration for all Presidents. While his Attorney General gathered names, Ford listened to Senators, House members and others. He considered suggestions from Senators Hugh Scott, James O. Eastland, Strom Thurmond, Mark Hatfield and Barry Goldwater. Names under consideration floated publicly included two future Supreme Court nominees: Robert Bork and Sandra Day O'Connor. When Judge Shirley Hufstedler's name appeared, Senator James McClure of Idaho wrote the President: "Her opinions from the bench lead us to believe that she is precisely the kind of judicial activist which has characterized recent difficulties with judicial decisions."[17] (She later became Secretary of Education under President Carter.)

Ideology entered into consideration to this extent: If the President did not feel comfortable with the person, he or she did not make the final list. Bork failed that test. Ford also insisted that the nominee "be of such known and obvious professional quality, experience, and integrity that valid opposition will not be possible."[18] One of those under final consideration, Senator Robert Griffin of Michigan, bothered Ford because of the fear of the charge leveled at LBJ of cronyism.

While the President weighed his decision, Senators Edward Kennedy of Massachusetts and James Abourezk of South Dakota, both Democrats, and Senator Charles Mathias of

Maryland, a Republican, convened a symposium on the "advice and consent" provision of the Constitution. They aimed to send a message to the President. Kennedy put it plainly: "Our hope is that the President will seek out the best and ablest person to fill the Douglas vacancy."[19] Abourezk commented: "If advice is to be anything but a sham, it must be received before a particular nominee is presented to the Senate for its consent."[20]

A memorandum from the Attorney General described the background of the eventual nominee, John Paul Stevens: Phi Beta Kappa graduate of the University of Chicago; majored in English, planning to be an English teacher; then changed his mind and went to Northwestern University Law School, graduating first in his class. Levi described him as "a judge of the first rank, highly intelligent, careful and energetic . . . a superb, careful craftsman." When named to the appellate court, the Bar Association praised him highly.

In its comprehensive search, the Ford administration submitted more than twenty names to the American Bar Association for review. The President checked with the Judiciary Committee chairman, Senator Eastland and Senator Charles Percy of Stevens's home state of Illinois. Senator Adlai Stevenson III of Illinois also enthusiastically endorsed him.

Praise for the nominee was not unanimous. Because two women had been considered, women's groups expressed their displeasure. Political commentator — and later presidential candidate — Patrick Buchanan found himself "disappointed in the choice."[21]

The Senate Judiciary Committee unanimously endorsed him, and two days later, he received a 98-0 vote in the Senate. Most Court-watchers consider him a valuable addition. The careful process that President Ford followed made the choice possible from among a large list of recommendations and gave him the opportunity to consult with key people, including members of the Senate.

It is of interest to note that Ford relied less on party affiliation in choosing federal judges for the lower courts than any President of the last half-century, through the Reagan administration.

Eighty-one percent of Ford's appointees were Republicans. Jimmy Carter had the next least partisan record, ninety percent. The most partisan were Ronald Reagan and Franklin D. Roosevelt, both at ninety-seven percent.[22]

Endnotes

1. Lewis Powell, Jr., Foreword to *Clement Haynsworth, the Senate, and the Supreme Court,* by John P. Frank (Charlottesville: University Press of Virginia, 1991).

2. Richard Harris, *Decision* (New York: E. P. Dutton, 1971), pp. 15-16.

3. Irwinton (Georgia) *Bulletin,* August 13, 1948, quoted in *Nomination of George Harrold Carswell,* Senate Judiciary Committee Hearings (Washington: Government Printing Office, 1970), p. 22.

4. Quoted in Richard Harris, p. 28.

5. Quoted in Richard Harris, p. 18.

6. Quoted in Richard Harris, p. 32.

7. John Frank, *Clement Haynsworth, the Senate, and the Supreme Court* (Charlottesville: University Press of Virginia, 1991), p. 102.

8. *Nomination of George Harrold Carswell,* Senate Judiciary Committee Hearings (Washington: Government Printing Office, 1970), pp. 277-278.

9. Quoted in *Congressional Record,* Senate, March 18, 1970, p. 7881.

10. *Congressional Record,* Senate, March 18, 1970, p. 7880.

11. *Congressional Record,* Senate, March 16, 1970, p. 7487.

12. "Haynsworth and Carswell: A New Senate Standard of Excellence," by Mitchell McConnell, Jr., *Kentucky Law Journal,* Vol. 59, 1970-71.

13. April 9, 1970, *Public Papers of Richard Nixon 1970* (Washington: Government Printing Office, 1971), p. 345.

14. Conversation of White House staff person with Paul Simon.

15. "The Case of Justice Stevens," by Victor Kramer, *Constitutional Commentary,* Vol. 7, 1990.

16. "Filling Justice William O. Douglas's Seat: President Gerald R. Ford's Appointment of Justice John Paul Stevens," by David M. O'Brien, *Supreme Court Yearbook, 1989* (Washington: Supreme Court Historical Society), p. 25.

17. *Ibid.,* p. 26.
18. *Ibid.,* p. 30.
19. *Advice and Consent on Supreme Court Nominations,* Sub-committee on Separation of Powers, Senate Committee on the Judiciary (Washington: Government Printing Office, 1976) p. 2.
20. *Ibid.,* p. 3.
21. O'Brien, p. 35.
22. "Background Paper," by David M. O'Brien, in *Judicial Roulette* (New York: Priority Press, 1988), p 37.

Part IV

Recommendations

18

Improving the Process

There is an old high-school debate question: "Can we learn from history, or are we destined to repeat our mistakes endlessly?" We can, of course, learn and sometimes we do.

In looking at the hearings, it is easy in hindsight to say we should have done things differently. There is some truth in a letter I received from a former staff member: "I understand that the process wasn't flawless . . . but that is true of everything in life. All things considered, the process is remarkable and . . . it served the nation well."[1] Endless Monday morning quarterbacking by political junkies can be a fascinating but useless endeavor. It is equally useless to pretend that no improvements can be made.

Let me first deal with the Anita Hill/Clarence Thomas hearings to suggest what might be done to improve that type of situation, and then look at the sweep of our two centuries of experiences to see what might be learned from that.

☐ *When an unproven charge is made that is serious in nature, the Judiciary Committee should either hold a non-public hearing, or give the nominee the option of doing that.*

In this case, the hearings would have been held in executive session, or held in that manner at the option of Clarence Thomas. I suggest this change as one who sponsored the act requiring open meetings of governmental units in Illinois when I served in the state legislature there. But I made an exception in the law for personnel matters because occasionally problems arise that are better handled quietly, with confidentiality.

The discussions at a "secret" meeting of the Committee would result in eventual disclosure to the press, either through leaks or through the Committee's formal action; but that is substantially different than international television coverage. The difficulty with television coverage on this type of charge is that it too easily and quickly deteriorates into a partisan exchange, rather than a search for truth. The cameras receive more attention than does truth-seeking. The nature of the coverage can do more to hide the truth than to illuminate it.

Suppose with the next nomination, someone who appears to be credible comes forward and says that ten years ago the nominee embezzled $50,000. The statute of limitations in that state means that prosecution is not possible. The FBI report, like all FBI reports, draws no conclusions but raises serious questions. Should the Committee ignore it? Should the Committee hold televised hearings on the charges? Or should the Committee, after careful investigation, hold closed hearings—a semi-trial, if you will—to determine what judgments can be drawn?

The last course would seem to be the wisest, unless there is a specific request by the nominee to make a hearing public.

☐ *When a sexual harassment charge is made, the Committee should first hear from experts on the patterns of conduct of those subjected to harassment.*

Most of us—I include myself—knew little about the typical pattern of behavior of those who are sexually harassed. Senator Biden offered Anita Hill's lawyers the opportunity to bring in such experts as "their" witnesses. It would be better for the Committee to initiate this, bringing in experts who are not tied to one side or the other. It became evident early in the hearings that some of my colleagues knew even less than I on this subject and drew conclusions from preconceptions that reflected ignorance more than partisanship or gender bias. Each of us on the Committee received letters from women that essentially said, "I understand Anita Hill's dilemma completely. I faced a similar situation. Here is my story." And they spelled out detailed life stories that were moving. Since the hearings I have learned more about sexual harassment, but it is accurate to say that when Anita Hill testified, the Committee—along with much of the American public—knew amazingly little about this troublesome problem in our society.

☐ *When a serious charge is made about a Supreme Court nominee, Committee hearings should not be rushed.*

Those of us who suggested a delay felt that we had achieved a significant breakthrough when we got a one-week postponement of the Senate vote. We had a clear understanding that within that week, the Committee would hold hearings and make a report to the Senate. Toward the end of the hearings, Senator DeConcini indicated that he thought the vote should be further delayed, that the Committee should not act in too great haste as it reviewed this information. DeConcini had earlier announced his support of Thomas and stuck with it. But he found himself struggling with two realities. One was the enormity of sexual harassment. He related,

I remember, as a young boy, my mother telling me about sexual harassment in her job and losing her job when she was twenty-two years old, so I grew up with that in my mind, and she mentioned it several times as I grew in age. I had dinner with her the night before last and she got choked up just telling me again about it sixty years later.[2]

At the same time, he sympathized with Judge Thomas being subjected to a leaked report. DeConcini had been the victim of a distorted, leaked report from someone with the Senate Ethics Committee, an action that did a real injustice to DeConcini. So DeConcini saw both sides and suggested that the Senate not rush to judgment.

In retrospect, he was right. We should have delayed, giving us time to hear a limited number of additional witnesses — such as Angela Wright — but giving the Senators and the public a chance to let the dust settle, to perhaps make a more rational decision. Several years before the Thomas hearings, Senator Byrd wrote: "From years of experience, I would say that we do the country a disservice by rushing any nomination, unless there is a clear record as to the nominee's integrity, capability, and qualifications, as well as an overriding need for speedy action."[3] In the Thomas case, we had no "overriding need for speedy action." Commenting after the hearing, Senator Specter said, "We were proceeding too fast."[4]

☐ *In this type of procedure, the committee would have been better served by getting professional counsel on each side who* **would** *ask questions, with less time allowed for questioning by the Senators.*

Professional counsel would have two advantages. The first is that they could devote full time to the endeavor and assume the main burden. Those of us in the Senate invariably are distracted by votes on the floor, problems that constituents have within our states and other committee assignments and duties. The second is that political considerations would less likely hamper vigorous pursuit of a line of inquiry.

In hindsight, following these suggestions would have helped, but not to the satisfaction of everyone. Senator Biden, who tried to be even-handed in the entire hearings, was correct in saying that there is no way to please everyone as we do our duties, and we should not try. Democracy is disorderly. We can learn, however, and do better.

History Lessons

The Senate should keep in mind these lessons from history:

1. While the Senate has turned down a few good nominees for the Court it should have approved, by far the greater sin over two centuries has been in approving nominees who were mediocre or worse, often by voice vote.

2. Senators should not commit themselves too early on a nominee.

A few senators felt encircled by their earlier speeches, which had applauded and endorsed Thomas. It takes special courage to reverse field as Senators Reid, Bryan and Lieberman did. Others did change their private opinions but took the easy way out, abiding by their public stand.

3. The Senate must be careful that our process does not encourage appointment of nominees with virtually no public record— who are mindless, voiceless ciphers—or that our process encourages evasion of the truth.

We should not expect nominees to tell us with precision their stands on too many issues, but the process should produce candor, rather than evasion. We are now producing evasion. It is a fine line for the Senate and the nominee between stating how he or she would rule on an issue or case, which no nominee should provide, and expressing frankly his or her philosophical moorings, which the nominee should provide.

4. The Senate not only can examine a nominee's philosophical base, but it has the obligation to do so.

That is the conclusion of virtually all who have examined this question seriously, including Chief Justice William Rehnquist. It has been part of our history and should continue to be practiced. Upon reflection, most people will recognize that examination of the base from which Justices emerge is essential because of the Court's immeasurable impact on the future of the nation. To use an extreme example, if the President were to nominate a Communist for the court, would anyone seriously question the right of Senators to question his or her philosophy? The historic path that includes examination of the views of the nominee is a path the Senate has followed for two hundred years and should continue to follow.

Presidential Advice

A brief glance through history would be helpful to a President and to the chief advisor to the President on Supreme Court nominations, usually the Attorney General. Such a study would tell us:

☐ *The President should take seriously the "advice" part of advice and consent that the Constitution mandates.*

The entire Thomas flap could have been avoided if the mandate of the Constitution had been followed. It wasn't. The Senate should not dominate the process, as it did for some years in the previous century. But the President would do well to follow the examples of several of our finest Presidents.

The President should ask Senators and others for suggestions and list several names as possibilities in conversations with Senators. It would not take a President long to determine which potential nominees would face difficulty with confirmation if that is done. It is not asking too much to require that the President follow the Constitution. The effort of those who wrote the Constitution to avoid excessive power in the hands of the executive is critically important for the Supreme Court. And giving **advice** suggests doing it **before** a nomination, not afterward. The Bush handling of the Thomas nomination is a classic example of how a President should not proceed.

There may be rare times when a President believes a nominee is so outstanding that a battle with the Senate is calculated and necessary. Wilson's appointment of Brandeis would be such an example. Wilson consulted with only one Senator, Robert Lafollette, and knew that the nomination would cause a furor. He correctly calculated Brandeis's presence on the Court to be worth it. But the Brandeis-type appointment is the rare exception. The common sense procedure for the President is to follow the Constitution; then he or she will serve the administration, the nation and the Court well.

☐ *The President should not rush into a decision.*

There are exceptions, but generally Presidents have served the nation best by taking time to look over the legal landscape carefully. George Washington, with two exceptions, did a superb job in selecting Justices. The two exceptions on the Court were Samuel Chase, whom he appointed against the counsel of several advisors, and John Rutledge, an appointment he made hastily without consulting others. Because of the enormity of the importance of the nomination, it is good for the legal community and the public to know that the President is looking at this carefully and thoughtfully.

It is also to the advantage of the President, who inevitably will receive some good suggestions that would not occur to either the President or the Attorney General. Lincoln waited almost a year in making three Supreme Court nominations. Even Jackson, not noted for his patience, waited months before nominating Taney as Chief Justice. Theodore Roosevelt used great care in selecting nominees, inquiring of many people, taking time but using it wisely. The result: auspicious nominations.

If the President is searching for an Assistant Secretary of Transportation, it is satisfactory — though maybe not wise — to rush to judgment. But a seat on the United States Supreme Court requires thoughtful, careful analysis. For the Thomas nomination, George Bush made the announcement five days after Justice Marshall announced his retirement, pulling names out of a readily available file for such an eventuality. I heard my colleagues of both parties privately praise the choice as "clever" or "politically adroit." But with the exception of Senator Danforth, I heard no Senator of either political party privately applaud the President's thoughtfulness or wisdom in his choice. A delay of thirty days or sixty days would at least give the appearance of thoughtfulness, but I hope it would give the nation much more than simply the appearance.

☐ *The President should have some criteria in mind as the selection is made.*

Integrity should be the base on which the other qualities build. The other criteria the President might seek include:

☐ *Outstanding legal ability*

It is astonishing how rarely this has been a significant consideration for Presidents. Yet when it has been made a priority, the service of the Court has been elevated. The President might ask twenty leaders whose judgment he or she trusts to list the ten people in the nation who, based solely on legal ability, would make the best Justices of the Court. Selecting one of the finest is something Theodore Roosevelt did when he selected Oliver Wendell Holmes Jr.; Woodrow Wilson did when he picked Louis Brandeis; Calvin Coolidge did when he named Harlan Stone; and Herbert Hoover did when he nominated Benjamin Cardozo and Charles Evans Hughes. If Coolidge and Hoover could make such selections, so could George Bush and his successors.

Some names likely to arise in this process would be well known, such as the late Paul Freund and Laurence Tribe, both of Harvard Law School; others might not be as widely known, such as Paul Gewirtz of the Yale Law School faculty. The search for a Supreme Court Justice should not be a clever political maneuver but a genuine search for the best in the nation for a Justice of distinction. A White House staff person complained to me that a Supreme Court nomination must now have a "Senate nanny," a Senator who guides and shields the nominee, as Senator Warren Rudman of New Hampshire did David Souter and Senator Danforth did Clarence Thomas. Souter might have made it without Rudman. Thomas would not have made it without Danforth. But a "Senate nanny" would not be necessary if the President conducted a more thorough search for quality.

☐ *Diversity*

George Washington sought geographical diversity, as did most presidents until Theodore Roosevelt. Ronald Reagan named a woman to the Court, Lyndon Johnson an African-American, Woodrow Wilson a Jew. It is important that people look to the Court as a symbol of justice, and diversity is helpful. We can achieve diversity without sacrificing quality. A magazine reporter wrote: "When I asked a senior aide of a conservative Republican on the Judiciary Committee why the administration didn't offer a black nominee with stronger qualifications, she answered bluntly, 'There aren't any.'"[5] That is simply untrue; a strong list of names could be provided. To suggest this about any ethnic or religious group is to demean them. The nominee to the Court should have a first-class legal mind; otherwise, both the Court and the cause of diversity are harmed.

☐ *Balance*

Too much attention has been paid to "fashioning" the Court in the mold of a President's philosophy. It is natural that the majority of nominations a President makes to the Court will at least partially fit that description, simply because a President wants to feel comfortable about the person named. But campaign promises to follow a certain philosophy are better not made. The law should not be a pendulum, swinging back and forth, depending on the political philosophy of the President making the appointments. This is more important today than a century ago, because there is much more litigation now and more of a role by the Court in determining the law. There is, as one writer puts it, a "fiction that the Court will somehow rise above politics if only the Senate does not focus on ideology."[6] There should be greater removal from partisan politics and a way found of achieving more philosophical balance on the Court. There should be fewer wide swings of the pendulum. Reaching a pre-nomination agreement with the Senate would foster both better relations and some assurance of greater balance on the Court. Attempts to "fashion" the Court in some special mold ultimately reduce the respect for, and the influence of, that body.

When the Senate refused to let FDR pack the Court, despite an overwhelming Democratic majority in the Senate, it did the Court and the nation a favor. If the President does not use good sense in providing balance on the Court, the Senate should use its prerogative and refuse to consent to a nomination. The Senate should refuse to let the President, in the words of journalist Leslie Gelb, "transform the Court into an ideological hit squad."[7] Court scholar Laurence Tribe may well be correct in stating that the Court is "more one-sided now ideologically than at any period in our nation's history."[8] Shortly before his second inauguration, President Dwight Eisenhower wrote in his diary: "The Attorney General and I agreed . . . . that so far as possible, we would try to get a balance on the Court between Democrats and Republicans . . . . I have [named] two Republicans and one Democrat."[9]

The *Decatur* (Illinois) *Herald and Review* had an editorial that reflects what many people expect: "Bush owes his election to people who believe in conservative values, including opposition to abortion. It's silly to expect him to appoint the type of nominees Lyndon B. Johnson placed on the high court. Johnson nominated Thurgood Marshall, a good liberal. Bush gave us Thomas, a conservative. That will continue until Democrats can convince people to put their candidates in the White House once again."[10] That editorial assumes the philosophical rigidity and lack of concern for balance that we have seen in the last few years. But Eisenhower nominated Brennan, as liberal as any Justice named by Lyndon Johnson. The two tagged "liberals" on the Court today, Blackmun and Stevens, were nominated by Nixon and Ford. Wilson nominated McReynolds, probably the most reactionary Justice ever to sit on the Court. Coolidge nominated Stone, and Hoover nominated Cardozo; both were conservative presidents, both were liberal Justices. Kennedy nominated White, Truman nominated Burton; both liberal Presidents, both conservative Justices. The Court should not be a place where presidents aim to place ideologues.

□ *Courage*

The Court, on occasion, must stand against public opinion, as it did not in 1942 in the *Korematsu* decision, as it did in the 1954 school desegregation case. Most Supreme Court decisions over two centuries on questions of separation of church and state have not been popular, but they have been good for both government and religious bodies. Freedom of religion has been preserved. The Court is the ultimate protector of our liberties, if the President and Congress falter. The Court should be composed of men and women with courage.

□ *Breadth of Understanding Beyond the Law*

Not everyone can be a Thomas Jefferson, but a good nominee should be one who knows a little about Plato and Beethoven, the Bible and the Koran, about Abraham Lincoln and Winston Churchill — one whose world is more than one-dimensional. The court system reflects life at its best and its worst. Some sense of perspective is needed by any good jurist, particularly one who sits on the highest court. In the debate on Hoover's nomination of Judge Parker, Senator Borah of Idaho observed: "Upon some judicial tribunals it is enough, perhaps, that there be men of integrity and of great learning in the law, but upon this tribunal something more is needed, something more is called for. Here the widest, broadest, deepest questions of government and governmental politics are involved."[11]

□ *Sensitivity to Civil Liberties*

Freedom is easier to give away than to preserve. The excuses for compromising our basic liberties are legion, and the reasons often seem good. But once given away, basic liberties are extremely difficult to recapture. The Court must be the defender of the unpopular, the minorities, those who sometimes appear not to deserve the freedom we give them. In the debate over

Parker, the great Republican Senator from Nebraska, George Norris, told the Senate:

> When we are passing on a judge . . . we ought not only to know whether he is a good lawyer, not only whether he is honest . . . but we ought to know how he approaches these great questions of human liberty.[12]

While I hope Congress and the President generally will champion the causes of liberty, both the legislative and executive branches of government are much too easily pressured into decisions that may help in the next election but diminish the nation's liberty down the road. The Court should be the guardian of freedom that does not worry about elections and is not swayed by public opinion polls. Unfortunately, an erosion of civil liberties is taking place under the present Court. A recent illustration is one of the worst decisions, *Rust v. Sullivan.* It is viewed by some as an abortion decision, but it goes far beyond that. The Court ruled 5-4 — Souter casting the decisive vote — that a physician working in a family planning clinic funded in part by the federal government could not tell patients about the legal option of abortion. They based their decision on a regulation adopted by the administration, not on a law passed by Congress. But whether law or regulation, the principle that the federal government can control what is said if it funds something goes far from our traditions. Because the federal government funds library construction, can that same government dictate what books are in the library? Because the federal government assists colleges and universities, can it dictate what courses are to be taught and what is to be taught in those courses?

Recently Justice Stevens spoke at the University of Chicago and noted: "While dozens of universities and communities throughout the land are celebrating the bicentennial of the Bill of Rights, an extraordinarily aggressive Supreme Court has reached out to announce a host of new rules narrowing the Federal Constitution's protection of individual liberties."[13] The battle for freedom is fought not once or twice or three times in the history of a nation. It is fought day after day after day, and we should have a Supreme Court that leads the fight for our fundamental freedoms, not a Court that sounds the trumpet of retreat.

☐ *Sensitivity to the Powerless*

Many will not agree with this final quality I mention, but it is vital for the political health of the nation that justice is available not simply for those who can employ the finest lawyers. Court historian Henry Abraham observed with accuracy: "The Court is infinitely more qualified to protect minority rights than the far more easily pressured, more impulsive, and more emotion-charged legislative and executive branches."[14]

On the opening day of the hearings on Clarence Thomas, I commented: "I am concerned that the Court is shifting from its role of being the champion of the less fortunate. It is easy for any government to become too cozy with the wealthy and powerful. Once on the Court, Justices do not rub shoulders with society's unsuccessful at Washington cocktail parties and dinners. But the test of whether we are a civilized society is not whether we treat the elite well, but how responsive we are to those who do not have the political or financial reins of power, the least fortunate among us."[15] A Supreme Court Justice should be someone who has had some experience with those in our society who struggle. Clarence Thomas brings that to the Court; whether he remembers those who struggle, we soon shall know.

When Justice David Souter came before the Committee, I expressed concern about the limited nature of his experiences and suggested that it would be helpful if he visited the West Side of Chicago, some of the poorest areas of that city, and visit an Indian reservation. A *New York Times* editorial scoffed at my suggestion. Reading the *Times* comments, I sensed that whoever wrote the editorial needed the same exposure. In a 1913 speech, Theodore Roosevelt said:

Our judges have been, on the whole, both able and upright public servants . . . . But their whole training and the aloofness of their position on the bench prevent their having, as a rule, any real knowledge of, or understanding sympathy with, the lives and needs of the ordinary hard-working toiler.[16]

Of the 1923 Court, journalist H. L. Mencken wrote: "The general tendency of all the recent decisions of the sapient and puissant Nine is toward shoving the man down and lifting the dollar up."[17] Once on the Supreme Court, Justices have contact primarily with the upper one percent of the population, both in income and in power. That was less true in the early years of our nation, when Supreme Court Justices "rode the circuit." Insensitivity of judges to the powerless has been a problem of all times and in all nations. Before the United States existed as a nation, the poet Alexander Pope wrote:

The hungry judges soon the sentence sign, And wretches hang that jury-men may dine.[18]

It becomes easy to forget those in need. The nation needs Justices who will not forget.

A President could easily follow these simple suggestions and elevate the quality of the Court and the quality of justice. In 1835, Horace Binney, a biographer of Chief Justice Marshall, wrote: "The world has produced fewer instances of truly great judges than it has of great men in almost every other department of civilized life." That may be true. But it is not inevitable.

With leadership in the White House and the Senate working together, "advice and consent" can become more than a meaningless phrase and justice more than a distant dream.

Endnotes

1. Sherry Hayes to Paul Simon, Oct. 17, 1991.

2. *Nomination of Judge Clarence Thomas,* op. cit., p. 111.

3. Robert Byrd, *The Senate, 1789-1989* (Washington: Government Printing Office, 1989), Vol. 2, p. 44.

4. "Senators Say Face-Off Was First Class Fiasco," by Judy Hasson, *USA Today,* Oct. 17, 1991.

5. "Nina Totenberg: Queen of the Leaks," by Ann Louise Bardach, *Vanity Fair,* Jan. 1992.

6. "The Evolving Role of Judicial Nominations," by Adam Mitzner, *Journal of Law and Politics,* Winter, 1989.

7. "Mr. Bush Packs the Court," by Leslie Gelb, *New York Times,* Oct. 13, 1991.

8. Laurence Tribe, conversation with Paul Simon, March 17, 1992.

9. *The Eisenhower Diaries,* (New York: Norton, 1981), p. 342.

10. "Simon Choice No Surprise," editorial, *Decatur Herald and Review,* Oct. 3, 1991.

11. Senator William Borah, quoted in "The Making of a Supreme Court Justice," by William Rehnquist, *Harvard Law Record,* Oct. 1959.

12. Quoted in *Congressional Record,* Senate, Oct. 21, 1987, p.14701.

13. "The Bill of Rights: A Century of Progress," by John Paul Stevens, unpublished manuscript of speech delivered Oct. 25, 1991.

14. Abraham, p. 342.

15. Nomination of Judge Clarence Thomas, Senate Judiciary Committee Hearings, unpublished transcript, morning session, Sept. 10, 1991, p. 78.

16. Theodore Roosevelt, speech in Santiago, Chile, November 22, 1913, printed by the Printing and Lithography Society of Santiago, San Diego State University Library.

17. Quoted in *The Spearless Leader,* by LeRoy Ashby, (Urbana: University of Illinois Press, 1972), p. 31.

18. *Rape of the Lock,* Canto III, 1.21.